Lecture Notes in Computer Science   12503

More information about this series at http://www.springer.com/series/7411

Cristina M. Pinotti · Alfredo Navarra ·
Amitabha Bagchi (Eds.)

Algorithms
for Sensor Systems

16th International Symposium on Algorithms and Experiments
for Wireless Sensor Networks, ALGOSENSORS 2020
Pisa, Italy, September 9–10, 2020
Revised Selected Papers

 Springer

Editors
Cristina M. Pinotti (iD)
Mathematics and Computer Science
University of Perugia
Perugia, Italy

Alfredo Navarra (iD)
Mathematics and Computer Science
University of Perugia
Perugia, Italy

Amitabha Bagchi (iD)
Computer Science and Engineering
Indian Institute of Technology Delhi
New Delhi, India

ISSN 0302-9743   ISSN 1611-3349   (electronic)
Lecture Notes in Computer Science
ISBN 978-3-030-62400-2   ISBN 978-3-030-62401-9   (eBook)
https://doi.org/10.1007/978-3-030-62401-9

LNCS Sublibrary: SL5 – Computer Communication Networks and Telecommunications

This Springer imprint is published by the registered company Springer Nature Switzerland AG
The registered company address is: Gewerbestrasse 11, 6330 Cham, Switzerland

Preface

This book constitutes revised selected papers from the 16th International Symposium on Algorithms and Experiments for Wireless Sensor Networks (ALGOSENSORS 2020), virtually held in Pisa, Italy, during Sepember 9–10, 2020. ALGOSENSORS 2020 was collocated with ALGO 2020.

The 12 full papers presented in this volume were carefully reviewed and selected from 27 submissions. For the first time, the submissions were collected in two rounds, 9 in the first round and 18 – out of which 3 were revised and resubmitted from the first round – in the second round. This special policy was arranged in view of the exceptional uncertainty due to the COVID-19 pandemic. The event was organized over two days on Microsoft Teams. For each paper, a pre-recorded presentation was made available followed by a live question and answer session.

ALGOSENSORS is an international symposium dedicated to the algorithmic aspects of wireless networks. Originally focused on sensor networks, in this edition, it covers algorithmic issues arising in wireless networks and all types of computational entities, static or mobile. The focus is on the design and analysis of algorithms and models of computation.

This year, two papers are in the area of classical wireless sensor networks: "Minimizing Total Interference in Asymmetric Sensor Networks" by A. Karim Abu-Affash, Paz Carmi, and Matthew Katz, and "Distributed Localization of Wireless Sensor Network Using Communication Wheel" by Kaustav Bose, Manash Kumar Kundu, Ranendu Adhikary, and Buddhadeb Sau. The first paper studies the problem of assigning a transmission range to each sensor – on a line or in the plane – such that the resulting network is strongly connected and the total interference of the network is minimized. The second paper deals with the problem of determining node locations of a dense wireless sensor network modeled as a unit disk graph. It proposes a distributed algorithm that starts localization from a strongly interior node and localizes all nodes of the network except some boundary nodes and isolated weakly interior nodes.

Two papers cover algorithms for emergent applications: "Covering users by a connected swarm efficiently" by Kiril Danilchenko, Michael Segal, and Zeev Nutov, and "VectorTSP: A Traveling Salesperson Problem with Racetrack-like acceleration constraints" by Arnaud Casteigts, Mathieu Raffinot, and Jason Schoeters. The first paper considers covering problems that arise in static and dynamic wireless networks powered by Unmanned Aerial Vehicles (UAVs). The second deals with a new version of the Euclidean TSP, called VectorTSP, where a mobile entity is allowed to move with no speed limitations and the inertia depends on the current velocity.

All the remaining eight papers consider autonomous moving computing entities, i.e., robots. The two papers "Connected Reconfiguration of Lattice-Based Cellular Structures by Finite-Memory Robots" by Sándor Fekete, Eike Niehs, Christian Scheffer, and Arne Schmidt, and "On Efficient Connectivity-Preserving Transformations in a Grid" by Abdullah Almethen, Othon Michail, and Igor Potapov propose algorithms for connected reconfigurations performed by robots with limited capabilitites. The first paper provides algorithmic methods for reconfiguration of lattice-based cellular structures by finite-state robots, motivated by large-scale constructions in space. The second paper considers reconfigurations on a one-dimensional lattice, the line, with devices equipped by a linear-strength mechanism that enables the movement of a whole line of consecutive devices in a single time-step.

The three papers "Live Exploration with Mobile Robots in a Dynamic Ring" by Subhrangsu Mandal, Anisur Rahaman Molla, and William K. Moses Jr., "Asynchronous Filling by Myopic Luminous Robots" by Tamas Lukovszki and Attila Hideg, and "Weighted Group Search on a Line" by Konstantinos Georgiou and Jesse Lucier deal with exploration and search-type problems with robots. The first paper requires a group of mobile robots, initially placed arbitrarily on the nodes of a graph, to work collaboratively to explore the graph such that each node is eventually visited by at least one robot and the robots must know when the exploration is completed. The second paper considers the exploration of an arbitrary connected graph by mobile luminous robots. In this problem, the robots enter the graph one-by-one and have to cover all vertices of the graph while avoiding collisions. The third paper introduces a new search problem on the line with two robots. The novelty is that the movements of the two robots have different costs.

Finally, the three papers "Fast Byzantine Gathering with Visibility in Graphs" by Avery Miller and Ullash Saha, "Efficient Dispersion on an Anonymous Ring in the Presence of Weak Byzantine Robots" by Anisur Rahaman Molla, Kaushik Mondal, and William K. Moses Jr., and "Conic Formation in Presence of Faulty Robots" by Debasish Pattanayak, Klaus-Tycho Förster, Partha Sarathi Mandal, and Stefan Schmid deal with faulty robots. The first paper considers the gathering task in an arbitrary graph by a team of synchronous mobile robots with IDs. The challenge is that the team includes a subset of Byzantine robots (say faulty-robots) that can behave arbitrarily and even have the ability to change their IDs to any value at any time. The second paper considers the dispersion task of a team of mobile robots some of whom are faulty. The robots, initially placed arbitrarily on the nodes of an anonymous graph, autonomously move to reach a final configuration where exactly each node has at most one non-faulty robot on it. The third paper considers the study of distributed pattern formation in situations when some robots can be faulty under the well-established look-compute-move model with oblivious, anonymous robots.

Keywords: wireless sensor networks, interference, localization, emergent applications, coverage, path planning, robots, transformation, exploration, faulty-nodes, gathering, dispersion, pattern-formation.

September 2020

Amitabha Bagchi
Alfredo Navarra
Cristina M. Pinotti

Organization

Program Committee

John Augustine	IIT Madras, India
Amitabha Bagchi	IIT Delhi, India
Stefano Carpin	University of California, Merced, USA
Jérémie Chalopin	LIS, CNRS, Aix-Marseille Université, Université de Toulon, France
Mattia D'Emidio	University of L'Aquila, Gran Sasso Science Institute (GSSI), Italy
Xavier Defago	Tokyo Institute of Technology, Japan
Irene Finocchi	LUISS Guido Carli University, Italy
Paola Flocchini	University of Ottawa, Canada
Leszek Gasieniec	The University of Liverpool, UK
Subrahmanyam Kalyanasundaram	IIT Hyderabad, India
Ralf Klasing	CNRS, University of Bordeaux, France
Irina Kostitsyna	Eindhoven University of Technology, The Netherlands
Euripides Markou	University of Thessaly, Greece
Miguel A. Mosteiro	Pace University, USA
Alfredo Navarra	Università degli Studi di Perugia, Italy
Theofanis P. Raptis	National Research Council, Italy
Dominik Pajak	Wroclaw University of Science and Technology, Poland
Cristina M. Pinotti	Università degli Studi di Perugia, Italy
Giuseppe Prencipe	Università di Pisa, Italy
Tomasz Radzik	King's College London, UK
Vlady Ravelomanana	Université Paris VII, France
Christian Scheideler	Paderborn University, Germany
Mordechai Shalom	Tel-Hai College, Israel
Christopher Thraves Caro	Universidad de Concepción, Chile
Dimitrios Zormpas	Tyndall National Institute, Ireland

Additional Reviewers

Adhikary, Ranendu	Gotfryd, Karol
Betti Sorbelli, Francesco	Kare, Anjeneya Swami
Bramas, Quentin	Leucci, Stefano
Das, Shantanu	Panolan, Fahad
Di Luna, Giuseppe Antonio	Schoeters, Jason

Contents

Contents

Minimizing Total Interference
in Asymmetric Sensor Networks

A. Karim Abu-Affash[1]([✉]), Paz Carmi[2], and Matthew J. Katz[2]

[1] Shamoon College of Engineering, 84100 Beer-Sheva, Israel
abuaa1@sce.ac.il
[2] Department of Computer Science, Ben-Gurion University, 84105 Beer-Sheva, Israel
{carmip,matya}@cs.bgu.ac.il

Abstract. The problem of computing a connected network with minimum interference is a fundamental problem in wireless sensor networks. Several models of interference have been studied in the literature. The most common model is the receiver-centric, in which the interference of a node p is defined as the number of other nodes whose transmission range covers p. In this paper, we study the problem of assigning a transmission range to each sensor, such that the resulting network is strongly connected and the total interference of the network is minimized.

For the one-dimensional case, we show how to solve the problem optimally in $O(n^3)$ time. For the two-dimensional case, we show that the problem is NP-complete and give a polynomial-time 2-approximation algorithm for the problem.

1 Introduction

Wireless sensor networks have received significant attention in the last two decades due to their potential civilian and military applications [7,10]. A wireless sensor network consists of numerous devices that are equipped with processing, memory, and wireless communication capabilities. This kind of network has no pre-installed infrastructure, rather all communication is supported by multi-hop transmissions, where intermediate nodes relay packets between communicating parties. Since each sensor has a limited battery and each transmission decreases the battery charge, energy consumption is a critical issue in wireless sensor networks. One way to conserve energy is to minimize the interference of the network. High interference increases the probability of packet collisions and therefore packet retransmission, which can significantly affect the effectiveness and the lifetime of the network.

In wireless networks design, the nodes are modeled as a set of points in the plane and each node u is assigned a transmission range $\rho(u)$. A node v can receive the signal transmitted by a node u if and only if $|uv| \leq \rho(u)$, where $|uv|$ is the

Work by A. K. Abu-Affash and P. Carmi was partially supported by Grant 2016116 from the United States – Israel Binational Science Foundation. Work by M. Katz was partially supported by grant 1884/16 from the Israel Science Foundation.

© Springer Nature Switzerland AG 2020
C. M. Pinotti et al. (Eds.): ALGOSENSORS 2020, LNCS 12503, pp. 1–16, 2020.
https://doi.org/10.1007/978-3-030-62401-9_1

Euclidean distance between u and v. There are two common ways to model the induced communication graph: symmetric and asymmetric. In the symmetric model [9,12,14,15,17], there is a non-directed edge between points p and q if and only if $|pq| \leq \min\{\rho(p), \rho(q)\}$, and in the asymmetric model [1–3,18], there is a directed edge from node p to node q if and only if $|pq| \leq \rho(p)$.

Several models of interference have been studied in the literature. Burkhart et al. [5] measures the number of nodes affected by the communication on a single edge. Moaveni-Nejad and Li [13] introduced the *sender-centric* model that measures the number of receiving nodes affected by the communication from a single sender. They showed that both problems can be solved optimally in polynomial-time, in the symmetric and asymmetric models.

Von Rickenbach et al. [18] argued that the sender-centric model of interference is not realistic, because the interference is actually felt by the receiver. Further, they argued that the model was overly sensitive to the addition of single nodes. Instead, they formulated the *receiver-centric* model; minimizing the maximum interference received at a node, where the interference received at a node p is the number of nodes q ($q \neq p$) such that $|pq| \leq \rho(q)$. In the one-dimensional case, i.e., when the points are located on a line, Von Rickenbach et al. [18] showed that one can always construct a network with $O(\sqrt{n})$ interference, in the symmetric model. Moreover, they showed that there exists an instance that requires $\Omega(\sqrt{n})$ interference, and gave an $O(n^{1/4})$ approximation algorithm for this case. Tan et al. [15] proved that the optimal network has some interesting properties and, based on these properties, one can compute a network with minimum interference in sub-exponential time. Brise et al. [3] extend this result for the asymmetric model.

In the two-dimensional case, the problem has been shown to be NP-hard [3,4]. Halldórsson and Tokuyama [9] showed how to construct a network with $O(\sqrt{n})$ interference for the symmetric model, extending the result of [18]. For the asymmetric model, Fussen et al. [8] showed that one can always construct a network with $O(\log n)$ interference.

Another model of interference is to minimize the total interference of the network. That is, given a set P of points in the plane, the goal is to assign ranges to the points to obtain a connected communication graph in which the total interference is minimized. For the symmetric model, Moscibroda and Wattenhofer [14] studied the problem in general metric graphs. They showed that the problem is NP-complete and cannot be approximated within $O(\log n)$, and they gave an $O(\log n)$ approximation algorithm for this problem. Lam et al. [12] proved that the problem is NP-complete for points in the plane. For the one-dimensional case, Tan et al. [15] showed how to compute an optimal network in $O(n^4)$ time.

For the asymmetric model, Bilò and Proietti [2] studied the problem of minimizing the total interference (sum of interference of each node) in general metric graphs. They gave a logarithmic approximation algorithm for the problem by reducing it to the power assignment problem in general graphs. Agrawal and Das [1] studied the problem in two-dimensions. They gave two heuristics with experimental results.

Our Results. In this paper, we consider the problem of minimizing the total interference in the asymmetric model. We first give an $O(n^3)$-time algorithm that solves the problem optimally, when the points are located on a line. Then, we show that the problem is NP-complete for points in the plane and give a 2-approximation algorithm for the problem. Our approach in the solution of the one-dimensional problem is somewhat unconventional and involves assigning to each point both a left range and a right range, see Sect. 3. We note that the approach of Tan et al. [15] (who considered the problem in the symmetric model) would yield a significantly worse time bound in our case, and that it would be interesting to check whether our approach can be applied also in their setting to obtain an improved running time.

2   Network Model and Problem Definition

Let P be a set of sensors in the plane. Each sensor $p \in P$ is assigned a transmission range $\rho(p)$. A sensor q can receive a signal from a sensor p if and only if q lies in the transmission area of p. We consider P as a set of points in the plane and the range assignment to the sensors as a function $\rho : P \to \mathbb{R}^+$. The communication graph induced by P and ρ is a *directed* graph $G_\rho = (P, E)$, such that $E = \{(p, q) : |pq| \leq \rho(p)\}$, where $|pq|$ is the Euclidean distance between p and q. G_ρ is *strongly connected* if, for every two points $p, q \in P$, there exists a directed path from p to q in G_ρ. A range assignment ρ is called *valid* if the induced graph G_ρ is strongly connected.

Given a communication graph $G_\rho = (P, E)$, in the *receiver-centric* interference model, the interference of a point p is defined as $RI(p) = |\{q \in P \setminus \{p\} : |pq| \leq \rho(q)\}|$. In the *sender-centric* interference model, the interference of a point p is defined as $SI(p) = |\{q \in P \setminus \{p\} : |pq| \leq \rho(p)\}|$. The *total interference* of G_ρ is defined as

$$I(G_\rho) = \sum_{p \in P} RI(p) = \sum_{p \in P} SI(p).$$

In the *Minimum Total Interference (MTIP)* problem, we are given a set P of points in the plane and the goal is to find a range assignment ρ to the points of P, such that the graph G_ρ induced by P and ρ is strongly connected and $I(G_\rho)$ is minimized.

3   *MTIP* in 1D

In this section, we present an exact algorithm that solves *MTIP* in $O(n^3)$ time in 1D. Let $P = \{p_1, p_2, \ldots, p_n\}$ be a set of n points located on a horizontal line. For simplicity, we assume that for every $i < j$, p_i is to the left of p_j.

For each $1 \leq i \leq j \leq n$, let $P_{[i,j]} \subseteq P$ be the set $\{p_i, p_{i+1}, \ldots, p_j\}$. A *sink tree* $T^x_{[i,j]}$ of $P_{[i,j]}$ rooted at p_x, where $x \in \{i, j\}$, is a directed tree that contains a directed path from each point $p \in P_{[i,j]} \setminus \{p_x\}$ to p_x. Let $\rho^x_{[i,j]}$ be a range assignment to the points in $P_{[i,j]}$, such that the graph induced by $\rho^x_{[i,j]}$ contains a sink tree $T_{[i,j]}^x$ of $P_{[i,j]}$ rooted at p_x, and let $I(T_{[i,j]}^x)$ denote the total interference of $T_{[i,j]}^x$. We say that $\rho_{[i,j]}^x$ is an optimal range assignment to the points in $P_{[i,j]}$ if and only if $I(T_{[i,j]}^x)$ is minimized.

Let $G = (P, E)$ be the complete directed graph on P. For each directed edge $(p_i, p_j) \in E$, we assign a weight $w(p_i, p_j) = |\{p_k \in P \setminus \{p_i\} : |p_i p_k| \leq |p_i p_j|\}|$. Let $G_{[i,j]}$ be the subgraph of G induced by $P_{[i,j]}$. Let $T_{[i,j]}^x$ be a sink tree rooted at p_x in $G_{[i,j]}$ and let $w(T_{[i,j]}^x) = \sum_{(p,q) \in T_{[i,j]}^x} w(p, q)$ denote its weight. Let $\rho_{[i,j]}^x$ be a range assignment to the points of $P_{[i,j]}$, such that its induced graph contains a sink tree $T_{[i,j]}^x$ rooted at p_x. Observe that if $\rho_{[i,j]}^x$ is an optimal range assignment to the points of $P_{[i,j]}$, then its induced graph contains a unique sink tree $T_{[i,j]}^x$.

Lemma 1. *$\rho_{[i,j]}^x$ is an optimal range assignment to the points of $P_{[i,j]}$ if and only if $T_{[i,j]}^x$ is a minimum-weight sink tree rooted at p_x in $G_{[i,j]}$.*

Proof. $T_{[i,j]}^x$ is a sink tree in $G_{[i,j]}$ and, by the way we assigned weights to the edges of G, $I(T_{[i,j]}^x)$ is equal to the weight of $T_{[i,j]}^x$ in $G_{[i,j]}$, i.e., $I(T_{[i,j]}^x) = w(T_{[i,j]}^x)$. On the other hand, let T be a sink tree rooted at p_x in $G_{[i,j]}$ of weight $w(T)$. We define a range assignment ρ' to the points of $P_{[i,j]}$ as follows: Set $\rho'(p_x) = 0$, and for each $(p_k, p_l) \in T$, set $\rho'(p_k) = |p_k p_l|$. Consider the graph induced by ρ'. Clearly, this graph contains T and $I(T) = w(T)$. This implies that $\rho_{[i,j]}^x$ is an optimal range assignment to the points of $P_{[i,j]}$ if and only if $T_{[i,j]}^x$ is a minimum-weight sink tree rooted at p_x in $G_{[i,j]}$. □

By Lemma 1, to compute an optimal range assignment $\rho_{[i,j]}^x$, it is sufficient to compute a minimum-weight sink tree rooted at p_x in $G_{[i,j]}$. In Sect. 3.1, we show how to compute a minimum-weight sink tree $T_{[i,j]}^x$ in $G_{[i,j]}$, for every $1 \leq i \leq j \leq n$ and for every $x \in \{i, j\}$. Then, in Sect. 3.2, we use these trees to devise a dynamic programming algorithm that solves *MTIP* in $O(n^3)$ time. Throughout this section, we will refer to a minimum-weight sink tree as *mwST*.

3.1   Computing All Sink Trees

In this section, we show how to compute a *mwST* rooted at p_i and a *mwST* rooted at p_j in $G_{[i,j]}$, for every $1 \leq i \leq j \leq n$, in $O(n^3)$ time. The following observation follows from the way we constructed G.

Observation 1. *Let p_i, p_j, and p_k be three points of P. If $|p_i p_j| < |p_i p_k|$, then $w(p_i, p_j) < w(p_i, p_k)$.*

Let $T_{[i,j]}^x$ be a *mwST* rooted at p_x in $G_{[i,j]}$, where $x \in \{i, j\}$, and let $OPT_{[i,j]}^x$ denote its weight. The following lemma reveals the special structure of $T_{[i,j]}^x$.

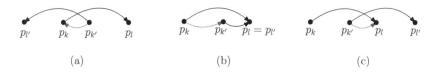

$$p_{l'} \quad p_k \quad p_{k'} \quad p_l \qquad\qquad p_k \quad p_{k'}\ p_l = p_{l'} \qquad\qquad p_k \quad p_{k'}\ p_l \quad p_{l'}$$

(a)   (b)   (c)

Fig. 1. Illustration of item (i) in the proof of Lemma 2

Lemma 2. *For every two distinct edges (p_k, p_l) and $(p_{k'}, p_{l'})$ in $T_{[i,j]}^x$, (i) if $k < k' < l$, then $k \leq l' < l$; and (ii) if $k < l' < l$, then $k < k' < l$.*

Proof

(i) Assume towards a contradiction that there exist two edges (p_k, p_l) and $(p_{k'}, p_{l'})$, such that $k < k' < l$, and $l' < k$ or $l' \geq l$; see Fig. 1. Notice that there is no path from p_l to $p_{k'}$ in $T_{[i,j]}^x$, otherwise, by replacing (p_k, p_l) by (p_k, p'_k) in $T_{[i,j]}^x$, we obtain a sink tree rooted at p_x in $G_{[i,j]}$ of weight less than $OPT_{[i,j]}^x$, which contradicts the minimality of $T_{[i,j]}^x$. Thus, the path from p_k to p_x in $T_{[i,j]}^x$ does not contain $p_{k'}$. We distinguish between two cases.

Case 1: $l' < k$; see Fig. 1(a). By Observation 1, $w(p_{k'}, p_k) < w(p_{k'}, p_{l'})$. Therefore, by replacing $(p_{k'}, p_{l'})$ by $(p_{k'}, p_k)$ in $T_{[i,j]}^x$, we obtain a sink tree rooted at p_x in $G_{[i,j]}$ of weight less than $OPT_{[i,j]}^x$, which contradicts the minimality of $T_{[i,j]}^x$.

Case 2: $l' \geq l$. If $l' = l$, then, by Observation 1, $w(p_k, p_{k'}) < w(p_k, p_l)$; see Fig. 1(b). Therefore, by replacing (p_k, p_l) by $(p_k, p_{k'})$ in $T_{[i,j]}^x$, we obtain a sink tree rooted at p_x in $G_{[i,j]}$ of weight less than $OPT_{[i,j]}^x$, which contradicts the minimality of $T_{[i,j]}^x$. And, if $l' > l$, then, by Observation 1, $w(p_{k'}, p_l) < w(p_{k'}, p_{l'})$; see Fig. 1(c). Therefore, by replacing $(p_{k'}, p_{l'})$ by $(p_{k'}, p_l)$ in $T_{[i,j]}^x$, we obtain a sink tree rooted at p_x in $G_{[i,j]}$ of weight less than $OPT_{[i,j]}^x$, which contradicts the minimality of $T_{[i,j]}^x$.

(ii) Assume towards a contradiction that there exist two edges (p_k, p_l) and $(p_{k'}, p_{l'})$, such that $k < l' < l$, and $k' \leq k$ or $k' \geq l$; see Fig. 2. We distinguish between two cases.

Case 1: $k' \leq k$. Since $T_{[i,j]}^x$ is a sink tree, the out-degree of each point in $T_{[i,j]}^x$ is at most 1. Hence, the case $k' = k$ cannot happen. Therefore, $k' < k$; see Fig. 2(a). In this case, there is no path from $p_{l'}$ to p_k in $T_{[i,j]}^x$, otherwise, by replacing $(p_{k'}, p_{l'})$ by $(p_{k'}, p_k)$ in $T_{[i,j]}^x$, we obtain a sink tree rooted at p_x in $G_{[i,j]}$ of weight less than $OPT_{[i,j]}^x$, which contradicts the minimality of $T_{[i,j]}^x$. Thus, the path from $p_{k'}$ to p_x in $T_{[i,j]}^x$ does not contain p_k. Moreover, by Observation 1, $w(p_k, p_{l'}) < w(p_k, p_l)$. Therefore, by replacing (p_k, p_l) by $w(p_k, p_{l'})$ in $T_{[i,j]}^x$, we obtain a sink tree rooted at p_x in $G_{[i,j]}$ of weight less than $OPT_{[i,j]}^x$, which contradicts the minimality of $T_{[i,j]}^x$.

Case 2: $k' \geq l$; see Fig. 2(b). Notice that, since $T_{[i,j]}^x$ is a sink tree, either no path from $p_{l'}$ to p_k or no path from p_l to $p_{k'}$ exists in $T_{[i,j]}^x$ (otherwise,

6   A. K. Abu-Affash et al.

(a)   (b)

Fig. 2. Illustration of item (ii) in the proof of Lemma 2.

$T^x_{[i,j]}$ contains a cycle). Assume, w.l.o.g., that there is no path from p_l to $p_{k'}$ in $T^x_{[i,j]}$, which also means that $k' > l$. Thus, the path from k to x in $T^x_{[i,j]}$ does not contain the point $p_{k'}$. By Observation 1, $w(p_{k'}, p_l) < w(p_{k'}, p_{l'})$. Therefore, by replacing $(p_{k'}, p_{l'})$ by $(p_{k'}, p_l)$ in $T^x_{[i,j]}$, we obtain a sink tree rooted at p_x in $G_{[i,j]}$ of weight less than $OPT^x_{[i,j]}$, which contradicts the minimality of $T^x_{[i,j]}$.

□

Consider a *mwST* $T^i_{[i,j]}$ of weight $OPT^i_{[i,j]}$ rooted at p_i in $G_{[i,j]}$. Let (p_j, p_k) be the edge connecting p_j to p_k in $T^i_{[i,j]}$. Thus, (p_j, p_k) partitions $T^i_{[i,j]}$ into two sub-trees T^i rooted at p_i and T^j rooted at p_j; see Fig. 3. By Lemma 2, T^i contains the points of $P_{[i,k]}$ and T^j contains the points of $P_{[k+1,j]}$. Moreover, since $T^i_{[i,j]}$ is a *mwST* rooted at p_i in $G_{[i,j]}$, T^i is a *mwST* rooted at p_i in $G_{[i,k]}$ and T^j is a *mwST* rooted at p_j in $G_{[k+1,j]}$. Therefore, $OPT^i_{[i,j]} = OPT^i_{[i,k]} + w(p_j, p_k) + OPT^j_{[k+1,j]}$. Similarly, $OPT^j_{[i,j]} = OPT^i_{[i,k-1]} + w(p_i, p_k) + OPT^j_{[k,j]}$.

Based on the aforementioned, to compute $OPT^i_{[i,j]}$ (resp., $OPT^j_{[i,j]}$), we compute $OPT^i_{[i,k]} + w(p_j, p_k) + OPT^j_{[k+1,j]}$ (resp., $OPT^i_{[i,k-1]} + w(p_i, p_k) + OPT^j_{[k,j]}$), for each $i \le k < j$ (resp., for each $i < k \le j$), and take the minimum over these values. That is,

$$OPT^i_{[i,j]} = \begin{cases} 0 & : \text{if } i = j \\ \min_{i \le k < j} \{OPT^i_{[i,k]} + w(p_j, p_k) + OPT^j_{[k+1,j]}\} & : \text{otherwise,} \end{cases}$$

(1)

and

$$OPT^j_{[i,j]} = \begin{cases} 0 & : \text{if } i = j \\ \min_{i < k \le j} \{OPT^i_{[i,k-1]} + w(p_i, p_k) + OPT^j_{[k,j]}\} & : \text{otherwise.} \end{cases}$$

(2)

Fig. 3. A *mwST* $T^i_{[i,j]}$ rooted at p_i. (p_j, p_k) partitions $T^i_{[i,j]}$ into T^i and T^j.

We compute $OPT_{[i,j]}^i$ and $OPT_{[i,j]}^j$, for each $1 \le i \le j \le n$, using dynamic programming as follows. We maintain two tables $\overleftarrow{S}$ and $\overrightarrow{S}$ each of size $n \times n$, such that $\overleftarrow{S}\,[i,j] = OPT_{[i,j]}^i$ and $\overrightarrow{S}\,[i,j] = OPT_{[i,j]}^j$, for each $1 \le i \le j \le n$.

Notice that, when we fill the cells $\overleftarrow{S}\,[i,j]$, all the cells $\overleftarrow{S}\,[i,k]$ and $\overrightarrow{S}\,[k+1,j]$, for each $i \le k < j$, are already computed, and when we fill the cells $\overrightarrow{S}\,[i,j]$, all the cells $\overleftarrow{S}\,[i,k-1]$ and $\overrightarrow{S}\,[k,j]$, for each $i < k \le j$, are already computed. Therefore, each cell in the table is computed in $O(n)$ time, and the whole table is computed in $O(n^3)$ time.

3.2 Solving *MTIP* in 1D

In this section, we present an $O(n^3)$-time algorithm that solves *MTIP* in 1D. That is, given a set $P = \{p_1, p_2, \ldots, p_n\}$ on an horizontal line, the algorithm computes a range assignment ρ for P, such that the graph G_ρ induced by ρ is strongly connected and $I(G_\rho)$ is minimized. For simplicity, we assume that for every $i < j$, p_i is to the left of p_j.

Given a range assignment $\rho : P \to \mathbb{R}^+$, the interference of a point $p \in P$, denoted by $I_\rho(p)$, is equal to the number of points in $P \setminus \{p\}$ of distance at most $\rho(p)$ from p (where $\rho(p)$ is the range assigned to p), i.e., $I_\rho(p) = |\{q \in P \setminus \{p\} : |pq| \le \rho(p)\}|$. The cost of an assignment ρ, is defined as $cost(\rho) = \sum_{p \in P} I_\rho(p)$. Notice that, $cost(\rho) = I(G_\rho)$, where G_ρ is the graph induced by ρ.

Instead of assigning each point in P a range, we assign each point two directional ranges, *left range assignment*, $\rho^l : P \to \mathbb{R}^+$, and *right range assignment*, $\rho^r : P \to \mathbb{R}^+$. A pair of assignments (ρ^l, ρ^r) is called a *left-right assignment*. Let (ρ^l, ρ^r) be a left-right assignment. The graph $G_{\rho^{lr}}$ induced by (ρ^l, ρ^r) contains a directed edge (p_i, p_j) if and only if one of the following holds: (i) $j < i$ and $|p_i p_j| \le \rho^l(p_i)$, or (ii) $j > i$ and $|p_i p_j| \le \rho^r(p_i)$. (ρ^l, ρ^r) is called *valid* if the graph induced by (ρ^l, ρ^r) is strongly connected. For each point $p \in P$, let $I_{\rho^l}(p) = |\{q \in P \setminus \{p\} : |pq| \le \rho^l(p)\}|$ and let $I_{\rho^r}(p) = |\{q \in P \setminus \{p\} : |pq| \le \rho^r(p)\}|$. The cost of (ρ^l, ρ^r), is defined as $cost(\rho^l, \rho^r) = \sum_{p \in P} \max\{I_{\rho^l}(p), I_{\rho^r}(p)\}$.

Notice that each left-right assignment (ρ^l, ρ^r) for P can be converted to a range assignment ρ with the same cost by assigning each point $p \in P$ a range $\rho(p) = \max\{\rho^l(p), \rho^r(p)\}$. On the other hand, each range assignment ρ for P can be converted to a left-right assignment with the same cost, by assigning each point $p \in P$, $\rho^l(p) = \rho^r(p) = \rho(p)$. To be more precise, either $\rho^l(p)$ or $\rho^r(p)$ should be reduced to $|pq|$, where q is the farthest point in the appropriate direction (see Observation 2). Therefore, instead finding an optimal range assignment, our algorithm finds a left-right assignment of minimum cost.

Given a left-right assignment (ρ^l, ρ^r), let $\overleftarrow{I}_{\rho^l}(p_i) = |\{p_j \in P : j < i \text{ and } |p_i p_j| \le \rho^l(p_i)\}|$ and $\overrightarrow{I}_{\rho^r}(p_i) = |\{p_j \in P : j > i \text{ and } |p_i p_j| \le \rho^r(p_i)\}|$. In addition to the *cost* function, we define $cost'(\rho^l, \rho^r) = \sum_{p \in P}(\overleftarrow{I}_{\rho^l}(p) + \overrightarrow{I}_{\rho^r}(p))$, and refine the notion of *optimal solution* to include only solutions (ρ^l, ρ^r) that minimize $cost'(\rho^l, \rho^r)$ among all solutions with minimum $cost(\rho^l, \rho^r)$.

Observation 2. *Let (ρ^l, ρ^r) be an optimal solution. Then, for every point $p_i \in P$, $\rho^l(p_i) = |p_j p_i|$, for some $j \leq i$, and $\rho^r(p_i) = |p_i p_k|$, for some $k \geq i$.*

For every $1 \leq i \leq j \leq n$, let $P_{[i,j]} \subseteq P$ be the set $\{p_i, p_{i+1}, \ldots, p_j\}$.

Lemma 3. *There exists an optimal solution (ρ^l, ρ^r) satisfying the following properties. Let p_i be a point in P, such that, $\rho^l(p_i) = |p_i p_j|$, for some $j < i - 1$, and $\rho^r(p_i) = |p_i p_{j'}|$, for some $j' > i + 1$. Then,*

(P1) *for each point $p_k \in P_{[j+1,i-1]}$, $\rho^l(p_k) < |p_k p_j|$;*
(P2) *for each point $p_k \in P_{[i+1,j'-1]}$, $\rho^r(p_k) < |p_k p_{j'}|$;*
(P3) *for each point $p_k \in P_{[j+1,i-1]}$, $\rho^r(p_k) \leq |p_k p_i|$; and*
(P4) *for each point $p_k \in P_{[i+1,j'-1]}$, $\rho^l(p_k) \leq |p_k p_i|$;*

Proof

(P1) Assume towards a contradiction that there exists a point $p_k \in P_{[j+1,i-1]}$, such that $\rho^l(p_k) = |p_k p_t| \geq |p_k p_j|$, for some $t \leq j$; see Fig. 4(a,b). Let (ρ'^l, ρ'^r) be the assignment obtained from (ρ^l, ρ^r) by assigning p_i a range $\rho'^l(p_i) = |p_i p_k|$. Thus, (i) the graph induced by (ρ'^l, ρ'^r) is still strongly connected, (ii) $I_{\rho'^l}(p_i) < I_{\rho^l}(p_i)$ and $I_{\rho'^r}(p_i) = I_{\rho^r}(p_i)$, and (iii) $\overleftarrow{I_{\rho'^l}}(p_i) < \overleftarrow{I_{\rho^l}}(p_i)$. Therefore, (ρ'^l, ρ'^r) is a valid assignment, $cost(\rho'^l, \rho'^r) \leq cost(\rho^l, \rho^r)$, and $cost'(\rho'^l, \rho'^r) < cost'(\rho^l, \rho^r)$, which contradicts the minimality of $cost'(\rho^l, \rho^r)$.
(P2) The proof is symmetric to the proof of (P1).
(P3) Assume that there exists a point $p_k \in P_{[j+1,i-1]}$, such that $\rho^r(p_k) = |p_k p_{t'}| > |p_k p_i|$, for some $t' > i$; see Fig. 4(c). Assume, w.l.o.g., that $|p_j p_k| \leq |p_i p_{t'}|$. By (P1), $\rho^l(p_k) < |p_k p_j|$. Let (ρ'^l, ρ'^r) be the assignment obtained from (ρ^l, ρ^r) by assigning p_i a range $\rho'^l(p_i) = |p_i p_k|$ and assigning p_k a range $\rho'^l(p_k) = |p_k p_j|$. Thus, (i) the graph induced by (ρ'^l, ρ'^r) is still strongly connected, (ii) $I_{\rho'^l}(p_i) \leq I_{\rho^l}(p_i)$ and $I_{\rho'^l}(p_k) \leq I_{\rho^r}(p_k)$, and (iii) $\overleftarrow{I_{\rho'^l}}(p_i) + \overleftarrow{I_{\rho'^l}}(p_k) = \overleftarrow{I_{\rho^l}}(p_i)$. Therefore, (ρ'^l, ρ'^r) is a valid assignment, $cost(\rho'^l, \rho'^r) \leq cost(\rho^l, \rho^r)$, and $cost'(\rho'^l, \rho'^r) \leq cost'(\rho^l, \rho^r)$, which implies that (ρ'^l, ρ'^r) is an optimal solution satisfying the lemma.
(P4) The proof is symmetric to the proof of (P3). □

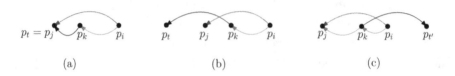

$p_t = p_j$ p_k p_i p_t p_j p_k p_i p_j p_k p_i $p_{t'}$

(a)   (b)   (c)

Fig. 4. Illustration of the proof of Lemma 3.

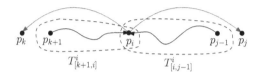

Fig. 5. Illustration of Corollary 1.

Let $G = (P, E)$ be the complete directed graph on P, in which $w(p_i, p_j) = |\{p_k \in P \setminus \{p_i\} : |p_i p_k| \le |p_i p_j|\}|$, for each directed edge $(p_i, p_j) \in E$. Let $G_{[i,j]}$ be the subgraph of G induced by $P_{[i,j]}$. Let $(\rho^l_{[i,j]}, \rho^r_{[i,j]})$ be an assignment for the points of $P_{[i,j]}$, such that the graph induced by $(\rho^l_{[i,j]}, \rho^r_{[i,j]})$ contains a sink tree $T^x_{[i,j]}$ rooted at p_x, where $x \in \{i, j\}$. In Lemma 1, we proved that, for any $x \in \{i, j\}$, $(\rho^l_{[i,j]}, \rho^r_{[i,j]})$ is an optimal assignment (i.e., $T^x_{[i,j]}$ is of minimum interference) if and only if $T^x_{[i,j]}$ is a *mwST* rooted at p_x in $G_{[i,j]}$. Combining this with Lemma 3, we have the following corollary.

Corollary 1. *Let (ρ^l, ρ^r) be an optimal solution satisfying the properties of Lemma 3. Let p_i be a point in P, such that, $\rho^l(p_i) = |p_i p_k|$, for some $k < i - 1$, and $\rho^r(p_i) = |p_i p_j|$, for some $j > i + 1$; see Fig. 5. Then, the graph induced by $(\rho^l_{[k+1,i-1]}, \rho^r_{[k+1,i-1]})$ is a mwST $T^i_{[k+1,i]}$ rooted at p_i in $G_{[k+1,i]}$, and the graph induced by $(\rho^l_{[i+1,j-1]}, \rho^r_{[i+1,j-1]})$ is a mwST $T^i_{[i,j-1]}$ rooted at p_i in $G_{[i,j-1]}$.*

Lemma 4. *Let (ρ^l, ρ^r) be an optimal solution satisfying the properties of Lemma 3 and let $G_{\rho^{lr}}$ be the strongly connected graph induced by (ρ^l, ρ^r). Let p_i be a point in P, such that, $\rho^l(p_i) = |p_i p_k|$, for some $k < i$, and $\rho^r(p_i) = |p_i p_j|$, for some $j > i$. Then, for each point $p_t \in P_{[j,n]}$, $\rho^l(p_t) \le |p_t p_{j-1}|$.*

Proof. Assume towards a contradiction that there exists a point $p_t \in P_{[j,n]}$, such that $\rho^l(p_t) = |p_t p_{j'}| \ge |p_t p_{j-2}|$. We distinguish between two cases.

Case 1: $j' \ge i$; see Fig. 6. Let $p_{i'} \in P_{[j'+1,j-1]}$. By (P1) in Lemma 3, $\rho^l(p_{i'}) < |p_{i'} p_{j'}|$, and by (P3) in Lemma 3, $\rho^r(p_{i'}) < |p_{i'} p_j|$. Thus, the points in $P_{[j'+1,j-1]}$ could not be connected to the points in $P_{[1,n]} \setminus P_{[j'+1,j-1]}$, which contradicts connectivity $G_{\rho^{lr}}$.

Case 2: $j' < i$. By (P1) in Lemma 3, $j' < k$; see Fig. 7. By Corollary 1, the graph induced by $(\rho^l_{[l+1,t-1]}, \rho^r_{[j'+1,t-1]})$ is a *mwST* $T^i_{[j'+1,t]}$ rooted at p_t. Therefore, since the out-degree of each point in $T^i_{[j'+1,t]}$ is at most one and (ρ^l, ρ^r) is of

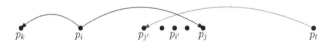

Fig. 6. Illustration of Case 1 in the proof of Lemma 4.

$p_{j'}$ p_k p_i p_j p_t

Fig. 7. Illustration of Case 2 in the proof of Lemma 4.

minimum $cost'$, either $\rho^l(p_i) = 0$ or $\rho^r(p_i) = 0$, which contradicts the assumption that $\rho^l(p_i) > 0$ and $\rho^r(p_i) > 0$. □

For each $1 \le k \le i \le n$, let $OPT(i, k)$ denote the cost of an optimal solution $(\rho^l_{[i,n]}, \rho^r_{[i,n]})$ for the sub-problem defined by the set $P_{[i,n]}$, in which $\rho^l(p_i) = |p_i p_k|$; see Fig. 8. Therefore, the cost of an optimal solution for the whole problem is $OPT(1, 1)$. For each $i \le j \le n$, let $\Delta(i, j, k) = \max\{0, w(p_i, p_j) - w(p_i, p_k)\}$ denote the difference between $w(p_i, p_j)$ and $w(p_i, p_k)$. That is,

$$\Delta(i, j, k) = \begin{cases} w(p_i, p_j) - w(p_i, p_k) & : \text{if } |p_i p_j| > |p_i p_k| \\ 0 & : \text{otherwise.} \end{cases} \qquad (3)$$

If $i = n$, then, clearly $OPT(i, k) = 0$. Otherwise, $\rho^r(p_i) > 0$ and thus there exists a point $p_j \in P_{[i+1,n]}$, such that $\rho^r(p_i) = |p_i p_j|$, and, by Lemma 3 and Lemma 4, there exists a point $p_t \in P_{[j,n]}$, such that $\rho^l(p_t) = |p_t p_{j-1}|$. Moreover, for $i+1 < j < t$, by Corollary 1, the graph induced by $(\rho^l_{[i+1,j-1]}, \rho^r_{[i+1,j-1]})$ is a *mwST* $T^i_{[i,j-1]}$ rooted at p_i in $G_{[i,j-1]}$, and the graph induced by $(\rho^l_{[j,t-1]}, \rho^r_{[j,t-1]})$ is a *mwST* $T^t_{[j,t]}$ rooted at p_t in $G_{[j,t]}$; see Fig. 8. If $j = i + 1$ and $t = j$, then $w(T^i_{[i,j-1]}) = w(T^t_{[j,t]}) = 0$. Therefore,
$OPT(i, k) = \Delta(i, j, k) + w(T^i_{[i,j-1]}) + w(p_t, p_{j-1}) + w(T^t_{[j,t]}) + OPT(t, j - 1)$.

Based on the aforementioned, to compute $OPT(i, k)$, we compute $\Delta(i, j, k) + w(T^i_{[i,j-1]}) + w(T^t_{[j,t]}) + w(p_t, p_{j-1}) + OPT(t, j - 1)$, for each $i < j \le n$ and for each $j \le t \le n$, and take the minimum over these values. That is, if $i = n$, then $OPT(i, k) = 0$, otherwise

$$OPT(i, k) = \min_{\substack{i < j \le n \\ j \le t \le n}} \left\{ \Delta(i, j, k) + w(T^i_{[i,j-1]}) + w(T^t_{[j,t]}) + w(p_t, p_{j-1}) + OPT(t, j - 1) \right\}.$$

For each $i < j \le n$, let $C(j) = \min_{j \le t \le n} \left\{ w(T^t_{[j,t]}) + w(p_t, p_{j-1}) + OPT(t, j - 1) \right\}$ and observe that $C(j)$ depends only on t. Therefore,

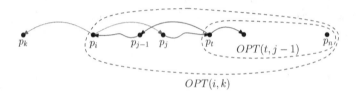

p_k p_i p_{j-1} p_j p_t $OPT(t, j - 1)$ p_n

$OPT(i, k)$

Fig. 8. Computing $OPT(i, k)$.

$$OPT(i,k) = \min_{i<j\leq n}\left\{\Delta(i,j,k) + w(T^i_{[i,j-1]}) + C(j)\right\}.$$

We compute $OPT(i,k)$, for each $1 \leq k \leq i \leq n$, using dynamic programming as follows. We maintain two tables M of size $n \times n$ and C of size $1 \times n$, such that $M[i,k] = OPT(i,k)$, for each $1 \leq k \leq i \leq n$, and $C[j] = C(j)$, for each $1 \leq j \leq n$. In Sect. 3.1, we computed two tables $\overleftarrow{S}$ and $\overrightarrow{S}$ each of size $n \times n$, such that $\overleftarrow{S}[i,j] = w(T^i_{[i,j]})$ and $\overrightarrow{S}[i,j] = w(T^j_{[i,j]})$, for each $1 \leq i \leq j \leq n$. Notice that, when we fill the cell $C[j]$, the cells $M[t,j-1]$ are already computed, for each $i < t \leq n$ and for each $1 < j \leq i$. Moreover, when we fill the cell $M[i,k]$, the cell $C[j]$ is already computed. Since for each $i < j \leq n$, the cell $C[j]$ is filled $n-1$ times (for each $1 \leq i < n$) and computed by taking the minimum over $\overrightarrow{S}[j,t] + w(p_t,p_{j-1}) + M[t,j-1]$, for each $j \leq t \leq n$, the total time for filling the table C is $O(n^3)$. Moreover, each cell $M[i,k]$ is computed by taking the minimum over $\Delta + \overleftarrow{S}[i,j-1] + C[j]$, for each $i < j \leq n$. Thus, each cell $M[i,k]$ is computed in $O(n)$ time, and the whole table is computed in $O(n^3)$ time. The following theorem summarizes the result of this section.

Theorem 3. *Let P be a set of n points located on a horizontal line. Then, one can compute in $O(n^3)$ time a range assignment ρ to the points of P, such that the induced graph G_ρ is strongly connected and its total interference is minimized.*

4   *MTIP* in 2D

In this section, we prove that *MTIP* is NP-complete in 2D and present a polynomial-time 2-approximation algorithm for the problem.

Theorem 4. *MTIP in 2D is NP-complete.*

Proof. Given a range assignment ρ as a certificate, it is easy to verify in polynomial-time whether the graph induced by ρ is strongly connected and whether its total interference is bounded by a given value I. This implies that *MTIP* is in NP.

To prove hardness of *MTIP*, we show a polynomial-time reduction from the problem of deciding whether a grid graph contains a Hamiltonian cycle, which is known to be NP-hard [11]. A grid graph is a graph whose vertex set is a subset of the integer grid $\mathbb{Z} \times \mathbb{Z}$, and two vertices are connected by an edge if and only if the distance between them is equal to 1.

Let $G = (V,E)$ be a grid graph, where $V = \{v_1, v_2, \ldots, v_n\}$. We construct in polynomial-time a set P of $5n$ points in the plane, and show that G contains a Hamiltonian cycle iff there exists a range assignment ρ such that the induced graph G_ρ is strongly connected and $I(G_\rho) = 9n$. We assume that the degree of each vertex in G is at least 2, otherwise G cannot contain a Hamiltonian cycle.

We first transform the vertices of G to a set $C = \{c_1, c_2, \ldots, c_n\}$ of n points on a grid of side length 3.4, such that two vertices v_i and v_j are adjacent in G if and only if c_i and c_j (the points corresponding to v_i and v_j) are adjacent in the

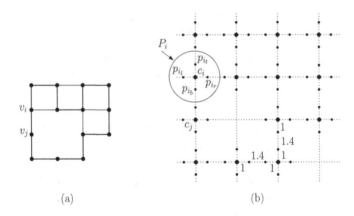

Fig. 9. (a) A grid graph G. (The bold edges form a Hamiltonian cycle.) (b) The resulting set P. Each set $P_i \subseteq P$ corresponds to a vertex v_i in G and consists of 5 points $\{c_i, p_{i_r}, p_{i_l}, p_{i_t}, p_{i_b}\}$.

new grid; see Fig. 9. Then, for each point $c_i \in P$, we locate four points $p_{i_r}, p_{i_l}, p_{i_t}$, and p_{i_b} on the grid edges incident to c_i, such that the distance between c_i and each one of them is equal to 1; see Fig. 9(b). Put $P_i = \{c_i, p_{i_r}, p_{i_l}, p_{i_t}, p_{i_b}\}$. We will refer to c_i as the center of P_i and to the other four points as connectors. Let $P = \bigcup_{v_i \in V} P_i$ be the resulting set. Clearly, $|P| = 5n$ and P can be constructed in polynomial-time.

Lemma 5. *Let ρ be a valid range assignment of P and let G_ρ be the graph induced by ρ. Then, for each $1 \le i \le n$, $SI(P_i) = \sum_{p \in P_i} SI(p) \ge 9$.*

Proof. Since ρ is a valid assignment, for each $p \in P_i$, we have $\rho(p) \ge 1$. Hence, $SI(c_i) \ge 4$ and $SI(p) \ge 1$, for each $p \in P_i \setminus \{c_i\}$. Moreover, since G_ρ is strongly connected, the transmission range of at least one of the points of P_i must cover at least one point from $P \setminus P_i$, which means that either $\rho(c_i) \ge 2.4$ or $\rho(p) \ge 1.4$ for

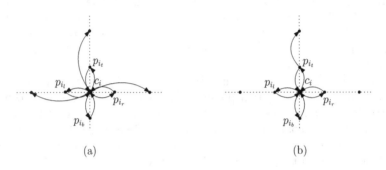

Fig. 10. $SI(P_i) \ge 9$.

at least one connector $p \in P_i$. If $\rho(c_i) \geq 2.4$, then $SI(c_i) \geq 6$ (since the degree of each vertex in G is at least 2), and therefore, $SI(P_i) \geq 10$; see Fig. 10(a). Otherwise, at least one connector $p \in P_i$ has $\rho(p) \geq 1.4$. Then, $SI(p) \geq 2$, and therefore $SI(P_i) \geq 9$; see Fig. 10(b). $\square$

Corollary 2. *Let ρ be a valid range assignment of P. Then, if $SI(P_i) = 9$, for some $1 \leq i \leq n$, then $\rho(c_i) < 2.4$, exactly one connector $p \in P_i$ has $1.4 \leq \rho(p) < \sqrt{2}$, and each of the other three connectors $p' \in P_i$ has $1 \leq \rho(p') < 1.4$.*

Proof. During the proof of Lemma 5, we showed that if $\rho(c_i) \geq 2.4$, then $SI(c_i) \geq 6$, and hence $SI(P_i) \geq 10$. Thus, $\rho(c_i) < 2.4$ and $SI(c_i) = 4$. Moreover, for each point $p \in P_i \setminus \{c_i\}$, $\rho(p) \geq 1$, and if $1.4 \leq \rho(p) < \sqrt{2}$, then $SI(p) = 2$. Since $SI(P_i) = 9$, exactly one point $p \in P_i \setminus \{c_i\}$ has $1.4 \leq \rho(p) < \sqrt{2}$, which completes the proof of the lemma. $\square$

We now prove the correctness of the reduction. Suppose that G contains a Hamiltonian cycle C. We compute a valid range assignment ρ to the points of P, such that $I(G_\rho) = 9n$. Consider C as a directed cycle, such that, each vertex in C has in-degree 1 and out-degree 1. For each vertex v_i in G we assign ranges to the points of P_i as follows. We assign 1 to the center c_i, assign 1.4 to one of the connectors (according to the outgoing edge incident to v_i in C), and assign 1 to each of the other three connectors. Since C is a Hamiltonian cycle, the graph induced by ρ is strongly connected. Moreover, $SI(P_i) = 9$, for each $1 \leq i \leq n$, and therefore $I(G_\rho) = 9n$.

Conversely, suppose that there exists a valid range assignment ρ to the points of P, such that $I(G_\rho) = 9n$. By Lemma 5, $SI(P_i) \geq 9$, for each $1 \leq i \leq n$. Since $I(G_\rho) = 9n$, we conclude that $SI(P_i) = 9$, for each $1 \leq i \leq n$. Moreover, by Corollary 2, in each set P_i, exactly one connector p has $1.4 \leq \rho(p) < \sqrt{2}$ (where $\rho(c_i) < 2.4$ and each of the other connectors p' has $1 \leq \rho(p') < 1.4$). We construct a Hamiltonian cycle C in G as follows. For every two sets P_i and P_j, we add the edge (v_i, v_j) to C if and only if the connector $p \in P_i$ assigned range $1.4 \leq \rho(p) < \sqrt{2}$ covers a point in P_j. Thus, C is a subgraph of G, and, since G_ρ is strongly connected, C is connected. Moreover, since each set P_i has exactly one point which reaches a point not in P_i, the degree of each vertex in C is exactly 2. Therefore, C is a Hamiltonian cycle in G. $\square$

5   Approximation Algorithm for *MTIP* in 2D

Let P be a set of n points in the plane. Let ρ^* be an optimal range assignment to the points of P. Let G_{ρ^*} be the graph induced by ρ^*, and put $OPT = I(G_{\rho^*})$. In this section, we present a polynomial-time approximation algorithm that computes a valid range assignment ρ, such that $I(G_\rho) \leq 2 \cdot OPT$.

Let s be a point of P. A *broadcast* tree for P rooted at s is a directed tree rooted at s, which contains a directed path from s to each point $p \in P \setminus \{s\}$. A *sink* tree for P rooted at s is a directed tree rooted at s, which contains a directed path from each point $p \in P \setminus \{s\}$ to s. We introduce two variants of

$MTIP$, namely $MTIP_1$ and $MTIP_2$. In $MTIP_1$, the goal is to compute a range assignment ρ_1 to the points of P, such that the graph induced by ρ_1 contains a broadcast tree T_{ρ_1} for P rooted at s of minimum total interference. And, in $MTIP_2$, the goal is to compute a range assignment ρ_2 to the points of P, such that the graph induced by ρ_2 contains a sink tree T_{ρ_2} for P rooted at s of minimum total interference.

Let ρ_1 and ρ_2 be optimal range assignments for $MTIP_1$ and $MTIP_2$, respectively, and let T_{ρ_1} and T_{ρ_2} be the corresponding broadcast and sink trees. We compute a new range assignment ρ as follows. For each point $p \in P$, we set $\rho(p) = \max\{\rho_1(p), \rho_2(p)\}$. Let G_ρ be the graph induced by ρ. Then, G_ρ is strongly connected, since given two points $p, q \in P$, one can get from p to q by first following the directed path in T_{ρ_2} from p to s and then following the directed path in T_{ρ_1} from s to q. In the next lemma we bound $I(G_\rho)$.

Lemma 6. $I(G_\rho) \leq 2 \cdot OPT$.

Proof. Consider the graph G_{ρ^*}. Since G_{ρ^*} is strongly connected, there exists a directed path from s to each of the points in $P \setminus \{c\}$ and vice versa. Thus, G_{ρ^*} contains broadcast and sink trees rooted at s. Let T_1 and T_2 be such broadcast and sink trees, respectively. Clearly, $I(T_1) \leq OPT$ and $I(T_2) \leq OPT$. Since T_{ρ_1} is a broadcast tree of minimum total interference and T_{ρ_2} is a sink tree of minimum total interference, we have $I(T_{\rho_1}) \leq I(T_1)$ and $I(T_{\rho_2}) \leq I(T_2)$. Moreover, since $I(G_\rho) \leq I(T_{\rho_1}) + I(T_{\rho_2})$, we have $I(G_\rho) \leq 2 \cdot OPT$.   □

We now show how to solve $MTIP_1$ and $MTIP_2$ optimally, and therefore, by Lemma 6, we can obtain a valid range assignment ρ, such that $I(G_\rho) \leq 2 \cdot OPT$.

Solving $MTIP_1$. An optimal range assignment ρ_1 for $MTIP_1$ can be found easily. We assign s the range $\rho_1(s) = \max_{p \in P} |sp|$, and for each point $p \in P \setminus \{s\}$, we assign p the range $\rho_1(p) = 0$. Clearly, ρ_1 induces a broadcast tree T_{ρ_1} rooted at s and $I(T_{\rho_1}) = n - 1$, which is optimal.

Solving $MTIP_2$. The algorithm in this case is more involved. Let $G = (P, E)$ be the complete weighted directed graph on P, such that the weight of $(p, q) \in E$ is $w(p, q) = |\{z \in P \setminus \{p\} : |pz| \leq |pq|\}|$. Let $T = (P, E_T)$ be a sink tree rooted at s in G, and let $w(T) = \sum_{(p,q) \in E_T} w(p, q)$ denote its weight. Let ρ_2 be a range assignment to the points of P, such that the induced graph contains a sink tree T_{ρ_2} rooted at s. Observe that if ρ_2 is an optimal range assignment for $MTIP_2$, then the induced graph contains a unique sink tree T_{ρ_2} rooted at s. The following lemma generalizes Lemma 1 and its proof is identical.

Lemma 7. ρ_2 *is an optimal range assignment for* $MTIP_2$ *if and only if* T_{ρ_2} *is a minimum-weight sink tree rooted at* s *in* G.

By Lemma 7, to compute an optimal range assignment ρ_2 for $MTIP_2$, it is sufficient to compute a minimum-weight sink tree rooted at s in G. We compute a minimum-weight sink tree rooted at s in G using Edmonds' algorithm [6] (for finding minimum directed spanning trees in directed graphs).

We construct the (inverse) complete weighted directed graph $G' = (P, E')$, such that the weight of $(p, q) \in E'$ is $w'(p, q) = w(q, p) = |\{z \in P \setminus \{q\} : |qz| \leq |qp|\}|$. Clearly, T' is a broadcast tree rooted at s in G' of weight W if and only if T (the tree obtained by inverting the edges of T') is a sink tree rooted at s in G of weight W. Thus, in order to compute a minimum-weight sink tree rooted at s in G, it suffices to compute a minimum-weight broadcast tree rooted at s in G'. Since a minimum-weight broadcast tree rooted at s in G' can be computed in $O(n^2)$ time [16] using Edmonds' algorithm, we can compute a minimum-weight sink tree rooted at s in G in $O(n^2)$ time. Moreover, since G and G' can be constructed in $O(n^2)$ time, we can solve $MTIP_2$ in $O(n^2)$ time (applying Lemma 7). The following theorem summarizes the result of this section.

Theorem 5. *Let P be a set of n points in the plane. Then, one can compute in $O(n^2)$ time a valid range assignment ρ to the points of P, such that the graph G_ρ induced by ρ is strongly connected and its total interference is at most $2 \cdot OPT$.*

References

1. Agrawal, P., Das, G.K.: Improved interference in wireless sensor networks. In: Hota, C., Srimani, P.K. (eds.) ICDCIT 2013. LNCS, vol. 7753, pp. 92–102. Springer, Heidelberg (2013). https://doi.org/10.1007/978-3-642-36071-8_6
2. Bilò, D., Proietti, G.: On the complexity of minimizing interference in ad-hoc and sensor networks. Theor. Comput. Sci. **402**(1), 43–55 (2008)
3. Brise, Y., Buchin, K., Eversmann, D., Hoffmann, M., Mulzer, W.: Interference minimization in asymmetric sensor networks. In: Gao, J., Efrat, A., Fekete, S.P., Zhang, Y. (eds.) ALGOSENSORS 2014. LNCS, vol. 8847, pp. 136–151. Springer, Heidelberg (2015). https://doi.org/10.1007/978-3-662-46018-4_9
4. Buchin, K.: Minimizing the maximum interference is hard. CoRR, abs/0802.2134 (2008)
5. Burkhart, M., von Rickenbach, P., Wattenhofer, R., Zollinger, A.: Does topology control reduce interference? In: MOBIHOC, pp. 9–19 (2004)
6. Edmonds, J.: Optimum branchings. J. Res. Nat. Bur. Stand. **71B**(4), 233–240 (1967)
7. Estrin, D., Govindan, R., Heidemann, J., Kumar, S.: Next century challenges: scalable coordination in sensor networks. In: MOBICOM, pp. 263–270 (1999)
8. Fussen, M., Wattenhofer, R., Zollinger, A.: Interference arises at the receiver. In: WirelessComBur (2005)
9. Halldórsson, M., Tokuyama, T.: Minimizing interference of a wireless ad-hoc network in a plane. Theor. Comput. Sci. **402**(1), 29–42 (2008)
10. Hubaux, J.-P., Gross, T., Boudec, J.-Y.L., Vetterli, M.: Towards self-organized mobile ad-hoc networks: the terminodes project. IEEE Commun. Mag. **39**(1), 118–124 (2001)
11. Itai, A., Papadimitriou, C.H., Szwarcfiter, J.L.: Hamilton paths in grid graphs. SIAM J. Comput. **11**(4), 676–686 (1982)
12. Lam, N.X., Nguyen, T.N., Huynh, D.T.: Minimum total node interference in wireless sensor networks. In: Zheng, J., Simplot-Ryl, D., Leung, V.C.M. (eds.) ADHOC-NETS 2010. LNICST, vol. 49, pp. 507–523. Springer, Heidelberg (2010). https://doi.org/10.1007/978-3-642-17994-5_35

13. Moaveni-nejad, K., Li, X.Y.: Low-interference topology control for wireless ad hoc networks. Ad Hoc Sens. Wirel. Netw. **1**, 41–64 (2005)
14. Moscibroda, T., Wattenhofer, R.: Minimizing interference in ad hoc and sensor networks. In: DIALM-POMC, Cologne, Germany, pp. 24–33 (2005)
15. Tan, H., Lou, T., Wang, Y., Hua, Q.-S., Lau, F.C.M.: Exact algorithms to minimize interference in wireless sensor networks. Theor. Comput. Sci. **412**(50), 6913–6925 (2011)
16. Tarjan, R.E.: Finding optimum branchings. Networks **7**(1), 25–35 (1977)
17. von Rickenbach, P., Schmid, S., Wattenhofer, R., Zollinger, A.: A robust interference model for wireless ad-hoc networks. In: IPDPS (2005)
18. von Rickenbach, P., Wattenhofer, R., Zollinger, A.: Algorithmic models of interference in wireless ad hoc and sensor networks. IEEE/ACM Trans. Netw. **17**(1), 172–185 (2009)

Distributed Localization of Wireless Sensor Network Using Communication Wheel

Kaustav Bose[1] ⓘ, Manash Kumar Kundu[2](✉) ⓘ, Ranendu Adhikary[1] ⓘ,
and Buddhadeb Sau[1] ⓘ

[1] Department of Mathematics, Jadavpur University, Kolkata, India
{kaustavbose.rs,ranenduadhikary.rs,buddhadeb.sau}@jadavpuruniversity.in
[2] Gayeshpur Government Polytechnic, Kalyani, India
manashkrkundu.rs@jadavpuruniversity.in

Abstract. We study the *network localization problem*, i.e., the problem of determining node positions of a wireless sensor network modeled as a unit disk graph. In an arbitrarily deployed network, positions of all nodes of the network may not be uniquely determined. It is known that even if the network corresponds to a unique solution, no polynomial-time algorithm can solve this problem in the worst case, unless RP = NP. So we are interested in algorithms that efficiently localize the network partially. A widely used technique that can efficiently localize a uniquely localizable portion of the network is *trilateration*: starting from three *anchors* (nodes with known positions), nodes having at least three localized neighbors are sequentially localized. However, the performance of trilateration can substantially differ for different choices of the initial three anchors. In this paper, we propose a distributed localization scheme with a theoretical characterization of nodes that are guaranteed to be localized. In particular, our proposed distributed algorithm starts localization from a *strongly interior node* and provided that the subgraph induced by the strongly interior nodes is connected, it localizes all nodes of the network except some *boundary nodes* and *isolated weakly interior nodes*.

Keywords: Wireless sensor network · Range-based localization · Anchor-free localization · Unit disk graph · Communication wheel · Trilateration

1 Introduction

A *wireless sensor network* (WSN) is a wireless network consisting of a large number of small autonomous sensors spatially distributed in a region to monitor physical or environmental parameters. The sensor nodes are low-cost, low-power, autonomous, multi-functional devices equipped with sensing, processing, and communication capabilities. The knowledge of the physical location of sensor nodes is essential in many applications where the geographical information of the

ⓒ Springer Nature Switzerland AG 2020
C. M. Pinotti et al. (Eds.): ALGOSENSORS 2020, LNCS 12503, pp. 17–31, 2020.
https://doi.org/10.1007/978-3-030-62401-9_2

sensed data is important, for example, event detection, environment and habitat monitoring, target tracking, pervasive medical care, etc. The positional information of the nodes also supports many fundamental location-aware protocols, like geographic routing, topology control, coverage, etc. One method of determining the location of the nodes is by equipping the sensor nodes with Global Positioning System (GPS). However, the installation of GPS on each node of a large scale WSN is expensive and the power consumption of GPS reduces the battery life of the sensor nodes. Moreover, it is not suitable in dense forests, underground or indoor environment where GPS signals are unavailable. Therefore, novel schemes have been proposed to determine the positions of the nodes in a network where only some special nodes called *anchors* are aware of their positions with respect to some global coordinate system (e.g., [1,4,5,7,22,25]). In these schemes, the nodes can measure the distances to their neighboring nodes and using these distance information they try to determine their positions. This process of computing the positions of the nodes is called *range-based network localization* or simply *network localization*.

The network localization problem can be abstracted as the following: given a weighted graph with edge weights equal to the distances between the respective nodes and coordinates of some nodes, called anchors, with respect to some coordinate system, we have to compute the coordinates of all other nodes in that coordinate system. A network, with the given positions of anchors and distances between adjacent nodes, is said to be *uniquely localizable* if all nodes of the network have unique positions consistent with the given data, i.e., there is a unique solution. Obviously, if the given instance corresponds to multiple feasible solutions, the actual positions of the nodes can not be determined. The unique localizability of a network is completely determined by certain combinatorial properties of the network graph and the number of anchors. *Graph rigidity theory* [9,14,15] provides the following necessary and sufficient condition for unique localizability [9]: a network is uniquely localizable if and only if it has at least 3 anchors and the network graph is *globally rigid* (see Sect. 2.3 for definition). However, unless a network is highly dense and regular, it is unlikely that the network is globally rigid. But even if a network is not globally rigid as a whole, a large portion of the network may be globally rigid. For the remaining nodes, there are multiple feasible solutions and hence, their actual positions can not be determined. In the decision version of the problem, also known as GRAPH EMBEDDING or GRAPH REALIZATION problem, given a weighted graph we have to determine whether there is an embedding of the graph in Euclidean plane so that the distances between the adjacent vertices are equal to the edge weights. This problem has been shown to be strongly NP-hard [26]. In [9], it is shown that the problem remains NP-hard even when the graph is globally rigid. However, these results are for general graphs. In a sensor network, only nodes that are within a certain communication range, say r, can measure their relative distances. Therefore, the network can be better modeled as a unit disk graph: two nodes are adjacent if and only if their distance is $\leq r$. In this version of the problem, apart from the coordinates of the anchors and the distances between the adjacent nodes, we have a third type of information: the distances between the non-adjacent nodes are $> r$. The decision version of this problem, also known as UNIT DISK GRAPH RECONSTRUCTION problem, is that given a weighted graph with weights $\leq r$, we have to determine whether there is an embedding of the graph in Euclidean plane so that 1) the distances between the adjacent vertices are equal to the edge weights, and 2) the distance between any pair of non-adjacent nodes is $> r$. It is shown in [2] that UNIT DISK GRAPH RECONSTRUCTION is NP-hard. Therefore, there is no efficient algorithm that solves the localization problem in the worst case unless $P = NP$. It is further shown in [2] that a similar result holds even for instances that have unique reconstructions: there is no efficient randomized algorithm that solves the localization problem even for instances that have unique reconstructions unless $RP = NP$.

Since a real life instance may not have unique solution and even if it has, it is unlikely that there is an efficient algorithm that solves the problem, we are interested in efficient heuristics that partially localize the network. A very popular technique is *trilateration* which efficiently localizes a globally rigid subgraph of the network. It is based on the simple fact that the position of a node can be determined from its distance from three non-collinear nodes with known coordinates. The algorithm starts with at least three anchor nodes and then nodes adjacent to at least three nodes with known coordinates are sequentially localized. It is computationally efficient and very easy to implement in distributed setting, thus widely used in practice. In this paper, we are interested in *anchor-free localization*, i.e., there are no anchor nodes. Since for localization at least three anchor nodes are necessary, in the anchor-free case, some three mutually adjacent nodes of the network fix their coordinates (respecting their mutual distances) in some virtual coordinate system. These three nodes play the role of anchors. However, in case of trilateration, the performance of the algorithm can drastically differ for different choices of the initial three nodes. In this paper, we address this issue and propose a distributed anchor-free localization scheme with a theoretical characterization of nodes that are guaranteed to be localized. In our approach, a node, based on its local information, can categorize itself as either *strongly interior, non-isolated weakly interior, isolated weakly interior* or *boundary*. Provided that the *strong interior*, i.e., the subgraph induced by the set of strongly interior nodes, is connected, one strongly interior node is chosen by a leader election protocol. Our sequential localization algorithm starts from that strongly interior node, and it is theoretically guaranteed to localize all nodes except some boundary and isolated weakly interior nodes. Due to the space restrictions, it is not possible to present a comprehensive survey of the large number of works on localization (e.g., [1,3–5,7,10–13,16,18,22,23,25,27–29,33] etc.) in the literature. The readers are instead referred to the surveys [8,19,21,31] and the references therein.

2   Preliminaries

2.1   Basic Model and Assumptions

The mathematical model of wireless sensor network considered in this work is described in the following:

1. A set of n sensors is arbitrarily deployed in $\mathbb{R}^2$. Each sensor node has computation and wireless communication capabilities.
2. There is a constant $r > 0$, called the *communication range*, such that any two sensor nodes can directly communicate with each other if and only if the distance between them is $\leq r$. This implies that the corresponding communication network can be modeled as a *unit disk graph (UDG)*: two nodes are adjacent if and only if they are at most r distance apart. We assume that this graph is connected. Note that if the graph is not connected, then it is impossible to localize the entire network consistently.
3. The euclidean distance between a pair of sensors can be measured directly and accurately if and only if they are at most r distance apart. Hence, if a sensor node can directly communicate with another node, then it also knows the distance between them.
4. The sensor nodes are assumed to be in general positions, i.e., no three points are collinear. This is not a major assumption, as the nodes of a randomly deployed network are almost always in general positions.

2.2   Definitions and Notations

Let $\mathcal{V}$ be the set of n sensors at positions in $\mathbb{R}^2$. The corresponding wireless sensor network can be modeled as an undirected edge-weighted graph $\mathcal{G} = (\mathcal{V}, \mathcal{E}, w)$, where

1. $\mathcal{V} = \{v_1, \ldots, v_n\}$ is the set of sensors,
2. $(v_i, v_j) \in \mathcal{E}$, i.e., v_i is adjacent to v_j if and only if $d(v_i, v_j) \leq r$, where r is the communication range of the sensors,
3. the edge-weight $w : \mathcal{E} \longrightarrow \mathbb{R}$ is given by $w(v_i, v_j) = d(v_i, v_j)$.

We call $\mathcal{G}$ the *underlying network graph* of the wireless sensor network. As mentioned previously, we assume that the graph $\mathcal{G}$ is connected.

For any $v \in \mathcal{V}$, $\mathcal{Z}(v)$ is the disk $\{x \in \mathbb{R}^2 \mid d(x, v) \leq \frac{r}{2}\}$. We shall say that a node $v \in \mathcal{V}$ *covers* a point $p \in \mathbb{R}^2$, if $p \in \mathcal{Z}(v)$. For $v \in \mathcal{V}$, its *neighborhood* is the set $\mathcal{N}(v) = \{v' \in \mathcal{V} \setminus \{v\} \mid d(v', v) \leq r\} = \{v' \in \mathcal{V} \setminus \{v\} \mid \mathcal{Z}(v') \cap \mathcal{Z}(v) \neq \emptyset\}$.

A sensor node $v \in \mathcal{V}$ is called an *interior node* if for every point $z \in \partial(\mathcal{Z}(v))$, where $\partial(\mathcal{Z}(v))$ is the boundary of $\mathcal{Z}(v)$, we have $z \in \mathcal{Z}(v')$ for some $v' \in \mathcal{V} \setminus \{v\}$. If $v \in \mathcal{V}$ is not an interior node, then it is called a *boundary node*. An interior node $v \in \mathcal{V}$ is said to be *a strongly interior node* if every node in $\mathcal{N}(v)$ is an interior node. An interior node $v \in \mathcal{V}$ is said to be *a weakly interior node* if at least one node in $\mathcal{N}(v)$ is a boundary node. A weakly interior node is said to be *isolated* if it is not adjacent to any strongly interior node. The subgraph of

$\mathcal{G}$ induced by the set of all interior nodes is called the *interior* of $\mathcal{G}$. Similarly, the subgraph of $\mathcal{G}$ induced by the set of all strongly interior nodes is called the *strong interior* of $\mathcal{G}$.

If $v, v' \in \mathcal{V}$ are adjacent to each other, then we shall refer to the intersections of $\partial(\mathcal{Z}(v))$ and $\partial(\mathcal{Z}(v'))$ as their *boundary intersections*. We shall denote these boundary intersections as $CW(v, v')$ and $CCW(v, v')$ according to the following rule: if one traverses from $CCW(v, v')$ to $CW(v, v')$ along $\partial(\mathcal{Z}(v))$ in clockwise direction, it sweeps an angle $< \pi$ about the center v.

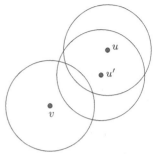

Given a node v, we define a partial order relation $\preceq_v$ on $\mathcal{N}(v)$ as following: for $u, u' \in \mathcal{N}(v)$, $u \preceq_v u'$ if and only if $\mathcal{Z}(u) \cap \partial(\mathcal{Z}(v)) \subseteq \mathcal{Z}(u') \cap \partial(\mathcal{Z}(v))$. See Fig. 1. A node $u \in \mathcal{N}(v)$ is said to be a *maximal* neighbor of v if it is a maximal element in $\mathcal{N}(v)$ with respect to $\preceq_v$, i.e., there is no $u' \in \mathcal{N}(v) \setminus \{u\}$, such that $u \preceq_v u'$.

Fig. 1. u is not a maximal neighbor of v as $u \preceq_v u'$.

2.3   Some Results from Graph Rigidity Theory

In this section, we present some basic definitions and results in graph rigidity. For a detailed exposition on graph rigidity, the readers are referred to [15].

A d-dimensional *framework* is a pair (G, ρ), where $G = (V, E)$ is a connected simple graph and the *realization* ρ is a map $\rho : V \longrightarrow \mathbb{R}^d$. Two frameworks (G, ρ_1) and (G, ρ_2) are said to be *equivalent* if $d(\rho_1(u), \rho_1(v)) = d(\rho_2(u), \rho_2(v))$, for all $(u, v) \in E$. Frameworks (G, ρ_1) and (G, ρ_2) are said to be *congruent* if $d(\rho_1(u), \rho_1(v)) = d(\rho_2(u), \rho_2(v))$, for all $u, v \in V$. In other words, two frameworks are said to be congruent if one can be obtained from another by an isometry of $\mathbb{R}^d$. A realization is *generic* if the vertex coordinates are algebraically independent over rationals. The framework (G, ρ) is *rigid* if $\exists$ an $\varepsilon > 0$ such that if (G, ρ') is equivalent to (G, ρ) and $d(\rho(u), \rho'(u)) < \varepsilon$ for all $u \in V$, then (G, ρ') is congruent to (G, ρ). Intuitively, it means that the framework can not be continuously deformed. (G, ρ) is said to be *globally rigid* if every framework which is equivalent to (G, ρ) is congruent to (G, ρ). It is known [32] that rigidity is a *generic property*, that is, the rigidity of (G, ρ) depends only on the graph G, if (G, ρ) is generic. The set of generic realizations is dense in the realization space and thus almost all realizations of a graph are generic. So, we say that a graph G is rigid in $\mathbb{R}^2$ if every generic realization of G in $\mathbb{R}^2$ is rigid.

Theorem 1 [15]. *A graph G is* globally rigid *in $\mathbb{R}^2$ if and only if either G is a complete graph on at most three vertices or G is 3-connected, rigid and remains rigid even after deleting an edge.*

Theorem 2 [9]. *If a network has at least 3 anchors and the underlying network graph is globally rigid, then it is uniquely localizable.*

The condition of having at least 3 anchors is also necessary for unique localizability in order to rule out the trivial transformations. Since we are considering anchor-free localization, some three mutually adjacent nodes of the network will play the role anchors by fixing their coordinates (respecting their mutual distances) in some virtual coordinate system. The remaining nodes of the network have to find their position according to this coordinate system. It should be noted here that for networks that do not satisfy the condition that two nodes are adjacent if and only if they are within some fixed distance, the condition of having globally rigid underlying network graph is also necessary. In our model, where two nodes are adjacent if and only if the distance between them is at most r, the network can be uniquely localizable even if its underlying network graph is not globally rigid.

3   Construction of a Globally Rigid Subgraph Using Communication Wheels

In this section, we show that if the strong interior is connected, then the network has a globally rigid subgraph containing all strongly interior nodes, and all non-isolated weakly interior nodes. We first present two results that will be frequently used in the paper. They follow from elementary geometric arguments.

Lemma 1. *If u and u' are two distinct neighbors of $v \in \mathcal{V}$ such that $u \preceq_v u'$, then $d(u, v) > d(u', v)$.*

Lemma 2. *For distinct $v, u \in \mathcal{V}$, u is a maximal neighbor of v if and only if v is a maximal neighbor of u.*

A *wheel graph* [30] of order n or simply an *n-wheel*, $n \geq 3$, is a simple graph which consists of a cycle of order n and another vertex called the *hub* such that every vertex of the cycle is connected to the hub. The vertices on the cycle are called the *rim vertices*. An edge joining a rim vertex and the hub is called a *spoke*, and an edge joining two consecutive rim vertices is called a *rim edge*. By Theorem 1, it follows that a wheel is globally rigid.

The most crucial part of our algorithm is the construction of a special structure called the *communication wheel*. The definition of communication wheel closely resembles to that of *sensing wheel* used in [24], where the authors devised a wheel based centralized sequential localization algorithm for a restricted class of sensing covered networks over a convex region.

Communication Wheel: For any interior node $v \in \mathcal{V}$, we define a *communication wheel* of v as a subgraph W of $\mathcal{G}$ such that

1. W is a wheel graph with v as the hub and the rim nodes $\{v_1, \ldots, v_m\}$ being maximal neighbors of v
2. $CCW(v, v_i) \in \mathcal{Z}(v_{i+1})$ and $CW(v, v_i) \in \mathcal{Z}(v_{i-1})$, for $i = 1, \ldots, m$, where v_{m+1} means v_1 and v_0 means v_m.

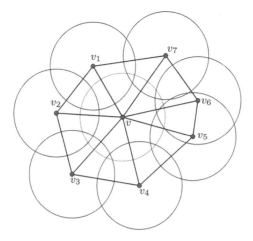

Fig. 2. A communication wheel of v with rim nodes $v_1, v_2, v_3, v_4, v_5, v_6$ and v_7.

For a rim node v' of a communication wheel W of v, we can denote the two neighboring rim nodes of v' as $CCW_W(v')$ and $CW_W(v')$ so that $CCW(v, v') \in \mathcal{Z}(CCW_W(v'))$ and $CW(v, v') \in \mathcal{Z}(CW_W(v'))$. See Fig. 2 for an illustration of communication wheel.

Due to space constraints, the proofs of the following results are omitted. The readers are referred to the extended version [6] of the paper for details. Our localization algorithm presented in Sect. 4 are based on these results.

Theorem 3. *If $v \in \mathcal{V}$ is an interior node and v_1 a maximal neighbor of v, then v has a communication wheel W having v_1 as a rim node.*

Corollary 1. *$v \in \mathcal{V}$ is an interior node if and only if it has a communication wheel.*

Lemma 3. *Let $v \in \mathcal{V}$ be an interior node and W be a communication wheel of v. If $u \in \mathcal{V}$ is a neighbor of v, then u is either a rim node of W or adjacent to some rim node of W.*

Lemma 4. *Let $v \in \mathcal{V}$ be an interior node and W be a communication wheel of v. If $u \in \mathcal{V}$ is a neighbor of v, which is adjacent to exactly one rim node of W, say u', then $u \preceq_v u'$.*

Theorem 4. *If $v \in \mathcal{V}$ is a strongly interior node, then there is a subgraph $\mathcal{H}_v$ of $\mathcal{G}$ containing v such that 1) $\mathcal{H}_v$ contains all neighbors of v, 2) $\mathcal{H}_v$ is globally rigid.*

Theorem 5. *If the strong interior of $\mathcal{G}$ is connected, then $\mathcal{G}$ has a globally rigid subgraph $\mathcal{R}$ which contains 1) all strongly interior nodes, 2) all non-isolated weakly interior nodes.*

Algorithm 1: COMMUNICATIONWHEEL

{ *The node v constructs a communication wheel. If it successfully constructs a communication wheel, it declares itself as an interior node, or otherwise a boundary node.*}

Procedure COMMUNICATIONWHEEL(v)

1    $w = [\,]$;
2    $v.position \longleftarrow$ origin;
3    $w_0 \longleftarrow$ closest neighbor of v ;
4    $w_0.position \longleftarrow$ on the X-axis according to the distance between v and w_0;
5    $w_1 \longleftarrow$ the common neighbor of v and w_0 closest to v that covers a boundary-intersection of v and w_0, such that $w_1 \not\leq_v w_0$;
6   **if** *(no such w_1 is found)* **then**
7      $v.type \longleftarrow$ *boundary*;
8   **break**;
9   **else**
10      $w_1.position \longleftarrow$ one of the two possible positions preserving the distances from v and w_0 such that w_1 has positive Y-coordinate;
11      $CCW(v, w_0) \longleftarrow$ the boundary-intersection of v and w_0 covered w_1
12      $i = 1$;
13   **do**
14        $i + +$;
15   NEXTRIM(v, w_{i-1}, w_{i-2});
16   **while** *($w_i \neq null$ & w_i does not cover $CW(v, w_0)$)*;
17   **if** *($w_i = null$)* **then**
18        $v.type \longleftarrow$ *boundary*;
19   **else**
20        $v.type \longleftarrow$ *interior*;

Algorithm 2: NEXTRIM

{ *Given two consecutive rim nodes w_{i-1} and w_{i-2}, the node v searches for the next rim node.*}

Function NEXTRIM(v, w_{i-1}, w_{i-2})

1    $D \longleftarrow r$;
2   **for** *($u \in \mathcal{N}(w_{i-1}) \cap \mathcal{N}(v)$)* **do**
3   **if** *(distance between u and $v \leq D$)* **then**
4   **if** *(u is adjacent to w_{i-2})* **then**
5   Find the unique position of u using its distances from v, w_{i-1} and w_{i-2};
6   **if** *(u covers $CCW(v, w_{i-1})$ and $CCW(v, u)$ is not covered by w_{i-1})* **then**
7            $w_i \longleftarrow u$;
8            $w_i.position \longleftarrow$ the unique position of u determined using its distances from v, w_{i-1} and w_{i-2};
9            $D \longleftarrow$ the distance between u and v;
10   **else**
11   Find two possible positions of u using its distances from v and w_{i-1};
12   **if** *(for any of the two possible positions, u covers $CCW(v, w_{i-1})$ and $CCW(v, u)$ is not covered by w_{i-1})* **then**
13            $w_i \longleftarrow u$;
14            $w_i.position \longleftarrow$ the one of the two possible positions of u for which it covers $CCW(v, w_{i-1})$;
15            $D \longleftarrow$ the distance between u and v;

---

4   The Localization Algorithm

In this section, we present our localization algorithm. The algorithm leads to the main result of the paper stated in Theorem 6.

Theorem 6. *If the strong interior of the network is connected then there is an efficient anchor-free localization algorithm that localizes all nodes of the network except some boundary nodes and isolated weakly interior nodes.*

In the beginning, each node messages its neighbor list along their distances form itself to all its neighbors. Therefore, every node $u \in \mathcal{V}$ knows the neighbors of all its neighbors and also if v is a neighbor of u and w is a neighbor of v, then u knows $d(v, w)$ as well. The three main stages of our algorithm are 1) construction of communication wheel, 2) leader election, and 3) propagation. They are discussed in detail in the following subsections.

4.1 Construction of Communication Wheel

Each sensor node v starts off computations by executing the COMMUNICATION-WHEEL algorithm. The algorithm finds if the node is interior or boundary, and also constructs a communication wheel if it is interior. A pseudocode description of the procedure is presented in Algorithm 1. Due to space constraints, we only give a brief description of the procedure. For a detailed proof of correctness and further details, the readers are referred to [6]. To construct a communication wheel of a node v, if it exists, we first need to find a maximal neighbor. In view of Lemma 1, the closest neighbor of a node is guaranteed to be a maximal neighbor. After finding the closest neighbor, call it w_0, v assigns its position on the X-axis and itself at the origin. Then it searches for a common neighbor of v and w_0 that covers a boundary-intersection of v and w_0. If no such node is found, then v is a boundary node. If more than one of such nodes are found, the one closest to v is to be taken. Let us call this node w_1. Now the distance of w_1 from v and w_0 is known. From this data, there are two possible coordinates for w_1, one with positive Y-coordinate and one with negative Y-coordinate. Choose the position for w_1 so that its Y-coordinate is positive. In other words, v sets its local coordinate system in such a way that w_1 gets positive Y-coordinate. Also set the boundary-intersection of v and w_0 that is covered by w_1 as $CCW(v, w_0)$. In other words v sets 'counterclockwise' to be the direction in which if one rotates a ray, from the origin towards the positive direction of the X-axis, by $\frac{\pi}{2}$, it coincides with the positive direction of the Y-axis. While discussing Algorithm 1, 'counterclockwise' and 'clockwise' will always be with respect to the local coordinate system of node executing the algorithm. Note that since w_0 is a maximal neighbor of v, $CW(v, w_0)$ is not covered by w_1. After fixing the positions of w_0 and w_1, the subroutine NEXTRIM is recursively called to find the subsequent rim nodes of the communication wheel. Given two consecutive rim nodes w_{i-1} and w_{i-2}, having positions fixed, NEXTRIM(v, w_{i-1}, w_{i-2}) finds the next rim node w_i. The program terminates when either NEXTRIM reports a failure or returns a node that covers $CW(v, w_0)$. A pseudocode description of the NEXTRIM function is presented in Algorithm 2.

4.2 Leader Election

Once a node identifies itself as interior or boundary, it announces the result to all its neighbors. Hence, every node can determine if it is a strongly interior node or not. Since the strong interior is connected and the nodes have unique id's, the strongly interior nodes can elect a leader among themselves by executing a leader election protocol [20].

4.3   Propagation

Starting from the leader, different nodes will gradually get localized via message passing. The correctness of the process will follow from the discussions in this subsection and the proofs of Theorem 4 and 5. There are five types of messages that a sensor node can send to another node:

1. *"I am at ..."*
2. *"You are at ..."*
3. *"Construct wheel with me at ... and v at ..."*
4. *"Construct wheel with me at ..., you at ..., v at ... and find u"*
5. *"u is at ..."*.

The nodes of the network will be localized in the local coordinate system of the leader v_l set during its execution of Algorithm 1. Henceforth, this coordinate system will be referred to as the *global coordinate system*. So the leader first localizes itself by setting its coordinates to $(0,0)$. Any non-leader node u is localized by either receiving a *"You are at ..."* message or receiving at least three *"I am at ..."* messages. In the first case, some node has calculated the coordinates of u and has sent it to u. In the second case, u receives the coordinates of at least three neighbors and therefore, can calculate its own coordinates. When a node is localized, it announces its coordinates to all its neighbors. After setting its coordinates to $(0,0)$ and v_l initiates the localization of $\mathcal{H}_{v_l}$ (see Theorem 4). It first announces its coordinates to all its neighbors via the message *"I am at $(0,0)$"*. During the construction of its communication wheel, v_l had assigned coordinates to the rim nodes. So v_l sends these coordinates to the corresponding rim nodes via the message *"You are at ..."*. Let us denote the communication wheel of v_l as $\mathcal{W}(v_l)$ and the set of all rim nodes as $\mathcal{R}im(v_l)$. When a rim node receives this message, it sets its coordinates accordingly and announces it to all its neighbors via the message *"I am at ..."*. Notice that a rim node does not need to send this message to v_l. There are multiple such modifications that can be made to reduce the number of messages used in the algorithm. But we do not mention them for simplicity of the description. Now if a neighbor of v_l is adjacent to at least two nodes of $\mathcal{R}im(v_l)$, then it can localize itself, since it will receive *"I am at ..."* messages from at least three nodes, i.e., one from v_l and at least two from $\mathcal{R}im(v_l)$. But if a neighbor of v_l is adjacent to only one vertex from $\mathcal{R}im(v_l)$, then it may not be localized. To resolve this, v_l computes $|\mathcal{N}(u) \cap \mathcal{R}im(v_l)|$ for all $u \in \mathcal{N}(v_l)$. If it finds a $u \in \mathcal{N}(v_l)$ with $\mathcal{N}(u) \cap \mathcal{R}im(v_l) = \{v_i\}$, it sends the message *"Construct wheel with me at ... and v_{i+1} at ..."* to v_i, where v_{i+1} is a neighboring rim node of v_i in $\mathcal{W}(v_l)$. When v_i receives this message from v_l, it does the following. Since v_l is a strongly interior node, v_i must be an interior node. Therefore, v_i has already computed the communication wheel $\mathcal{W}(v_i)$ and coordinates of each of its nodes with respect to its local coordinate system. Since v_l is a maximal neighbor of v_i (by Lemma 2), it is adjacent to at least two nodes of $\mathcal{R}im(v_i)$ (by Lemma 4). Hence, v_i can compute the coordinates of v_l with respect to its local coordinate system. Let $\mathcal{W}'$ be the globally rigid graph $v_l \cup \mathcal{W}(v_i)$. Now, from the proof of Theorem 4 (see [6]), it is known that v_{i+1} is adjacent to at least three nodes of $\mathcal{W}'$. Hence, v_i can also compute the coordinates of v_{i+1} with respect to its local coordinate system. So, v_i has the coordinates of all nodes of $\mathcal{W}'' = v_{i+1} \cup \mathcal{W}'$ with respect to its local coordinate system. Now, v_i will compute the positions of all nodes of $\mathcal{W}''$ with respect to the global coordinate system set by v_l. Let us call them the *true positions* of the nodes. Note that v_i knows the true positions of at least three nodes of $\mathcal{W}''$, namely, itself, v_l, and v_{i+1}. With this information, v_i can determine the formula that transforms its local coordinate system to the global coordinate system. Hence, v_i computes the true positions of all nodes in $\mathcal{W}''$ and informs them via "*You are at ...*" messages. Hence, all nodes in $\mathcal{W}''$ will be localized and will announce their locations to all their neighbors. Since u is adjacent to at least three nodes in $\mathcal{W}''$, it will also get localized. Therefore, we see that every neighbor of v_l eventually gets localized.

The localization propagates as each strongly interior node localizes its neighbors. However, a strongly interior node v can compute the positions of its neighbors only with respect to its local coordinate system. Hence, in order to compute the true positions (i.e., to perform coordinate transformation), it needs to know its true position and that of at least two neighbors. Hence, when a localized strongly interior node v receives at least two "*I am at ...*" messages, it starts to localize its neighbors in the following way. Let u be a neighbor of v. If u is adjacent at least two nodes of $\mathcal{R}im(v)$, then v can compute the position of u in terms of its local coordinate system. Otherwise, if $\mathcal{N}(u) \cap \mathcal{R}im(v) = \{v_i\}$, then v sends the message "*Construct wheel with me at ..., you at ..., v_{i+1} at ... and find u*" to v_i, where v_{i+1} is a neighboring rim node to v_i in $\mathcal{W}(v)$, and positions mentioned in the message are given in local coordinates of v. Again, as v_i is a maximal neighbor of v, by Lemma 2 and 4, v is either in $\mathcal{W}(v_i)$ or adjacent to at least three nodes in $\mathcal{W}(v_i)$. Also, v_{i+1} is either in $\mathcal{W}' = \mathcal{W}(v_i) \cup v$ or adjacent to at least three nodes in $\mathcal{W}'$. Hence, from the data received from v, v_i can compute the positions of all the nodes in $\mathcal{W}'' = \mathcal{W}' \cup v_{i+1}$ in terms of the local coordinates of v. Since u is either in $\mathcal{W}''$ or adjacent to at least three nodes in $\mathcal{W}''$, v_i can compute the position of u in terms of the local coordinate system of v, and then sends the information back to v via the message "*u is at ...*". Hence, v computes the positions of all its neighbors in its local coordinate system. So, v now knows the positions of three nodes (namely, itself and the two nodes from which it has received "*I am at ...*" message) with respect to both its local coordinate system and the global coordinate system set by the leader. Hence, v can find the formula that transformations its local coordinate system to the global coordinate system. Hence, v computes the true positions of all its neighbors and then informs them via "*You are at ...*" messages. However, it still remains to prove that every non-leader localized strongly interior node v always receives at least two "*I am at ...*" messages, that triggers the propagation. Since v is localized, either it has received three "*I am at ...*" messages or one "*You are at* ..." message. If it is the first case, then we are done. In the later case, v receives the "*You are at* ..." message from a localized interior node, say v'. Then by Lemma 3, v is either in the communication wheel of v', or adjacent to at least one of its rim nodes. Observe that v' is localized and has also localized all its rim nodes. So, v will get least two "*I am at* ..." messages, as all localized nodes announce their positions. Therefore, all strongly interior and non-isolated weakly interior nodes get localized, while some boundary nodes and isolated weakly interior nodes may not get localized. Therefore, all strongly interior and non-isolated weakly interior nodes get localized. Also, if a localized weakly interior node receives "*I am at* ..." messages from at least two nodes, it can localize all the rim nodes and also neighbors that are adjacent to at least two rim nodes.

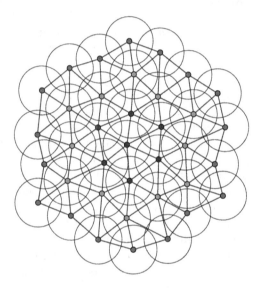

Fig. 3. The red, green and blue nodes are respectively boundary, weakly interior and strongly interior nodes. It is easy to see that trilateration does not progress beyond the base step for any choice of the initial triangle. However, our algorithm always localizes all the nodes of the network from any initial strongly interior node. This structure can be extended arbitrarily. Hence for any $n \in \mathbb{N}$, we have a network of size $\geq n$, such that 1) it is always entirely localized by our algorithm, 2) but trilateration fails to localize more than 3 nodes for any choice of the initial triangle. (Color figure online)

5   Concluding Remarks

Our algorithm works under the condition that the strong interior of the network is connected. Relaxing this condition, it would be interesting to characterize the conditions under which localization starting from different components of the strong interior can be stitched together. It would be also interesting to study impact noisy distance measurement on our algorithm. Our algorithm also works under the strong assumption of uniform communication range. An important direction of future research would be to see if our approach can be extend to networks with sensors having irregular communication range, e.g., quasi unit disk networks [17]. Another problem is to compare the class of networks that are fully localized by our algorithm to those that are fully localized by trilateration. The example in Fig. 3 shows a class of network in which trilateration does not progress beyond the base step for any choice of the initial triangle, but our algorithm always localizes all the nodes from any initial strongly interior node.

Acknowledgements. The first author is supported by NBHM, DAE, Govt. of India and the third author is supported by CSIR, Govt. of India. This work was done when the second author was at Jadavpur University, Kolkata, India, supported by UGC, Govt. of India. We would like to thank the anonymous reviewers for their valuable comments which helped us to improve the quality and presentation of the paper.

References

1. Albowicz, J., Chen, A., Zhang, L.: Recursive position estimation in sensor networks. In: 9th International Conference on Network Protocols (ICNP 2001), Riverside, CA, USA, 11–14 November 2001, pp. 35–43. IEEE Computer Society (2001). https://doi.org/10.1109/ICNP.2001.992758
2. Aspnes, J., Goldenberg, D., Yang, Y.R.: On the computational complexity of sensor network localization. In: Nikoletseas, S.E., Rolim, J.D.P. (eds.) ALGOSENSORS 2004. LNCS, vol. 3121, pp. 32–44. Springer, Heidelberg (2004). https://doi.org/10.1007/978-3-540-27820-7_5
3. Baggio, A., Langendoen, K.: Monte Carlo localization for mobile wireless sensor networks. Ad Hoc Netw. **6**(5), 718–733 (2008). https://doi.org/10.1016/j.adhoc.2007.06.004
4. Biswas, P., Liang, T.-C., Wang, T.-C., Ye, Y.: Semidefinite programming based algorithms for sensor network localization. ACM Trans. Sens. Netw. **2**(2), 188–220 (2006). https://doi.org/10.1145/1149283.1149286
5. Biswas, P., Toh, K.-C., Ye, Y.: A distributed SDP approach for large-scale noisy anchor-free graph realization with applications to molecular conformation. SIAM J. Sci. Comput. **30**(3), 1251–1277 (2008). https://doi.org/10.1137/05062754X
6. Bose, K., Kundu, M.K., Adhikary, R., Sau, B.: Distributed localization of wireless sensor network using communication wheel. CoRR, abs/2008.00739 (2020). https://arxiv.org/abs/2008.00739
7. Bulusu, N., Heidemann, J.S., Estrin, D.: GPS-less low-cost outdoor localization for very small devices. IEEE Wirel. Commun. **7**(5), 28–34 (2000). https://doi.org/10.1109/98.878533
8. Chowdhury, T.J.S., Elkin, C., Devabhaktuni, V., Rawat, D.B., Oluoch, J.: Advances on localization techniques for wireless sensor networks: a survey. Comput. Netw. **110**, 284–305 (2016). https://doi.org/10.1016/j.comnet.2016.10.006
9. Eren, T., et al.: Rigidity, computation, and randomization in network localization. In: Proceedings IEEE INFOCOM 2004, the 23rd Annual Joint Conference of the IEEE Computer and Communications Societies, Hong Kong, China, 7–11 March 2004, pp. 2673–2684. IEEE (2004). https://doi.org/10.1109/INFCOM.2004.1354686

10. Fang, J., Cao, M., Morse, A.S., Anderson, B.D.O.: Sequential localization of sensor networks. SIAM J. Control. Optim. **48**(1), 321–350 (2009). https://doi.org/10. 1137/070679144
11. Goldenberg, D.K., et al.: Localization in sparse networks using sweeps. In: Gerla, M., Petrioli, C., Ramjee, R. (eds.) Proceedings of the 12th Annual International Conference on Mobile Computing and Networking, MOBICOM 2006, Los Angeles, CA, USA, 23–29 September 2006, pp. 110–121. ACM (2006). https://doi.org/10. 1145/1161089.1161103
12. Goldenberg, D.K., et al.: Network localization in partially localizable networks. In: INFOCOM 2005. 24th Annual Joint Conference of the IEEE Computer and Communications Societies, Miami, FL, USA, 13–17 March 2005, pp. 313–326. IEEE (2005). https://doi.org/10.1109/INFCOM.2005.1497902
13. He, T., Huang, C., Blum, B.M., Stankovic, J.A., Abdelzaher, T.: Range-free localization schemes for large scale sensor networks. In: Johnson, D.B., Joseph, A.D., Vaidya, N.H. (eds.) Proceedings of the Ninth Annual International Conference on Mobile Computing and Networking, MOBICOM 2003, San Diego, CA, USA, 14–19 September 2003, pp. 81–95. ACM (2003). https://doi.org/10.1145/938985.938995
14. Hendrickson, B.: Conditions for unique graph realizations. SIAM J. Comput. **21**(1), 65–84 (1992). https://doi.org/10.1137/0221008
15. Jackson, B., Jordán, T.: Connected rigidity matroids and unique realizations of graphs. J. Comb. Theory Ser. B **94**(1), 1–29 (2005). https://doi.org/10.1016/j. jctb.2004.11.002
16. Ji, X.: Sensor positioning in wireless ad-hoc sensor networks with multidimensional scaling. In: Proceedings IEEE INFOCOM 2004, the 23rd Annual Joint Conference of the IEEE Computer and Communications Societies, Hong Kong, China, 7–11 March 2004, pp. 2652–2661. IEEE (2004). https://doi.org/10.1109/INFCOM.2004. 1354684
17. Kuhn, F., Wattenhofer, R., Zollinger, A.: Ad hoc networks beyond unit disk graphs. Wirel. Netw. **14**(5), 715–729 (2008). https://doi.org/10.1007/s11276-007-0045-6
18. Lederer, S., Wang, Y., Gao, J.: Connectivity-based localization of large-scale sensor networks with complex shape. ACM Trans. Sens. Netw. **5**(4), 31:1–31:32 (2009). https://doi.org/10.1145/1614379.1614383
19. Liu, Y., Yang, Z., Wang, X., Jian, L.: Location, localization, and localizability. J. Comput. Sci. Technol. **25**(2), 274–297 (2010). https://doi.org/10.1007/s11390-010-9324-2
20. Lynch, N.A.: Distributed Algorithms. Elsevier, Amsterdam (1996)
21. Mao, G., Fidan, B., Anderson, B.D.O.: Wireless sensor network localization techniques. Comput. Netw. **51**(10), 2529–2553 (2007). https://doi.org/10.1016/ j.comnet.2006.11.018
22. Moore, D.C., Leonard, J.J., Rus, D., Teller, S.J.: Robust distributed network localization with noisy range measurements. In: Stankovic, J.A., Arora, A., Govindan, R (eds.) Proceedings of the 2nd International Conference on Embedded Networked Sensor Systems, SenSys 2004, Baltimore, MD, USA, 3–5 November 2004, pp. 50–61. ACM (2004). https://doi.org/10.1145/1031495.1031502
23. Peng, R., Sichitiu, M.L.: Angle of arrival localization for wireless sensor networks. In: Proceedings of the Third Annual IEEE Communications Society Conference on Sensor, Mesh and Ad Hoc Communications and Networks, SECON 2006, Reston, VA, USA, 25–28 September 2006, pp. 374–382. IEEE (2006). https://doi.org/10. 1109/SAHCN.2006.288442

24. Sau, B., Mukhopadhyaya, K.: Length-based anchor-free localization in a fully covered sensor network. In: 2009 First International Communication Systems and Networks and Workshops, pp. 1–10, January 2009. https://doi.org/10.1109/COMSNETS.2009.4808851

25. Savvides, A., Han, C.C., Strivastava, M.B.: Dynamic fine-grained localization in ad-hoc networks of sensors. In: Rose, C. (ed.) MOBICOM 2001, Proceedings of the Seventh Annual International Conference on Mobile Computing and Networking, Rome, Italy, 16–21 July 2001, pp. 166–179. ACM (2001). https://doi.org/10.1145/381677.381693

26. Saxe, J.B.: Embeddability of weighted graphs in k-space is strongly NP-hard. In: Proceedings of 17th Allerton Conference in Communications, Control and Computing, Monticello, IL, pp. 480–489 (1979)

27. Shang, Y., Ruml, W.: Improved MDS-based localization. In: Proceedings IEEE INFOCOM 2004, The 23rd Annual Joint Conference of the IEEE Computer and Communications Societies, Hong Kong, China, 7–11 March 2004, pp. 2640–2651. IEEE (2004). https://doi.org/10.1109/INFCOM.2004.1354683

28. Shang, Y., Ruml, W., Zhang, Y., Fromherz, M.P.: Localization from mere connectivity. In: Proceedings of the 4th ACM International Symposium on Mobile Ad Hoc Networking and Computing, MobiHoc 2003, Annapolis, Maryland, USA, 1–3 June 2003, pp. 201–212. ACM (2003). https://doi.org/10.1145/778415.778439

29. Sorbelli, F.B., Das, S.K., Pinotti, C.M., Silvestri, S.: Range based algorithms for precise localization of terrestrial objects using a drone. Pervasive Mob. Comput. **48**, 20–42 (2018). https://doi.org/10.1016/j.pmcj.2018.05.007

30. Tutte, W.T.: Graph Theory. Cambridge Mathematical Library. Cambridge University Press, Cambridge (2001)

31. Wang, J., Ghosh, R.K., Das, S.K.: A survey on sensor localization. J. Control Theory Appl. **8**(1), 2–11 (2010). https://doi.org/10.1007/s11768-010-9187-7

32. Whiteley, W.: Some matroids from discrete applied geometry. Contemp. Math. **197**, 171–312 (1996)

33. Yang, Z., Liu, Y., Li, X.-Y.: Beyond trilateration: on the localizability of wireless ad hoc networks. IEEE/ACM Trans. Netw. **18**(6), 1806–1814 (2010). https://doi.org/10.1109/TNET.2010.2049578

Covering Users by a Connected Swarm Efficiently

Kiril Danilchenko[1(✉)], Michael Segal[1], and Zeev Nutov[2]

[1] School of Electrical and Computer Engineering,
Ben-Gurion University of the Negev, Beersheba, Israel
{kirild,segal}@bgu.ac.il
[2] Open University of Israel, Ra'anana, Israel
nutov@openu.ac.il

Abstract. In this paper we study covering problems that arise in wireless networks with Unmanned Aerial Vehicles (UAVs) swarms. In the general setting we want to place a set of UAVs that should cover a given set of planar users under some constraints and we want to maintain the solution efficiently in a static and dynamic fashion. Specifically, for a set S of n non-negative weighted points in the plane, we consider a set P of m disks (or squares) of radius R_{COV} where the goal is to place (and maintain under dynamic updates) their location such that the sum of the weights of the points in S covered by disks from P is maximized. In the connected version, we also require that the graph imposed on P should be connected. Moreover, for the static connected version we improve the results from [1] and we obtain a constant factor approximation algorithm. In order to solve our problem under various requirements, we use a variety of techniques including dynamic grid, a reduction to Budgeted Subset Steiner Connected Dominating Set problem, tree partition, and others. We present several simple data structures that maintain an $O(1)$-approximate solution efficiently, under insertions and deletions of points to/from S where each update operation can be performed in logarithmic time.

Keywords: Budgeted covering · Approximation algorithm · Dynamic data structure · Tree partition

1 Introduction

Unmanned aerial vehicles (UAVs or drones) have been the subject of concerted research over the past few years. UAV swarms have many potential applications in wireless communication systems [16]. The performance of the UAV-based network heavily depends on the deployment of UAVs. The researchers have focused on deployment strategies based on minimizing the number of UAVs required to

K. Danilchenko and M. Segal—This research has been supported by the grant from Pazy Foundation.

C. M. Pinotti et al. (Eds.): ALGOSENSORS 2020, LNCS 12503, pp. 32–44, 2020.
https://doi.org/10.1007/978-3-030-62401-9_3

provide wireless coverage to all ground users. Opposite to most existing work where the number of UAVs is assumed to be at least as a number of ground users [10–12], in this paper we consider a more realistic scenario. We focus on the situation where the number of UAVs is given, and this number is significantly smaller than the number of ground users. This assumption is reasonable in emergency cases or battlefields where the number of ground users (for example, soldiers or firefighters) is more than the number of UAVs. As a result, we face a problem that not all users will necessarily be covered. Additionally, we assume that each ground user has a *rank* that reflects the importance of user's coverage. The number, rank, and location of ground users may be changed from time to time. Thus, we are facing the most crucial question "Who should be covered and who should not, at any point of time?" For a given particular time snapshot, this problem is known to be NP-hard [2]. Additionally, we deal with two cases of connectivity between the drones: third party (e.g., satellite) that provides connectivity (see Fig. 1a) or drones provide connectivity among themselves (see Fig. 1b). In this paper, we assume that all UAVs fly at the same, fixed altitude, and have same covering radius (R_{COV}) and communication radius (R_{COM}).

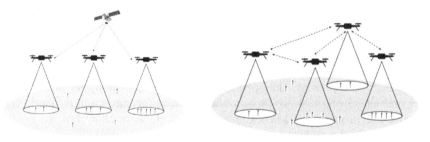

(a) A third party (e.g., satellite) that provides connectivity.

(b) The drones provide connectivity among themselves.

Fig. 1. Coverage of ground users by UAVs.

Formally, we consider a set S of n points distributed in the plane, where each point $s_i \in S, i = 1, \ldots, n$, has a positive weight $w(s_i)$. Also consider a set P of m objects (normally, L_2 or L_∞ disks) of radius R_{COV}, where set C contains the centers of these objects. We start with covering problems, where the connectivity is provided by the third party. Denote this model as *Maximum Weight Covering With Connectivity (MWCC)*.

Static-max(S,m)($max_*(S, m)$): Given a set S, place the disks from the set P such that the total weight of points from the set S covered by the disks is maximized.

Dynamic-max(S,m)($Dmax_*(S, m)$): Given a set S, maintain the disks from the set P such that the sum of the weights of the points in S covered by the disks from P is maximized under insertions and deletions of points to/from S.

Here "$*$" symbolizes which covering shape is in use ($\square$ stands for square and $\bigcirc$ stands for disk).

In this paper we present a first non-trivial algorithm for $Dmax_*(S, m)$ which achieves $1/4$ approximation solution in $O(\log n)$ time. In order to solve $Dmax_*(S, m)$ we use the solution for $max_*(S, m)$ and maintain it under insertion and deletion to/from set S. For the $max_*(S, m)$ problem there is known a PTAS in the literature [5,9].

Next, we continue with the covering problems where UAVs provide connectivity between themselves. Denote this model as *Maximum Weight Covering With Internal Connectivity (MWCIC)*.

Connected max(S,m)($Cmax_*(S, m)$): Given a set S and a parameter R_{COM}, place the disks from the set P such that:

1. The total weight of points from the set S covered by the disks is maximized.
2. The undirected graph $G = (C, E)$ imposed on P should be connected, where an edge $(u, v) \in E$ if $d(u, v) \le R_{COM}$, for $d(u, v)$ being the L_∞ (L_2) distance between the centers $v, u \in C$.

Similarly to the above, the **Connected-Dynamic max(S,m)**($CDmax_*(S, m)$) problem aims to maintain the disks from P under dynamic updates of S.

We show how to obtain an $O(1)$-approximate solution to the optimal solution for $Cmax_*(S, m)$. By deteriorating the number of drones (by factor of $\sqrt{m}$), we were able to maintain $O(1)$ approximation dynamically.

The rest of the paper is organized as follows. Next section reviews the related work. Section 3 presents the approach for calculating the upper bound value of our problem. In Sect. 3, we present the solutions for static and dynamic version of covering problem for MWCC model. In Sect. 4 we show how to deal with the static and dynamic version of covering problems for MWCIC model. Finally, Sect. 5 concludes the paper and discusses the future work.

2   Related Work

The paper [10] provides wireless coverage for a group of ground terminals, ensuring that each ground terminal is within the communication range of at least one UAV with minimal number of UAVs. The authors presented a polynomial-time algorithm with successive UAVs placement, where the UAVs are placed sequentially starting from the area perimeter of the uncovered ground terminals along a spiral path towards the center, until all ground terminals are covered. The paper [11] considers the optimal deployment of UAVs, such that the total coverage area is maximized. The UAVs were assumed to be equipped with directional antennas. The authors of [12] and [18] have shown the drones deployments in which a given set of objects should be covered by the sensing range of at least one drone. Each object should be monitored for a certain amount of time. The authors consider minimizing the number of drones to cover the target and the total energy consumption of the drones. A challenging problem of how to deploy multiple

UAVs for on-demand coverage while at the same time maintaining the connectivity among UAVs was investigated in [17]. The paper [14] utilizes autonomous mobile base stations (MBSs) to maintain network connectivity while minimizing the number of MBNs that are deployed. They [14] formulate the problem of reducing the number of MBSs and refer to it as the Connected Disk Cover (CDC) problem. They show that it can be decomposed into the Geometric Disk Cover (GDC) problem and the Steiner Tree Problem with Minimum Number of Steiner Points (STP-MSP). They proved that if these subproblems can be solved separately by γ-approximation and δ-approximation algorithms, respectively, then the approximation ratio of the joint solution is $\gamma + \delta$. The main difference from our result is that they tried to cover all users by minimal number of drones while we are interested to cover the maximum weight set users by given number of drones.

Our problem under the $MWCC$ model with m disks was given some attention in the past. The authors of [2] presented the problem of covering the maximum number of points in the point set S with m unit disks, without the demand for disks connectivity. They gave a $(1 - \varepsilon)$-approximation algorithm with time complexity $O(n\varepsilon^{-4m+4}) \log^{2m-1}(\frac{1}{\varepsilon})$. The problem to place m rectangles such that the sum of the weights of the points in P covered by these rectangles is maximized is considered in [9]. For any fixed $\varepsilon > 0$, the authors present efficient approximation schemes that can find a $(1 - \varepsilon)$-approximation to the optimal solution in $O(\frac{n}{\varepsilon} \log(\frac{1}{\varepsilon}) + m(\frac{1}{\varepsilon})^{O(\min(\sqrt{m}, \frac{1}{\varepsilon}))})$ runtime. In [5] the authors presented a PTAS for a more general case different covering shapes (disks, polygons with $O(1)$ edges), running in $O(n\frac{1}{\varepsilon}^{O(1)} + \frac{m}{\varepsilon} \log m + m(\frac{1}{\varepsilon})^{O(\min(m, \frac{1}{\varepsilon}))})$ time.

The authors of [1] consider the $Cmax_*(S, m)$ problem under $MWCIC$. They gave $O(\frac{1}{\sqrt{m}})$ with time complexity $O(\beta^2 mn \log n)$, where $\beta \cdot R_{COM} = d_{max}$ and d_{max} be the largest L_∞ distance defined by a pair of points in S. The authors of [13] solve the relevant problem to place two disks in the plane to ensure both maximum covering and full connectivity. By providing two algorithms having $O(n^4)$ and $O(n^3 \log n)$ time complexity, respectively. Another related problem is presented in [4,8]. In these works, the authors formulate the following problem: given a set of n discs in the plane, select a subset of k disks that maximize the area of their union, under the constrain that this union is connected. However, in our work, we want to place the disks such that maximize the weight of the points they cover. To the best of our knowledge, $CDmax_*(S, m)$ problem under $MWCIC$ model was not considered before.

3 MWCC Model

In this section we consider our problem under the $MWCC$ model.

3.1 Approximate Solution for $max_*(S, m)$

We note that our primary goal is to find a dynamic solution (under insertions/deletions of weighted points from S). Unfortunately, it is impossible to make dynamic solutions based on the techniques presented in [5,9] for achieving PTAS. Since after each insertion/deletion, we have to recalculate the provided solution. Therefore, we first present the solution for the static case and then show how to make it work in the dynamic setting. Now, we focus on the square case $max_\square(S, m)$. Denote by G_r the square grid with cell size r such that the vertical and the horizontal lines are defined as follows:

$$G_r = \left\{(x, y) \in \mathbb{R}^2 \mid x = k \cdot r, k \in \mathbb{Z}\right\} \bigcup \left\{(x, y) \in \mathbb{R}^2 \mid y = k \cdot r, k \in \mathbb{Z}\right\}$$

Given a point $s_i \in S$ we call the integer pair $\left(\left\lfloor \frac{x}{r} \right\rfloor, \left\lfloor \frac{y}{r} \right\rfloor\right)$ as *cell index* (the cell in which s_i is located). Each nonempty cell in G_r will be identified by *index*. We calculate the *cell index* (a_i, b_i) for each point $s_i \in S$ and use (a_i, b_i) to find *index* $\pi(a_i, b_i)$. The *index* $\pi(a_i, b_i)$ is a result of Cantor pair function [15], where the *cell index* (a_i, b_i) is input of this function. Cantor pairing function is a recursive pairing function $\pi : \mathbb{N} \times \mathbb{N} \to \mathbb{N}$ defined by $\pi(x, y) = \frac{(x+y+1)(x+y)}{2} + y$.

Next, we present our heuristic solution of the $max_\square(S, m)$ and $Rmax_\square(S, m)$. Denote this solution as $Hmax_\square(S, m)$. We divide the area that contains the set S into grid with cell size $r = 2R_{COV}$. We place the set of m squares of P in the cells having maximal weight, such that the squares fit the cells of G_r.

Algorithm 1. $Hmax_*(S, m)$

Input: G_r, m

Output: Set P covering m cells having largest weight

1 Sort the weights of G_r cells in non decreasing order.

2 Place the set P in the m cells having largest weight.

Lemma 1. *The $Hmax_*(S, m)$ algorithm provides $1/4$-approximate solution to $max_\square(S, m)$ and $1/7$-approximate solution to $max_\bigcirc(S, m)$.*

Proof. Define the optimal solution of $max_\square(S, m)$ by OPT and the solution that is achieved by $Hmax_\square(S, m)$ as SOL. Additionally, denote the total weight of points covered by OPT and SOL as $W(OPT)$ and $W(SOL)$, respectively. Each of the squares in OPT may overlap with at most 4 cells from G_r. In this case grid G_r divides each square into four rectangles. In Fig. 2a grid G_r divides one of the squares from OPT, R_o into four rectangles: o_1, o_2, o_3 and o_4. As already mentioned, each square from OPT is divided by at most four rectangles. Therefore the number of cells in G_r overlapping with the squares from OPT is $4\,m$. Define the set of sorted cells that overlap with OPT, as Q, and the weight of this set as $W(Q)$. Additionally, define the set of m cells having maximal weight from set Q as Q_m and the weight of this set as $W(Q_m)$. Obviously, the weight of $W(Q_m) \geq \frac{W(Q)}{4}$. It is easy to see that the equality holds only in the case of uniform distribution of weight among the cells from Q; in any other case, the inequality holds. On the other side, the weight of SOL is greater than or equal to the weight of any other set of cells from G_r with the same amount of cells. Therefore $W(SOL) \geq W(Q_m) \geq \frac{W(Q)}{4}$.

Now, we focus on the case of disks. We change the size of cell in grid G_r to be $r = \sqrt{2}R_{COV}$. All the rest remain the same. The $Hmax_\circ(S, m)$ algorithm provides 1/7-approximate solution to $max_\circ(S, m)$. The proof is similar to the proof of square case with a slight difference. Each of the disks in OPT may overlap with at most 7 cells from G_r. See Fig. 2a. Thus, set Q may overlap with 7 m cells. Using similar arguments as in Lemma 1 we can see that the approximation ration is 1/7.

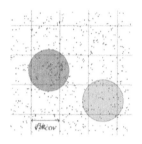

(a) Overlapping between the square from OPT and the grid G_r.

(b) Location of disk from optimal solution and $HSmax_\circ(S, m)$, left and right disks, respectively.

Fig. 2. Overlapping between optimal solution and the grid.

In order to find our solution, we build a balanced binary search tree T where each node has two fields: key and value. The key field is an *index* of non-empty cell in grid G_r and value is a total weight of points covered by this cell. For each point $s_i \in S$ we calculate *cell index* (a_i, b_i) and use (a_i, b_i) to find $\pi(a_i, b_i)$. For each point s_i we insert node with key $\pi(a_i, b_i)$ in T, and if it is necessary update the value of this node.

For each cell in G_r we calculate the total weight of points belonging to this cell; this calculation takes $O(n \log n)$ runtime. Note that the number of non-empty cells is at most n. The runtime required to built T is $O(n \log n)$ and to find m most weighted cells takes $O(m \log n)$ runtime.

Maintenance of Dynamic Covering Set. In this section, we deal with a dynamic set of points S. From time to time, a point is added to S, deleted from S, or its weight may be updated. In the dynamic version of the $Dmax_*(S, m)$ problem we want to maintain dynamically a set P of disks (squares) to maximize the total weight of covered points from S.

Theorem 1. *Let S be a set of weighted (non-negative) points on the plane, and assume that the size of S never exceeds $O(n)$. It is possible to construct in time $O(n \log n)$ a data structure D of size $O(n)$ that enables to maintain a set* *of m disks (squares), under insertions and deletions of points to/from S, that covers a subset of m cells having largest weights in given G_r, in time $O(\log n)$ per update. The approximation ratio of algorithms that solve $Dmax_\square(S,m)$ and $Dmax_O(S,m)$ by using data structure D, on dynamic set of points S is $\frac{1}{4}$ or $\frac{1}{7}$, respectively.*

First, we focus on the case of squares. To deal with the dynamic set S, we offer the following approach. After each change in S, we check if the square $p_i \in P$ that covers points having minimal total weight over all squares from P after the set update needs to change its location in order to cover points of larger total weight. At the start of the algorithm, we place the set P by $Hmax_*(S,m)$ from the previous section. For simplicity, we also assume that all the points from S are in general position.

We construct a data structure D of size $O(n)$ that will allow us to update the set S and to maintain the location of P dynamically. Among the non-empty cells of grid G_r and covered cells by set P, we select the cell $minC$ having the minimum weight. Also, among the non-empty cells of grid G_r and not covered cells by set P, we select the cell $maxC$ having the maximum weight. We define the weight of the cell in G_r with *index* $\pi(a,b)$ as $\rho_{\pi(a,b)}$.

The proposed data structure D is a combination of two data structures. The first data structure keeps the set S, and the second data structure contains the set C of square centers and weights of points covered by each $p_i \in P$. We denote these data structures by D_1 and D_2, respectively. The first data structure D_1 is a balanced binary search tree built on the x-coordinate of the points in S. The second data structure D_2 is a combination of three balanced binary search trees T_1, T_2 and T_3. The balanced binary search tree T_1 is a tree where each node corresponds to the weight of the cell from G_r covered by the square from set P. Therefore if cell with *index* $\pi(a,b)$ is covered by the square from P, then node with key $\rho_{\pi(a,b)}$ belongs to T_1. The balanced binary search tree T_2 is a tree where each node corresponds to the weight of nonempty cell in G_r, which is not covered by any square from set P. Therefore if nonempty cell with *index* $\pi(a,b)$ is not covered by any square from P, then node with key $\rho_{\pi(a,b)}$ belongs to T_2.

The balanced binary search tree T_3 is a tree where each node has key and value. The key is an *index* $\pi(a,b)$ of the non-empty cell in G_r, and the value is $c_i \in C$ if the cell is covered by square $p_i \in P$ or $NULL$ if the cell is not covered by square from set P. Additionally, each node in T_3 has a pointer to node in T_1 or T_2, accordingly if the cell is covered or not. We note that there is no need to store any information for empty cells. The data structure D uses $O(n)$ storage and it can be constructed in $O(n \log n)$ time.

Insertion. Let s_n be a new point to be added to S. The insertion of point s_n into D_1 takes $O(\log n)$ runtime. Next we calculate *cell index* of point s_n. We find the *cell index* (a,b) of the point s_n and use (a,b) to find the *index* $\pi(a,b)$. We insert node with key $\pi(a,b)$ in T_3 (or not if $\pi(a,b)$ exist), and update T_1 or T_2. There are two options depending on whether exist a node in T_3 with key $\pi(a,b)$. In the first case a node with key $\pi(a,b)$ does not exist in T_3. We will insert a node with key $\pi(a,b)$ into T_3, and node with key $\rho_{\pi(a,b)}$ is inserted into T_2. Also, node with key $\pi(a,b)$ from T_1 has a pointer to node with key $\rho_{\pi(a,b)}$ from tree T_2. The insertion of a new node in T_1 and T_3 takes $O(\log n)$ runtime. In the second case a node with key $\pi(a,b)$ exists in T_3. Two options possible: the cell is covered by one of the squares from set P or not. Therefore we need to update node with key $\rho_{\pi(a,b)}$ in T_1 or T_2. The update takes $O(\log n)$ runtime.

Let $p' \in P$ be the square covering $minC$. We need to check whether or not the location of $p' \in P$ should be changed to cover $maxC$ cell instead of $minC$. If the weight of $minC$ is greater than the $maxC$ weight, we finish. In another case, $maxC > minC$, we have to replace the square p' to cover the cell $maxC$. As the result of this, we have to update the data structure D_2. The update of D_2 includes the change the value of v_{cell} from c' to $NULL$, update the value of node $v \in T_1$ from $minC$ to $maxC$, and delete from T_2 the node associated with the cell $maxC$ and inserting new node associated with the cell $minC$ to T_2. The runtime is $O(\log n)$. In this case the update operation takes $O(\log n)$ runtime.

Deletion. Let s_d be a point to be deleted from S. The required runtime to delete s_d from D_1 is $O(\log n)$. Next we calculate the *cell index* (a,b) of s_d and use (a,b) to find the *index* $\pi(a,b)$. We find node with key $\pi(a,b)$ in T_3. Next, we update T_1 or T_2, depending on the value (center of covering square or NULL) of node with key $\pi(a,b)$. Assume w.l.o.g. that the cell with *cell index* (a,b) is covered by square $p' \in P$. We update the node with key $\rho_{\pi(a,b)}$ in T_1. We may need to rebalance the T_1 structure too, in $O(\log n)$ time.

Additionally, we need to check whether or not the location of square which covers $minC$ should be changed to cover $maxC$ cell instead of $minC$. The approach of replacing the $minC$ by $maxC$ is described in previous section.

Now, we focus on the case of disks. To deal with dynamic set S, when the covering shape is disk, we perform the following changes. At the start of the algorithm, we place set P of m disks by $Hmax_\bigcirc(S,m)$. The disks in our solution may overlap. Therefore we have to exclude double counting of the weight of point covered by more than one disk. For this, when we calculate the weight of a disk, we take into account only the points located in the cell, which is circumscribed by the disk. The rest remains the same.

Thus, regarding the proof of Theorem 3, following our explanations and the result from Lemma 1, we may conclude that we can achieve approximation ratio for $Dmax_\square(S,m)$ or $Dmax_\bigcirc(S,m)$ to be $\frac{1}{4}$ or $\frac{1}{7}$, respectively.

4   MWCIC Model

In this section we consider our problem under *MWCIC* model. Our algorithms work when $R_{COM} \geq 2R_{COV}$. For ease of explanation, in the rest of the paper we assume that $R_{COM} = 2R_{COV}$. This requirement can be easily relaxed and does not influence our suggested solutions.

4.1   Static Version

Recall that the set C contains the centers of the disks from the set P. The *profit* of each point $c_i \in C$ is the total weight of points from the set S covered by the disk p_i. We claim that we can solve $Cmax_*(S, m)$ by the algorithm to the following problem.

Max-Profit Budgeted Subset Steiner Connected Dominating Set:

> Given: a graph $G = (V, E)$ and a set $R \subseteq V$ of independent terminals, node profits $\{p_v : v \in R\}$, node weights $\{w_v : v \in V \setminus R\}$, and a budget k.
> Find: a subtree $T = (S, F)$ of $G[V \setminus R]$ such that $w(S) \leq k$ and $p(N(S) \cap R)$ is maximum, where $N(S)$ is the set of neighbors of S in G.

We will consider instances with the following special properties:

1. Every $v \in R$ is a leaf of G, namely, has a unique neighbor in $V \setminus R$.
2. We have unit weights, namely, $w_v = 1$ for all $v \in V \setminus R$.

By properties 1, 2, this reduces to the following problem:

Max-Profit k-MST: Given a graph $G = (V, E)$, profits of each node $\{\rho_v : v \in R\}$ and budget k. Find a subtree $T = (S, F)$ of G such that $|F| \leq k$ and $\rho(S)$ is maximum.

Theorem 2. *Max-Profit k-MST admits ratio $1/3$ in general graph. The problem also admits a bicriteria $(1, 2)$-approximation algorithm, that computes a tree of profit at least the maximum possible (among subtrees with k edges), and has at most $2k$ edges. By using Max-Profit k-MST we can solve $Cmax_*(S, m)$ with $O(1)$-approximation ratio.*

In next subsections we provide the proof of this theorem and show how to use the solution for Max-Profit k-MST for our needs.

The Algorithm and Its Analysis. A related "dual" problem to Max-Profit k-MST is:

Quota Steiner Tree: Given a graph $G = (V, E)$, profits of each node $\{\rho_v : v \in R\}$, costs of each edge $\{c_e : e \in E\}$ and a parameter quota q. Find a subtree $T = (S, F)$ of G such that $\rho(S) \geq q$ and $c(F)$ is minimum.

In the k-MST problem we need to find a min-cost subtree with k nodes/edges. Johnson et al. [6] showed that ratio γ for k-MST implies ratio γ for this problem, while Garg [3] give ratio 2 for k-MST. Thus combining we have (see also [7]).

Theorem 3 ([3,6]). *Quota Steiner Tree admits ratio 2.*

Assume for a moment that we know the optimal value q of a given Max-Profit k-MST instance. If we apply the Theorem 3 algorithm, it will return a tree with at most $2k$ edges. So we have a bicriteria $(1,2)$-approximation for MAX-PROFIT k-MST – the algorithm will return a tree that has maximum possible profit (among subtrees with k edges), an has at most $t \le 2k$ edges. If $t \le k$ then we are done, so we will assume that $t \ge k + 1$. Our goal will be to "prune" this tree, namely, to show that it contains a subtree with at most k edges that has large enough profit. This is given in the following two lemmas, which we believe are known as a folklore.

Lemma 2. *Let $k \ge 2$ be an integer and let S be a set of positive integers in the range $1, \ldots, k$ that sum to at most $2k$. Then S can be partitioned into at most 3 sets that sum to at most k each.*

Proof. We may assume that $\sum_{s \in S} s = 2k$. Initiate 3 bins B_1, B_2, B_3 of capacity k each. The residual capacity of a bin B_j w.r.t. a set A of numbers in the bin is defined by $\mathsf{rc}(B_j) = k - \sum_{s \in A} s$. Now apply the following algorithm.

Algorithm 2. DISTRIBUTE$(S; B_1, B_2, B_3)$

---
1 Sort the numbers in S in a decreasing order, say $s_1 \ge s_2 \ge \cdots \ge s_\ell$
2 **for** $i = 1$ to ℓ **do**
3 | **if** $s_i \le \mathsf{rc}(B_j)$ for some bin B_j **then** move s_i from S to B_j
4 **end**

We claim that $S = \varnothing$ at the end of the algorithm. Otherwise, at some iteration there is $s \in S$ such that $s \ge k - \alpha + 1$, where $\alpha = \min_{j=1,2,3} \mathsf{rc}(B_j)$ is the minimum residual bin capacity at this iteration. The sum of s and the numbers in the bins is at most $2k$ and at least $s + 3\alpha \ge k - \alpha + 1 + 3\alpha = k + 2\alpha + 1$; hence $2k \ge k + 2\alpha + 1$ and thus $\alpha \le \frac{k-1}{2}$. This implies $s \ge k - \alpha + 1 \ge \frac{k+1}{2} + 1 > \alpha$, contradicting a decreasing order sort of the numbers.

Lemma 3. *Let $T = (S, F)$ be a tree with $t = |F|$ edges, where $k + 1 \le t \le 2k$. Then one can find in polynomial time at most 3 subtrees of T with at most k edges each, such their edge sets partition F.*

Proof. For a node r of T, the r-subtrees (of T) are the inclusion maximal subtrees of T containing exactly one edge incident to r. Root T at an arbitrary node r. If there is an r-subtree with at least $k + 1$ edges, then set $r \leftarrow$ the neighbor of r in this subtree. The maximum number of edges in an r-subtree decreases by at least one, hence eventually we will find a node r such that every r-subtree has at most k edges. Let s_i be the number of edges in an r-subtree T_i. Applying the previous lemma we get that there is a partition of the r-subtrees into at most 3 sets, such that the overall number of edges in each part is at most k. For each part, taking the union of the subtrees in the part, gives at most 3 subtrees of T as required. The polynomial time implementation is obvious.

Theorem 2 (except the last part) easily follows from Lemma 3. Let opt denote the optimal value of a given MAX-PROFIT k-MST instance. Using binary search we find a "locally maximal" integer q such that the algorithm in Theorem 3 returns a tree with at most $2k$ edges; namely, for q the algorithm returns a tree with at most $2k$ edges, but for $q + 1$ it returns a tree with at least $2k + 1$ edges. Note that $q \geq$ opt. We then partition this tree into at most 3 edge-disjoint subtrees with at most k edges each, using the algorithm of Lemma 3. The most profitable subtree has profit at least opt/3.

The following lemma presents the relation between the general optimal solution and the optimal solution that we are looking for while the squares are constrained to cover the exact cells of the grid G_r.

Lemma 4 [1]. *Consider the weight s^* of an optimal solution for $Cmax_*(S, m)$ problem with n points and m connected squares (discs). Consider grid G_r and weight g of the optimal solution in G_r. Then $g \geq s^*/6$ or $g \geq s^*/8$ for $Cmax_\square(S, m)$ or $Cmax_\circ(S, m)$, respectively.*

The last part of Theorem 2 follows Lemma 4 and the fact that we can find a solution for G_r having weight of at least $g/3$.

4.2   Dynamic Version

A static solution from [1] inspires our proposed algorithm, we extend it for the dynamic version. We can solve our problem for grid, by considering all $(2m - 1) \times (2m - 1)$ large cells of grid each containing $O(m^2)$ square cells and considering the problem separately for each large cell assuming that the center of such cell is a root of connected tree containing m nodes (that correspond to drones). Then we chose the best computed solution.

Theorem 4. *The approximation ratio of algorithms that solve $CDmax_*(S, m)$ using $O(m\sqrt{m})$ drones, on dynamic set of points S is $O(1)$. It is possible to construct in time $O(\beta^2 mn \log n) + n^2 \log n)$ a data structure that used by these algorithms to maintain a set of drones, under insertions and deletions of points to/from S in time $O(\log n)$ per update, where $\beta \cdot R_{COM} = d_{max}$.*

Proof. We explain our algorithm for one separate large cell L. Note that once we computed the best solution that belongs to some large cell L', this cell defines a new partition of grid G_r by large cells that are not overlapping with each other. We will maintain the best solution for each of the large cells obtained by such partition and choose the solution having the maximum weight each time. For a specific large cell L we greedily chose the set of m small cells such that these small cells have maximal weights. From Theorem 1 we get that the approximation ratio of algorithms that solve $Dmax_\square(S, m)$ and $Dmax_\circ(S, m)$, on dynamic set of points S is $1/4$ or $1/7$, respectively. This will result in (L_2 or L_∞) disks (centered in these cells) that are not necessarily connected. In order to connect them, we perform 2 stages from Theorem 7 in [1]. Therefore, we solve the $Cmax_*(S, m)$ with approximation ratio $O(1)$ for both cases.

In order to maintain the best solution for $CDmax_*(S, m)$ in G_r we use the data structure D from Sect. 2 with a slight change. By using the same data structures D_1 from Sect. 2 we can update the weight of each point from S in time $O(\log n)$ per update. For each non-empty large cell L we build D_2 data structure. In order to determine to which large cell point s_i belongs, we create a binary search tree T_4 where each node corresponds to the *index* $\pi(a, b)$ of non-empty large cells in G_r. Additionally, each node in T_4 has a pointer to the corresponding D_2. We also create a balanced binary search tree T_5 where each node corresponds to the weight of nonempty large cells in G_r. In this case, the weight of cell L is the total weight of m most weighted small cells that belong to L. In order to calculate this weight we use the total weight of T_1 from corresponding D_2. After any change in set S, the runtime which is required to find a large cell L with maximal weight is $O(\log n)$. This change affects only one large cell L. The required runtime to find this cell in T_4 is $O(\log n)$ and to recalculate the weight of m most weighted small cells in L is also $O(\log n)$ according to Theorem 1. At the end, we need to update the tree T_5. Unfortunately, the large cell having maximal total weight of m most weighed small cells is not necessarily the best one. That is since after each change in S, the current grid may need to be shifted to choose the better large cell. We claim that the weight of the best solution in the shifted grid is at most 4 times greater than in given fixed grid. The reason of that is similar to the claim in 1. Using Theorem 4 we know that best solution for grid archives $O(1)$ approximation ratio for $Cmax_*(S, m)$. Therefore, the approximation ratio of algorithms that solve $CDmax_*(S, m)$ in the case of squares and discs, on dynamic set of points S is $O(1)$. Regarding the construction time of our solution, we observe that finding the optimal solution for large cell L takes $O(mn \log n)$ time. The number of times we perform this action is bounded by β^2. The cell L' defines a new partition of grid G_r by large cells, with the number of non empty large cells in this partition being at most n. The total time it takes to create D_2 structure for all non empty large cells is $O(n \log n^n) = O(n^2 \log n)$. Additionally, the construction time of T_4 and T_5 is $O(n \log n)$. Thus, the total construction time is $O(\beta^2 mn \log n + n^2 \log n)$.

5   Conclusion

In this paper, we dealt with the problem of dynamic maintenance of UAVs' swarm in order to cover ground users. We consider two models of connectivity among the drones: in the first model the connectivity is provided by third party, while in the second UAVs provide connectivity between themselves. For the first model, we presented a heuristic algorithm that provides $\frac{1}{4}$ or $\frac{1}{7}$ approximation of the optimal solution, in static and dynamic scenarios (with logarithmic update time), when the covered shapes of UAVs are squares or disks, respectively. For the second model, we presented a heuristic algorithm that provides $O(1)$ approximation of the optimal solution, for both cases of covering objects. The update time remains $O(\log n)$ but the solution requires to increase the number of covering UAVs.

References

1. Danilchenko, K., Segal, M.: Connected ad-hoc swarm of drones. In: Proceedings of the 6th ACM Workshop on Micro Aerial Vehicle Networks, Systems, and Applications, DroNet 2020, New York, NY, USA. Association for Computing Machinery (2020). https://doi.org/10.1145/3396864.3399699
2. De Berg, M., Cabello, S., Har-Peled, S.: Covering many or few points with unit disks. Theory Comput. Syst. **45**(3), 446–469 (2009)
3. Garg, N.: Saving an epsilon: a 2-approximation for the k-MST problem in graphs. In: STOC, pp. 396–402 (2005)
4. Huang, C.-C., Mari, M., Mathieu, C., Mitchell, J.S.B., Mustafa, N.H.: Maximizing covered area in the Euclidean plane with connectivity constraint. In: Approximation, Randomization, and Combinatorial Optimization. Algorithms and Techniques (APPROX/RANDOM 2019). Schloss Dagstuhl-Leibniz-Zentrum fuer Informatik (2019)
5. Jin, K., Li, J., Wang, H., Zhang, B., Zhang, N.: Near-linear time approximation schemes for geometric maximum coverage. Theoret. Comput. Sci. **725**, 64–78 (2018)
6. Johnson, D.S., Minkoff, M., Phillips, S.: The prize collecting Steiner tree problem: theory and practice. In: SODA, pp. 760–769 (2000)
7. Khuller, S., Purohit, M., Sarpatwar, K.K.: Analyzing the optimal neighborhood: algorithms for budgeted and partial connected dominating set problems. In: SODA, pp. 1702–1713 (2014)
8. Kuo, T., Lin, K.C., Tsai, M.: Maximizing submodular set function with connectivity constraint: theory and application to networks. IEEE/ACM Trans. Netw. **23**(2), 533–546 (2015)
9. Li, J., Wang, H., Zhang, B., Zhang, N.: Linear time approximation schemes for geometric maximum coverage. In: International Computing and Combinatorics Conference, pp. 559–571 (2015)
10. Lyu, J., Zeng, Y., Zhang, R., Lim, T.J.: Placement optimization of UAV-mounted mobile base stations. IEEE Commun. Lett. **21**(3), 604–607 (2016)
11. Mozaffari, M., Saad, W., Bennis, M., Debbah, M.: Efficient deployment of multiple unmanned aerial vehicles for optimal wireless coverage. IEEE Commun. Lett. **20**(8), 1647–1650 (2016)
12. Di Puglia Pugliese, L., Guerriero, F., Zorbas, D., Razafindralambo, T.: Modelling the mobile target covering problem using flying drones. Optim. Lett. **10**(5), 1021–1052 (2015). https://doi.org/10.1007/s11590-015-0932-1
13. Soltani, S., Razzazi, M., Ghasemalizadeh, H.: The most points connected-covering problem with two disks. Theory Comput. Syst. **62**(8), 2035–2047 (2018)
14. Srinivas, A., Zussman, G., Modiano, E.: Construction and maintenance of wireless mobile backbone networks. IEEE/ACM Trans. Netw. **17**(1), 239–252 (2009)
15. Szudzik, M.: An elegant pairing function. In: Wolfram Research (ed.) Special NKS 2006 Wolfram Science Conference, pp. 1–12 (2006)
16. Zeng, Y., Zhang, R., Lim, T.J.: Wireless communications with unmanned aerial vehicles: opportunities and challenges. IEEE Commun. Mag. **54**(5), 36–42 (2016)
17. Zhao, H., Wang, H., Weiyu, W., Wei, J.: Deployment algorithms for UAV airborne networks toward on-demand coverage. IEEE J. Sel. Areas Commun. **36**(9), 2015–2031 (2018)
18. Zorbas, D., Di Puglia, L., Pugliese, T.R., Guerriero, F.: Optimal drone placement and cost-efficient target coverage. JNCA **75**, 16–31 (2016)

VectorTSP: A Traveling Salesperson Problem with Racetrack-Like Acceleration Constraints

Arnaud Casteigts$^{(\boxtimes)}$, Mathieu Raffinot$^{(\boxtimes)}$, and Jason Schoeters$^{(\boxtimes)}$

Univ. Bordeaux, Bordeaux INP, CNRS, LaBRI, UMR5800, 33400 Talence, France
{arnaud.casteigts,mathieu.raffinot,jason.schoeters}@u-bordeaux.fr

Abstract. We study a new version of the Euclidean TSP called VEC-TORTSP (VTSP for short) where a mobile entity is allowed to move according to a set of physical constraints inspired from the pen-and-pencil game *Racetrack* (also known as *Vector Racer*). In contrast to other versions of TSP accounting for physical constraints, such as Dubins TSP, the spirit of this model is that (1) no speed limitations apply, and (2) inertia depends on the current velocity. As such, this model is closer to typical models considered in path planning problems, although applied here to the visit of n cities in a non-predetermined order.

We motivate and introduce the VECTORTSP problem, discussing fundamental differences with previous versions of TSP. In particular, an optimal visit order for ETSP may not be optimal for VTSP. We show that VECTORTSP is NP-hard, and in the other direction, that VEC-TORTSP reduces to GROUPTSP in polynomial time (although with a significant blow-up in size). On the algorithmic side, we formulate the search for a solution as an interactive scheme between a high-level algorithm and a *trajectory oracle*, the former being responsible for computing the visit order and the latter for computing the cost (or the trajectory) for a given visit order. We present algorithms for both, and we demonstrate and quantify through experiments that this approach frequently finds a better solution than the optimal trajectory realizing an optimal ETSP tour, which legitimates the problem itself.

1 Introduction

The problem of visiting a given set of places and returning to the starting point, while minimizing the total cost, is known as the Traveling Salesperson Problem (TSP, for short). The problem was independently formulated by Hamilton and Kirkman in the 1800s and has been extensively studied since. Many versions of this problem exist, motivated by applications in various areas, such as delivery planning, stock cutting, and DNA reconstruction. In the classical version, an instance of the problem is specified as a graph whose vertices represent the *cities* (places to be visited) and weights on the edges represent the cost of moving from

Supported by ANR project ESTATE (ANR-16-CE25-0009-03).

© Springer Nature Switzerland AG 2020
C. M. Pinotti et al. (Eds.): ALGOSENSORS 2020, LNCS 12503, pp. 45–59, 2020.
https://doi.org/10.1007/978-3-030-62401-9_4

one city to another (the move is impossible if the edge does no exist). One is asked to find the minimum cost tour (optimization version) or to decide whether a tour having at most some cost exists (decision version) subject to the constraint that every city is visited *exactly* once. Karp proved in 1972 that the Hamiltonian Cycle problem is NP-hard, which implies that TSP is NP-hard [16]. TSP was subsequently shown to be inapproximable (unless $P = NP$) by Orponen and Manilla in 1990 [21]. On the positive side, while the trivial algorithm has a factorial running time (essentially, evaluating all permutations of the visit order), Held and Karp presented a dynamic programming algorithm [14] running in time $O(n^2 2^n)$, which as of today remains the fastest deterministic algorithm known (a faster randomized algorithm was proposed by Björklund [5]).

In many cases, the problem is restricted to more tractable settings. In Metric TSP, the costs must respect the triangle inequality, namely $cost(u,v) \leq cost(u,w) + cost(w,v)$ for all u, v, w, and the constraint of visiting a city exactly once is relaxed (or equivalently, it is not, but the instance is turned into a complete graph where the weight of every edge uv is the cost of a shortest *path* from u to v in the original instance). Metric TSP was shown to be approximable within factor 1.5 by Christofides [8]. Whether the factor is optimal is unknown, although it cannot be less than 1.0045 (unless $P = NP$) and so no PTAS exists for Metric TSP [22]. A particular case of Metric TSP is when the cities are points in the plane, and weights are the Euclidean distance between them, known as the Euclidean TSP (ETSP, for short). This problem, although still NP-hard (see Papadimitriou [23] and Garey *et al.* [13]), was shown to admit a PTAS by Arora [3] and Mitchell [18].

One attempt to add physical constraints to the ETSP is Dubins TSP (DTSP). This version of TSP, which is also NP-hard (Le Ny *et al.* [17]), accounts for inertia through bounding by a fixed radius the curvature of a trajectory. This approach offers an elegant (*i.e.* purely geometrical) abstraction to the problem. However, it does not account for speed variations; for example, it does not enable sharper turns when the speed is low, nor does it account for inertia beyond a fixed speed. More realistic models have been considered beyond TSP, such as in the context of the path planning problem, where one aims to find an optimal trajectory between two given points (with obstacles), while satisfying constraints on acceleration/inertia. More generally, the literature on *kinodynamics* is vast (see, e.g. [6,7,10] for some relevant examples). The constraints are often formulated in terms of the considered space's dimensions, a bounded acceleration and a bounded speed. The positions may either be considered in a discrete domain or continuous domain, the latter being more related to the fields of control theory and analytic functions (*e.g.* for a TSP with double integrator see [25]). In contrast, the discrete domain is naturally prone to algorithmic investigation.

In a recreative column of the *Scientific American* in 1973 [12], Martin Gardner presented a paper-and-pencil game known as *Racetrack* (not to be confused with a similarly titled TSP heuristic [27]). The physical model is as follows. In each step, a vehicle moves according to a discrete-coordinate vector (initially the zero vector), with the constraint that the vector at step $i + 1$ cannot differ from the vector at step i by more than one unit in each dimension. The game consists of finding the best trajectory (smallest number of vectors) in a given race track defined by start/finish areas and polygonal boundaries. A nice feature of such models is the ability to think of the state of the vehicle at a given time as a point in a double dimension *configuration space*, such as (x, y, dx, dy) when the original space is $\mathbb{Z}^2$. The optimal trajectory can then be found by performing a breadth-first search in the configuration graph (these techniques are described later on). These techniques were rediscovered many times, both in the racetrack context (see *e.g.* [4,11,20,26]) and in the kinodynamics literature (see *e.g.* [6,10])—we will consider them as folklore.

1.1   Contributions

In this paper, we introduce a version of the Traveling Salesperson Problem called VECTORTSP (or VTSP), in which a vehicle must visit a given set of points in some Euclidean space and return to the starting point, subject to racetrack-like constraints. The quality of a solution is the *number* of vectors (equivalently, of configurations) it uses. We start by presenting a generalized racetrack physical model, in Sect. 2, and reviewing some of its algorithmic features, including known techniques based on the graph of configurations. Then, we define the VTSP problem in a quite general setting, where the space may be discrete or continuous, in an arbitrary number of dimensions (namely, $\mathbb{Z}^d$ or $\mathbb{R}^d$). An instance may be parameterized by two additional parameters: the maximum speed at which a city is considered as visited (visit speed ν), the speed being otherwise unbounded; and the maximum distance at which a city is considered as visited (visit distance α). These parameters correspond to natural motivations. For example, if the aforementioned space mission consists of dropping or collecting passengers in given "city", then the vehicle might need to slow down (or stop) at visit time; if it consists of making quick measurements, then the visit speed is unconstrained and some distance from the visited city may even be tolerated.

In Sect. 3, we make a number of general observations about VTSP. In particular, optimizing the racetrack trajectory of an optimal ETSP tour may not result in an optimal VTSP solution: the visit order is impacted by acceleration. Another key observation is that even if the speed is unbounded, one can easily compute a loose bound on the maximal speed to be considered in the search for an optimal solution, with important consequences on the computational complexity of the problem. In fact, we prove that VTSP is NP-hard under a natural parameterization (and therefore, in general), and in the other direction, it polynomially reduces to GROUPTSP, however with a significant blow-up in the input size. On the algorithmic side, we present in Sect. 4 a modular approach to address VTSP based on an interactive scheme between a high-level algorithm and a trajectory oracle. The first is responsible for exploring the space of possible visit orders, while making queries to the second for knowing the cost (or full trajectory) associated with a given visit order. We present algorithms for both. The high-level algorithm adapts a known heuristic for ETSP, trying to gradually improve the solution through generating a set of 2-permutations (swaps of two cities) until a local optimum is found.

As for the oracle, we present an algorithm which adapts the A* framework to multipoint paths in the configuration space, using an original cost function based on unidimensional projections of the cities coordinates.

In Sect. 5, we present a few experimental results based on this algorithmic framework. Beyond demonstrating the practicality of our algorithms, our results motivate the problem itself, by showing empirical evidence that the optimum trajectory resulting from an optimal ETSP tour is unlikely to be optimal for VTSP, and so, in most natural settings. In particular, the probability that our algorithm improves upon such a trajectory seems to approach 1 as the number of cities increase in a fixed area. Proofs marked with ★ are deferred to the full version of this paper, available at https://arxiv.org/abs/2006.03666.

2   Model and Definitions

In this section, we present a generalized version of the racetrack model, highlighting some of its algorithmic features. Then, we define VECTORTSP in generality, making observations and presenting preliminary results that are used in the subsequent sections.

2.1   Generalized Racetrack Model

Let us consider a mobile entity (hereafter, the *vehicle*), moving in a discrete or continuous Euclidean space $\mathbb{S}$ of some dimension d (for example, $\mathbb{S} = \mathbb{Z}^2$ or $\mathbb{S} = \mathbb{R}^3$). The state of the vehicle at any time is given by a *configuration* c, which is a couple containing a position $pos(c)$ and a velocity $vel(c)$, both encoded as elements of $\mathbb{S}$. For example, if $\mathbb{S} = \mathbb{Z}^2$, then a configuration c is of the form $((x, y), (dx, dy))$. Furthermore, we write $speed(c)$ for $||vel(c)||$. Given a configuration c, the set of configurations being reachable from c in a single time step, *i.e.*, the successors of c, is written as $\mathtt{succ}(c)$ and is model-dependent.

The original model presented by Gardner [12] corresponds to the case that $\mathbb{S} = \mathbb{Z}^2$, and given two configurations c_i and c_j, written as above, $c_j \in \mathtt{succ}(c_i)$ if and only if $x_j = x_i + dx_i \pm 1$ and $dx_j = x_j - x_i$, and $y_j = y_i + dy_i \pm 1$ and $dy_j = y_j - y_i$. In other words, the velocity of a configuration corresponds to the difference between its position and the position of the previous configuration, and this difference may only vary by one unit in each dimension in one time step. In the following, we refer to this model as the 9-successor model, and to the case that at most one dimension can change in one time step as the 5-successor model. These models can be naturally extended to continuous space, by considering that the set of successors is infinite, typically amounting to choosing a point in a d-sphere, as illustrated on Fig. 1.

Definition 1 (Trajectory). *A trajectory (of length k) is a sequence of configurations $c_1, c_2, ..., c_k$. It is called* valid *if $c_{i+1} \in \boldsymbol{succ}(c_i)$ for all $i < k$.*

We define the inverse c^{-1} of a configuration c as the configuration that represents the same movement in the opposite direction. For example, if $\mathbb{S} = \mathbb{Z}^2$ and

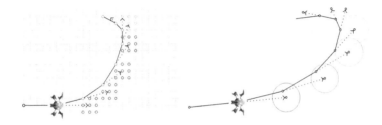

Fig. 1. Discrete and continuous space racetrack models.

$c = ((x, y), (dx, dy))$, then $c^{-1} = ((x+dx, y+dy), (-dx, -dy))$. A successor function is *symmetrical* if $c_j \in \texttt{succ}(c_i)$ if and only if $c_i^{-1} \in \texttt{succ}(c_j^{-1})$. Intuitively, this implies that if $(c_1, c_2, \ldots, c_k)$ is a valid trajectory, then $(c_k^{-1}, \ldots, c_2^{-1}, c_1^{-1})$ is also a valid trajectory: the trajectory is *reversible*. For simplicity, all the models considered in this paper use symmetrical successor functions.

2.1.1   Configuration Space

The concept of *configuration space* is a powerful and natural tool in the study of racetrack-like problems. This concept was rediscovered many times and is now considered as folklore. The idea is to consider the graph of configurations induced by the successor function as follows.

Definition 2 (Configuration graph). *Let $\mathcal{C}$ be the set of all possible configurations, then the* configuration graph *is the directed graph $G(\mathcal{C}) = (V, E)$ where $V = \mathcal{C}$ and $E = \{(c_i, c_j) \subseteq \mathcal{C}^2 : c_j \in \texttt{succ}(c_i)\}$.*

The configuration graph $G(\mathcal{C})$ is particularly useful when the number of successors of a configuration is bounded by a constant. In this case, $G(\mathcal{C})$ is sparse and one can search for optimal trajectories within it, using standard algorithms like breadth-first search (BFS). For example, in a $L \times L$ subspace of $\mathbb{Z}^2$, there are at most L^2 possible positions and at most $O(L)$ possible velocities (the speed cannot exceed $\sqrt{L}$ in each dimension without getting out of bounds [11]), thus $G(\mathcal{C})$ has $\Theta(L^3)$-many vertices and edges. More generally:

Observation 1 (Folklore). *A breadth-first search (BFS) in a $L \times L$ subspace of $\mathbb{Z}^2$ can find an optimum trajectory between two given configurations in time $O(L^3)$. A similar observation leads to time $O(L^{9/2})$ in $\mathbb{Z}^3$, and more generally $O(L^{3d/2})$ in dimension d.*

Note that the presence of obstacles (if any) results only in the graph having possibly less vertices and edges. (We do not consider obstacles in this paper.)

2.2   Definition of VECTORTSP

Informally, VECTORTSP is defined as the problem of finding a minimum length trajectory (optimization version), or deciding if a trajectory of at most a given length exists (decision version), which visits a given set of unordered cities (points) in some Euclidean space, subject to racetrack-like physical constraints. As explained in the introduction, we consider additional parameters to the problem, which are (1) *Visit speed* ν: maximum speed at which a city is visited; (2) *Visit distance* α: maximum distance at which a city is visited; and (3) *Vector completion* β: *(true/false)* whether the visit distance is evaluated only at the coordinates of the configurations, or also in-between configurations. The first two parameters are already discussed in the introduction. The visit distance is actually similar in spirit to the *TSP with neighborhood* [2]. The third parameter is more technical, although it could be motivated by having a specific action (sensing, taking pictures, etc.) being realized only at periodic times.

Considering Fig. 2, if ν is 7 or less, α is 2 or more, and $\beta = false$, then the city (circle) is considered as visited by the middle red vector. If either $\nu < 7$, $\alpha < 2$, or $\beta = true$, the city is not visited.

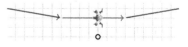

Fig. 2. A trajectory visiting a city.

We are now ready to define VECTORTSP. For simplicity, the definitions rely on discrete space ($\mathbb{S} = \mathbb{Z}^d$), to avoid technical issues with the representation of real numbers, in particular their impact on the input size. Similarly, we require the parameters ν and α to be integers and β to be a boolean. However, the problem might be adaptable to continuous space without much complications, possibly with the use of a *real RAM* abstraction [24].

Definition 3. VECTORTSP *(decision version)*

> ***Input:*** *A set of n cities (points) $P \subseteq \mathbb{Z}^d$, a distinguished city $p_0 \in P$, two integer parameters ν and α, a boolean parameter β, a polynomial-time-computable successor function* **succ**, *a positive integer k, and a trivial bound Δ encoded in unary.*
>
> ***Question:*** *Does there exist a valid trajectory $\mathcal{T} = (c_1, \ldots, c_k)$ of length at most k that visits all the cities in P, with $pos(c_1) = pos(c_k) = p_0$ and $speed(c_1) = speed(c_k) = 0$.*

The role of parameter Δ is to guarantee that the length of the optimal trajectory is polynomially bounded in the size of the input. Without it, an instance of even two cities could be artificially hard due to the sole distance between them [11,15]. As we will see, one can always find a (possibly sub-optimal) solution trajectory of $poly(L)$ configurations, where L is the maximum distance between two points in any dimension, and similarly, a solution trajectory must have length at least $\sqrt{L}$. Therefore, writing $\Delta = \texttt{unary}(\lfloor \sqrt{L} \rfloor)$ in the input is sufficient. The optimization version is defined analogously.

Tour *vs.* Trajectory (Terminology): In the Euclidean TSP, the term *tour* denotes both the visit order and the actual path realizing the visit, because both coincide. In VECTORTSP, a given visit order could be realized by many possible trajectories. To avoid ambiguities, we always refer to a visit order (*i.e.*, a permutation π of P) as a *tour*, while reserving the term *trajectory* for the actual sequence of racetrack configurations. Furthermore, we denote by racetrack(π) an optimal (*i.e.*, min-length) racetrack trajectory realizing a given tour π (irrespective of the quality of π).

Default Setting: In the rest of the paper, we call *default setting* the 9-successor model in two dimensional discrete space ($\mathbb{S} = \mathbb{Z}^2$), with unrestricted visit speed ($\nu = \infty$), zero visit distance ($\alpha = 0$), and non-restricted vector completion ($\beta = false$). Most of the results are however transposable to other values of the parameters and to higher dimensions.

3   Preliminary Results

In this section we make general observations about VECTORTSP, some of which are used in the subsequent sections. In particular, we highlight those properties which are distinct from Euclidean TSP.

Fact 2 (★). *The starting city has an impact on the cost of an optimal solution.*

This fact is the reason why an input instance of VECTORTSP is also parameterized by a starting city $p_0 \in P$. More generally, the cost of traveling between two given cities is impacted by the previous and subsequent positions of the vehicle and cannot be captured by a fixed cost, which is why VTSP does not straightforwardly reduce to classical TSP. The following fact strengthens the distinctive features of VTSP, showing that it does not straightforwardly reduce to ETSP either.

Fact 3. *Let $\mathcal{I}$ be a VTSP instance on a set of cities P, in the default setting. Let π be an optimal tour for an ETSP instance on the same set of cities P, then racetrack(π) may not be an optimal solution to $\mathcal{I}$.*

Example. Consider the following example, where the trajectories alternate between dashed red and plain blue vectors. On the left picture, the trajectory corresponds 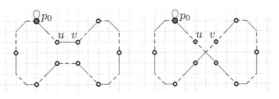 to an optimal realization of the optimal ETSP tour π, starting and ending at p_0 (whence the final deceleration loop). It it not hard to see that this trajectory is indeed optimal for π. In contrast, an optimal VTSP trajectory visiting the same cities (right picture) would use two configurations less, based on a non-optimal tour π' for ETSP. An example with visit speed $\nu = 0$ is given as well (★). □

Hence, solving VTSP does not reduce to optimizing the trajectory of an optimal ETSP solution: the visit order is impacted. Furthermore, we observe the following property:

Fact 4. *An optimal VTSP solution may self-cross.*

3.1   The Configuration Space Can Be Bounded

The spirit of the racetrack model is to focus on acceleration only, without bounding the speed. Nonetheless, we show here that a VECTORTSP trajectory in general (and an optimal one in particular) can always be found within a certain subgraph of the configuration graph, whose size is polynomially bounded in the size of the input. These results are formulated in the default setting for any discrete d-dimensional space.

Lemma 5 (Bounds on the solution length). *Let P be a set of cities and L be the largest distance in any dimension (over all d dimensions) between two cities of P. Then a solution trajectory must contain at least $\sqrt{L}$ configurations. Furthermore, there always exists a solution trajectory of $O(L^d)$ configurations.*

Proof. The lower bound follows from the fact that it takes at least $\sqrt{L}$ configurations to travel a distance of L (starting at speed 0), the latter being a lower bound on the total distance to be traveled. The upper bound can be obtained by exploring all the points of the d-dimensional rectangular hull containing the cities in P at unit speed, which amounts to $O(L^d)$ configurations.   □

Lemma 6 (Bounds on the configuration graph). *An (optimal) trajectory for VTSP can be found in a subgraph of the configuration graph with polynomially many vertices and edges (in the size of the input), namely $O(L^{(d^2)})$.*

Proof. First observe that if there exists a trajectory of $O(L^d)$ configurations, then this bound also applies to an optimal trajectory. Now, we know that a trajectory corresponds to a path in $G(\mathcal{C})$, thus an optimal trajectory can be found within the subgraph of $G(\mathcal{C})$ induced by the vertices at distance at most $O(L^d)$ from the starting point, which consists of $O(L^{(d^2)})$ vertices in total.   □

3.2   A Glimpse at Computational Complexity

Here, we present polynomial time transformations from VECTORTSP to other NP-hard problems and vice versa. Precisely, we establish NP-hardness of a particular parameterization of VECTORTSP (and thus, of the general problem) where the visit speed ν is zero. The reduction is from EXACTCOVER and is based on Papadimitriou's proof to show NP-hardness of ETSP. More interestingly, we present a general reduction from VECTORTSP to GROUPTSP. This reduction relies crucially on Lemma 6 above.

3.2.1   NP-hardness of VectorTSP

Let $\mathcal{U}$ be a set of m elements (the *universe*), the problem EXACTCOVER takes as input a set $\mathcal{F} = \{F_i\}$ of n subsets of $\mathcal{U}$, and asks if there exists $\mathcal{F}' \subseteq \mathcal{F}$ such that all sets in $\mathcal{F}'$ are *disjoint* and $\mathcal{F}'$ covers all the elements of $\mathcal{U}$.

Theorem 7 (★).   EXACTCOVER *reduces in polynomial time to* VECTORTSP *with $\nu = 0$.*

We consider default settings except for visit speed $\nu = 0$. It adapts Papadimitriou's proof for showing that ETSP is NP-hard [23]. Admittedly, the fact that Theorem 7 relies on a visit speed $\nu = 0$, although implying that VECTORTSP in general is NP-hard, is not satisfactory. The more natural question is whether VECTORTSP is NP-hard without constraining the visit speed (e.g. in the default setting).

Open question 1. *Is* VECTORTSP *NP-hard in the particular case of the default setting?*

3.2.2   Transformation from VECTORTSP to GROUPTSP

Here, we show that VTSP reduces in polynomial time to the so-called GROUPTSP (also known as SETTSP or GENERALIZEDTSP), where the input is a set of cities partitioned into groups, and the goal is to visit at least one city in each group.

Lemma 8. VTSP *reduces to* GROUP TSP *in polynomial time in the size of the input.*

Proof. Let $\mathcal{I}$ be the original VTSP instance and n the number of cities in $\mathcal{I}$. Each city in $\mathcal{I}$ can be visited in a number of different ways, each corresponding to a different configuration in $\mathcal{C}$ (the set of all possible configurations). The strategy is to create a city in $\mathcal{I}$' for each configuration that visits at least once city in $\mathcal{I}$, and group them according to which city of $\mathcal{I}$ they visit (the other configurations are discarded). Thus, visiting a city in each group of $\mathcal{I}$' corresponds to visiting all cities in $\mathcal{I}$. Depending on the parameters of the model (visit speed, visit distance, vector completion), it may happen that a same configuration visits several cities in $\mathcal{I}$, which implies that the groups may overlap; however, Noon and Bean show in [19] that a GTSP instance with overlapping groups can be transformed into one with mutually exclusive groups at the cost of creating k copies of a city when it appears originally in k different groups. Thus we proceed without worrying about overlaps. Let X be the set of cities in $\mathcal{I}$, and $\mathcal{C}(x) \subseteq \mathcal{C}$ be the configurations which visit city $x \in X$. Instance $\mathcal{I}$' is defined by creating a city for each configuration in $\cup_{x \in X} \mathcal{C}(x)$ and a group for each $\mathcal{C}(x)$. An arc is added between all couples (c_1, c_2) of cities in $\mathcal{I}$' such that c_1 and c_2 belong to different groups; the weight of this arc is the distance between c_1 and c_2 in the configuration graph. Thus, a trajectory using k configurations to visit all the cities in $\mathcal{I}$ corresponds to a tour of cost k visiting at least one city in each group in $\mathcal{I}$'. The fact that the reduction is polynomial (both in time and space) results from the facts that (1) there is a polynomial number of relevant configurations (Lemma 6), each one being copied at most n times; and (2) the distance between two configurations in the configuration graph can be computed in polynomial time (Observation 1).   □

Note that the reduction described in Lemma 8 implies a prohibitive blow-up in the number of cities. However, it is general in terms of the parameters: any combination ν, α, and β only impacts the set of vectors that visit each city.

4   Algorithms

In this section, we present an algorithmic framework for finding acceptable solutions to VTSP in practical polynomial time. It is based on an interaction between a high-level part that decides the visit order (tour), and a trajectory oracle that evaluates its cost.

4.1   Exploring Visit Orders (FlipVTSP)

A classical heuristic for ETSP is the so-called 2-opt algorithm [9], also known as Flip. It is a local search algorithm which starts with an arbitrary tour π. In each step, all the possible 2-permutations (*i.e.*, swaps of two cities, or simply flips) of the current tour π are generated. If such a flip π' improves upon π, it is selected and the algorithm recurses on π'. Eventually, the algorithm finds a local optimum whose quality is commonly admitted to be of reasonable quality, albeit without guarantees (the name 2-opt does not reflect an approximation ratio, it stands for 2-permutation local optimality). Adapting this algorithm seems like a natural option for the high-level part of our framework.

The main differences between our algorithm, called FlipVTSP, and its ETSP analogue are that (1) the cost of a tour is not evaluated in terms of distance, but in terms of the required number of racetrack configurations (through calls to the oracle); (2) the tours involving self-crosses are not discarded (see Fact 4); and (3) the number of recursions is polynomially bounded because new tours are considered only in case of improvement, and the length of a trajectory is itself polynomially bounded (Lemma 5). The resulting tour is a local optimum with respect to 2-permutations, also known as a 2-optimal tour.

Theorem 9 ($\bigstar$). *A 2-optimal VTSP tour is computable in time $O(n^2 L^d \tau(n, L))$, where n is the number of cities, L the largest distance between cities in a dimension, d the number of dimensions, and $\tau(n, L)$ the running time complexity of the oracle.*

4.2   Optimal Racetrack Given a Fixed Visit Order (Multipoint A*)

Here, we discuss the problem of computing an optimal racetrack trajectory that visits a set of points *in a given order*. A previous work of interest is Bekos *et al.* [4], which addresses the problem of computing an optimal racetrack trajectory in a so-called "Indianapolis" track, where the track has a certain width and right-angle turns. This particular setting limits the maximum speed at the turns, which makes it possible to decompose the computation in a dynamic programming fashion. In contrast, the space is open in VTSP, with no simple way to bound the maximum speed. Therefore, we propose a different strategy based on searching for an optimal path in the configuration graph using A*.

The Problem: Given an ordered sequence of points $\pi = (p_1, p_2, \ldots, p_n)$, compute (the cost of) an optimal trajectory realizing π, *i.e.*, visiting the points in order, starting at p_1 and ending at p_n at zero speeds. (In the particular case of VTSP, p_1 and p_n coincide.)

Finding the optimal trajectory between *two* configurations already suggests the use of path-finding algorithms like BFS, Dijkstra, or A* (see e.g. [26] and [4]). The difficulty in our case is to force the path to visit all the intermediary points in order, despite the fact that the space is open. Our contribution here is to design a cost function that guides A* through these constraints. In general, A* explores the search space by generating a set of successors of the current "position" (in our case, configuration) and estimate the cost of each successor using a problem-specific function. The successors are then inserted into a datastructure (in general, a priority queue) which makes it easy to continue exploration from the position which is globally the best estimated. The great feature of A* is that it is guaranteed to find an optimal path, provided that the cost function does not over-estimate the actual cost, and so, as fast as the estimation is precise.

4.2.1   Cost Estimation

For simplicity, we first present how the estimation works relative to the entire tour. Then we explain how to generalize it for estimating an arbitrary intermediate configuration in the trajectory (i.e. one that has already visited a certain number of cities and is located at a given position with given velocity). The key insight is that the optimal trajectory, whatever it be, must obey some pattern in each dimension. Consider, for example, the tour $\pi = \{(5, 10), (10, 12), (14, 7), (8, 1), (3, 5), (5, 10)\}$ shown on Fig. 3. In the x-dimension, the vehicle must move at least from 1 to 3, then stop at a *turning point*, change direction, and travel towards 5, then stop and change direction again, and travel back to 1. Thus, any trajectory realizing π can be divided into *at least* three subtrajectories in the x-dimension, whose cost is *at least* the cost of traveling along these segments, starting and

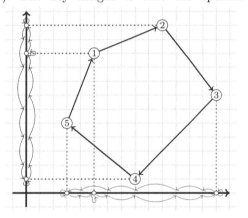

Fig. 3. Projection in each dimension.

ending at speed 0 at the turning points. Thus, in the above example, the vehicle must travel at least along distances 9, 11, and 2 (with zero speed at the endpoints), which gives a cost of at least 16 (*i.e.*, 6, 7, and 3, respectively). The same analysis can be performed in each dimension; then, the actual cost must be *at least the maximum* value among these costs, which is therefore the value we consider as estimation.

In general, the configurations whose estimation is required by A* are more general than the above case. In particular, it has an arbitrary position and velocity, and the vehicle may have already visited a number of cities. Therefore, the number of visited cities is stored along a configuration, and the dimensional cost is evaluated against the remaining sub-tour. The only technical difference is that one must carefully take into account the current position and velocity when determining where the next turning point is in the dimensional projection, which however poses no significant difficulty. Concretely, a case-based study of the initial configuration with respect to the first turning point, allows one to self-reduce the estimation to the particular case that the initial speed is zero (possibly at a different starting position). Consequently, the total cost amounts to a sum of costs between consecutive pairs of turning points with zero speed at these points.

Lemma 10. *The cost estimation of a subtour $\pi' = c, p_i, ..., p_n$, where c is the current configuration and $p_i, \ldots, p_n$ a suffix of π can be computed in $O(n)$ time.*

Proof. As explained, the subtour is first reduced to a subtour $\pi'' = p_{i-1}, p_i, \ldots, p_n$. The turning points in π'' are easily identified through a pass over π''. Their number is at most n because they are a subset of the points in π''. Finally, the cost between each pair of selected turning points can be computed in constant time [4] (if one neglects the encoding size of an integer representing a coordinate). □

The reader is referred to [4] for more on computing the cost between two configurations in one dimension. Let us now discuss the running time complexity of the resulting algorithm. In general, A* can have an exponential running time in the solution depth (thus, length of the trajectory). It is however possible, in our case, to make it polynomial.

Theorem 11. *The A* oracle runs in polynomial time $\widetilde{O}(L^{(d^2)}n^2)$.*

Proof. A "configuration" of the A* algorithm (let us call it a state, to avoid ambiguity) is made of a racetrack configuration c together with a number k of visited cities. There are at most $O(L^{(d^2)})$ configurations (Lemma 6) and n cities, thus A* will perform at most $O(L^{(d^2)}n)$ iterations, provided that it does not explore a state twice. Given that the states are easily orderable, the later condition can be enforced by storing all the visited states in an ordered collection that is searchable and insertable in logarithmic time (whence the $\widetilde{O}$ notation). Finally, each state is estimated in $O(n)$ time (Lemma 10). □

The combined use of `FlipVTSP` and `Multipoint A*` thus runs in polynomial time (Theorem 9 and Theorem 11). We also present a modified version of the oracle algorithm (★) which, as opposed to the presented computation with a complete view of the visit order, uses sequential smaller computations using limited views of the visit order (a trick also used in the indianapolis case [4]). This significantly improves practical running time but potentially loses optimality.

5   Experiments and Conclusion

In this section, we present a few experiments with the goal to (1) validate the algorithmic framework described in Sect. 4, and (2) motivate the VTSP problem itself, by quantifying the discrepancy between ETSP and VTSP. The instances were generated by distributing cities uniformly at random within a given square area. For each instance, Concorde [1] was used to obtain the reference optimal ETSP tour π. The optimal trajectory T realizing this tour was computed using Multipoint A* (with complete view). Then, FlipVTSP explored the possible flips (with limited view) until a local optimum is found. Such an outcome is not rare. Figure 4 shows some measures when varying (1) the number of cities in a fixed area; (2) the size of the area for a fixed number of cities; and (3) both at constant density. For performance, only the flips which did not deteriorate the tour distance by too much were considered (15 %, empirically). Thus, the plots tend to *under-estimate* the impact of VTSP (they already do so, by considering only *local* optima, and *limited view* in the flip phase).

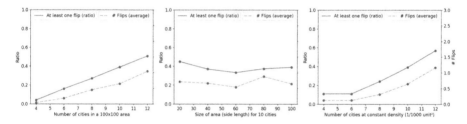

Fig. 4. Varying the number of cities (left), size of the area (middle), and both (right). The plots show the likelyhood of at least one flip and the average number of flips (over 100 instances).

The results suggest that an optimal ETSP tour becomes less likely to be optimal for VTSP as the number of cities increases (in a fixed area). The size of the area for a fixed number of cities (here, 10) does not seem to have a significant impact. Somewhat logically, scaling both parameters simultaneously (at constant density) seem to favor VTSP as well. Further experiments should be performed for a finer understanding. However, these results are sufficient to confirm that VTSP is a specific problem.

References

1. Applegate, D., Bixby, R., Chvatal, V., Cook, W.: Concorde TSP solver (2006)
2. Arkin, E.M., Hassin, R.: Approximation algorithms for the geometric covering salesman problem. Discrete Appl. Math. **55**(3), 197–218 (1994)

3. Arora, S.: Polynomial time approximation schemes for Euclidean TSP and other geometric problems. In: Proceedings of 37th Conference on Foundations of Computer Science, pp. 2–11. IEEE (1996)
4. Bekos, M.A., Bruckdorfer, T., Förster, H., Kaufmann, M., Poschenrieder, S., Stüber, T.: Algorithms and insights for racetrack. Theoret. Comput. Sci. **748**, 2–16 (2018)
5. Bjorklund, A.: Determinant sums for undirected Hamiltonicity. SIAM J. Comput. **43**(1), 280–299 (2014)
6. Canny, J., Donald, B., Reif, J., Xavier, P.: On the complexity of kinodynamic planning. IEEE (1988)
7. Canny, J., Rege, A., Reif, J.: An exact algorithm for kinodynamic planning in the plane. Discrete Comput. Geom. **6**(3), 461–484 (1991)
8. Christofides, N.: Worst-case analysis of a new heuristic for the travelling salesman problem. Carnegie-Mellon Univ Pittsburgh Pa Management Sciences Research Group, Technical report (1976)
9. Croes, G.A.: A method for solving traveling-salesman problems. Oper. Res. **6**(6), 791–812 (1958)
10. Donald, B., Xavier, P., Canny, J., Reif, J.: Kinodynamic motion planning. J. ACM (JACM) **40**(5), 1048–1066 (1993)
11. Erickson, J.: Ernie's 3d pancakes: "how hard is optimal racing?" (2009). http://3dpancakes.typepad.com/ernie/2009/06/how-hard-is-optimal-racing.html
12. Gardner, M.: Sim, chomp and race track-new games for intellect (and not for lady luck). Sci. Ame. **228**(1), 108–115 (1973)
13. Garey, M.R., Graham, R.L., Johnson, D.S.: Some NP-complete geometric problems, pp. 10–22 (1976)
14. Held, M., Karp, R.M.: A dynamic programming approach to sequencing problems. J. Soc. Ind. Appl. Math. **10**(1), 196–210 (1962)
15. Holzer, M., McKenzie, P.: The computational complexity of racetrack, pp. 260–271 (2010)
16. Karp, R.M.: Reducibility among combinatorial problems, pp. 85–103 (1972)
17. Le Ny, J., Frazzoli, E., Feron, E.: The curvature-constrained traveling salesman problem for high point densities. In: 46th IEEE Conference on Decision and Control, pp. 5985–5990. IEEE (2007)
18. Mitchell, J.S.: Guillotine subdivisions approximate polygonal subdivisions: a simple polynomial-time approximation scheme for geometric TSP, k-MST, and related problems. SIAM J. Comput. **28**(4), 1298–1309 (1999)
19. Noon, C.E., Bean, J.C.: An efficient transformation of the generalized traveling salesman problem. INFOR: Inf. Syst. Oper. Res. **31**(1), 39–44 (1993)
20. Olsson, R., Tarandi, A.: A genetic algorithm in the game racetrack (2011)
21. Orponen, P., Mannila, H.: On approximation preserving reductions: complete problems and robust measures (revised version). University of Helsinki, Department of Computer Science (1990)
22. Papadimitriou, C., Vempala†, S.: On the approximability of the traveling salesman problem. In: Conference Proceedings of the Annual ACM Symposium on Theory of Computing, vol. 26, pp. 101–120, February 2006. https://doi.org/10.1007/s00493-006-0008-z
23. Papadimitriou, C.H.: The Euclidean travelling salesman problem is NP-complete. Theoret. Comput. Sci. **4**(3), 237–244 (1977)
24. Márquez, A., Ramos, P., Urrutia, J. (eds.): EGC 2011. LNCS, vol. 7579. Springer, Heidelberg (2012). https://doi.org/10.1007/978-3-642-34191-5

25. Savla, K., Bullo, F., Frazzoli, E.: Traveling salesperson problems for a double integrator. IEEE Trans. Autom. Control **54**(4), 788–793 (2009)
26. Schmid, J.: Vectorrace - finding the fastest path through a two-dimensional track. http://schmid.dk/articles/vectorRace.pdf (2005)
27. Yuan, Y., Peng, Y.: RaceTrack: an approximation algorithm for the mobile sink routing problem. In: Nikolaidis, I., Wu, K. (eds.) ADHOC-NOW 2010. LNCS, vol. 6288, pp. 135–148. Springer, Heidelberg (2010). https://doi.org/10.1007/978-3-642-14785-2_11

Connected Reconfiguration of Lattice-Based Cellular Structures by Finite-Memory Robots

Sándor P. Fekete[1]🆔, Eike Niehs[1]🆔, Christian Scheffer[2]🆔, and Arne Schmidt[1(✉)]🆔

[1] Department of Computer Science, TU Braunschweig, Braunschweig, Germany
{s.fekete,e.niehs,arne.schmidt}@tu-bs.de
[2] Department of Computer Science, University of Münster, Münster, Germany
christian.scheffer@uni-muenster.de

Abstract. We provide algorithmic methods for reconfiguration of lattice-based cellular structures by finite-state robots, motivated by large-scale constructions in space. We present algorithms that are able to detect and reconfigure arbitrary polyominoes, while also preserving connectivity of a structure during reconfiguration; we also provide mathematical proofs and performance guarantees. Specific results include methods for determining a bounding box, scaling a given arrangement, and adapting more general algorithms for transforming polyominoes.

1 Introduction

Developing algorithmic methods for building and modifying large-scale structures is an important objective motivated by a vast array of applications. In many cases, the use of autonomous robots promises significant advantages, but also a number of additional difficulties. Particularly intriguing challenges arise in space, with difficulties of expensive supply chains, scarcity of building materials, dramatic costs and consequences of even small errors, and the limitations of outside intervention in case of malfunctions posing a vast array of extreme problems.

As described in parallel, practically oriented work [34], and visualized in our video [1], a number of significant advances have been made to facilitate overall breakthroughs; see Fig. 1 for an illustration. One important step has been the development of ultra-light and scalable composite lattice materials [28] that allow the construction of modular, reconfigurable, lattice-based structures [31]. A second step has been the design of simple autonomous robots [30,32] that are able to move on the resulting lattice structures and move their elementary cell components, thereby allowing the reconfiguration of the overall edifice. Combining such materials and robots in space promises to vastly increase the dimensions of constructible facilities and spacecraft, as well as offering to extend mission capabilities with reconfiguration and re-use [27].

C. M. Pinotti et al. (Eds.): ALGOSENSORS 2020, LNCS 12503, pp. 60–75, 2020.
https://doi.org/10.1007/978-3-030-62401-9_5

In this paper, we provide algorithmic foundations for addressing the next step in this hierarchy: enabling extremely simple robots, i.e., finite automata, to perform a more complex spectrum of construction tasks for cellular structures in space, such as computing a bounding box for a cellular arrangement, scaling up a given seed construction, and a number of other design operations.

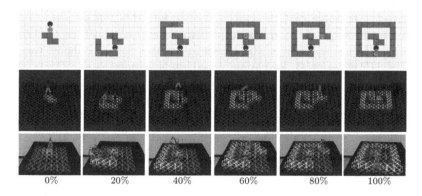

0%   20%   40%   60%   80%   100%

Fig. 1. Snapshots from building a bounding box for a Z-shaped polyomino using 2D simulator, 3D simulator, and staged hardware robots, synchronized so all are shown at steps {0, 24, 48, 72, 96, 120}.

1.1   Our Results

We present the following results.

1. We show how just two finite-state robots suffice to construct a bounding box for a given connected planar arrangement of grid cells (a *polyomino P*) in a limited number of steps.
2. We provide an algorithmic method that enables two finite-state robots to construct (for a polyomino P with a surrounding bounding box) a scaled-up copy of P in a limited number of steps, while preserving connectivity of intermediate arrangements.
3. We give an alternative, more efficient method for scaling a monotone polyomino P, while preserving connectivity of intermediate arrangements.
4. We describe how other arbitrary reconfiguration can be adapted to our connected scenario.

1.2   Related Work

There has been a considerable amount of classic algorithmic work dealing with robots or agents on graphs. Blum and Kozen [3] showed that two finite automata can jointly search any unknown maze. Other work has focused on exploring general graphs (e.g., [5, 18, 21, 33, 35]), as a distributed or collaborative problem using multiple agents (e.g. [2,4,7,19]) or with space limitations (e.g. [15,20–23]). From an algorithmic perspective, we are interested in different models representing programmable matter and further recent results. Inspired by the single-celled amoeba, Derakhshandeh et al. [9] introduced the Amoebot model and later a generalized variant, the general Amoebot model [13]. The Amoebot model provides a framework based on a triangular lattice and active particles that can occupy a single lattice vertex or a pair of adjacent vertices. With just a few possible movements, these particles can be formed into different shapes like lines, triangles or hexagons [11], and perform distributed tasks such as leader election [8,13]. (Leader election in the somewhat weaker SILBOT model was presented by D'Angelo et al. [6].) A universal shape formation algorithm within the Amoebot model was described by Di Luna et al. in [14]. An algorithm for solving the problem of coating an arbitrarily shaped object with a layer of self-organizing programmable matter was presented in [12] and analyzed in [10]. Other models with active particles were introduced in [36] as the Nubot model and in [29] with modular robots. Gmyr et al. [26] introduced a model with two types of particles: active robots acting like a deterministic finite automaton and passive particles. Furthermore, they presented algorithms for shape formation [25] and shape recognition [24]. Based on this model, Fekete et al. [16] presented algorithms to bound a given shape and for counting the number of particles or corners. They also introduced more complex geometric algorithms for copying, reflecting, rotating and scaling a given polyomino as well as an algorithm for constructing a bounding box surrounding a polyomino; however, this work did not account for connectivity of the particle configurations, which is critical for many applications.

For an overview of practically oriented previous research, see our application-oriented paper [34].

2   Preliminaries

In the following, we introduce models, general definitions as well as a description of the underlying limitations.

2.1   Model

We consider an infinite *square grid graph* $G = (V, E)$, where $V = \mathbb{Z}^2$ is the set of *pixel*, and two pixels p_1 and p_2 are adjacent when $||p_1 - p_2||_1 = 1$. We call two pixels a *diagonal pair* when both their x-coordinates and their y-coordinates differ by one. We use the compass directions (N, E, S, W) for orientation when moving on the grid and may use up, right, down and left synonymously.

Every pixel of G is either *occupied* by a passive particle (i.e., a tile) or *empty*. Passive particles cannot move or manipulate themselves. The maximal connected set of occupied pixels is called a *polyomino*.

The *boundary* of a polyomino P is denoted by ∂P and includes all particles of P that are adjacent to an empty pixel or that form a diagonal pair with an empty pixel (see also Fig. 2 (a)). Polyominoes can have *holes*, i.e., finite maximal connected sets of empty pixels (see Fig. 2 (b)). Polyominoes without holes are called *simple*; otherwise, they are *non-simple*. The *bounding box* $bb(P)$ of a given polyomino P is defined as the boundary of the smallest axis-aligned rectangle enclosing but not touching P; see Fig. 2 (d). Because the bounding box and polyomino are comprised of indistinguishable particles, we use a gap to differentiate the two.

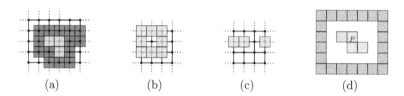

Fig. 2. (a) Dark blue tiles indicate the boundary ∂P of the polyomino P (dark and light blue). (b) A non-simple polyomino with one hole. (c) Tiles on the grid induce two separate connected components. (d) A polyomino P and $bb(P)$ (gray). (Color figure online)

We use *robots* as active particles. These robots work like *finite deterministic automata* that can move around on the grid and manipulate the polyomino. A robot has the ability to move along the edges of the grid graph and to change the state of the current pixel by placing or removing a particle on it (in particular, we assume that the robot can create and destroy particles). Robots work in a series of Look-Compute-Move steps. Depending on the current state of the robot and the pixel it is positioned on (Look), the next step is computed according to a specific transition function δ (Compute), which determines the future state of robot and pixel and the actual movement (Move). In the case of multiple robots (Fig. 3 (b)), we assume that they cannot be placed on the same pixel at the same time. Communication between robots is limited to adjacent pixels and can be implemented by expanding the Look phase by the states of all adjacent robots. It is not necessary to assume that the system is fully synchronous; coordinating the two robots in an asynchronous setting is straightforward in most parts, and briefly sketched for computing the bounding box.

In the following, we assume that connectivity is ensured if the union of all placed particles and all used robots is completely connected. Accordingly, a robot can hold two components together, e.g., as shown in Fig. 3 (c).

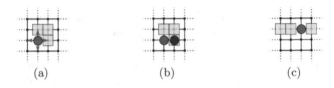

(a)   (b)   (c)

Fig. 3. (a) One robot and its possible moves. (b) Two robots on the grid. (c) Robots can hold separate connected components together.

3   Constructing a Bounding Box

Fekete et al. [16] showed how to construct a bounding box around a polyomino. However, that algorithm does not guarantee connectivity. We describe an algorithm to construct the bounding box, maintaining connectivity after each step. Due to space constraints, we only sketch technical details; see our full version [17] for full details. To accomplish the required connectivity, we specify without loss of generality that the connection between $bb(P)$ and P must be on the south side of the boundary. For easier distinction, we show the tiles of the original polyomino in blue, while those of the bounding box (which is composed of additional tiles that are added during the process) are shown in gray. Note that this is for illustrative purposes only; the robots cannot distinguish between those particles. (We follow a similar convention in the illustrations throughout this paper: Original tiles are shown in blue, while additional tiles are shown in gray.)

In the following, we assume that two robots are placed adjacent to each other on an arbitrary particle of the polyomino P, and that the first robot R_1 (marked red in the figures) is the leader.

The construction can be split into three phases: (1) finding a start position, (2) constructing the bounding box, and (3) clean-up. To find a suitable start position, we search for a locally y-minimal pixel that is occupied by a particle. This can be achieved by scanning the current row and moving **down** whenever possible. The search is carried out by the leader robot R_1, followed by R_2 (because we are in an asynchronous setting, R_1 always waits for R_2 to catch up before making the next move). Then R_2 positions itself on the first pixel beneath this locally y-minimal pixel. Afterwards, R_1 starts the bounding box construction one pixel further down. This brings us to phase (2).

The construction of the bounding box is performed clockwise around P, i.e., whenever possible, R_1 makes a right turn. At some point, R_1 finds a particle either belonging to P or to the bounding box. To decide whether a particle t belongs to P or the current bounding box, we start moving around the boundary of the shape t belongs to. At some point, R_1 reaches R_2. If R_1 is above R_2 then t is a particle of P, otherwise t is a particle of the bounding box. To find t again, we move below R_2 and follow the construction until we cannot move any further. From there we can carry on building $bb(P)$.

Now consider the two cases: If the particle does not belong to P, we are done with phase (2) and can proceed with phase (3). If it is a particle belonging to P, we need to shift the current line outwards until there is no more conflict, then continue the construction (see Fig. 4). If there are particles blocking the shift process, then we deconstruct $bb(P)$ until we can shift again or until we can proceed adding particles to the current line. If the line to shift is the first line of the constructed bounding box, we know that there exists a particle of P that has the same y-coordinate as the current starting position. Therefore, we build a bridge to traverse this gap, as shown in Fig. 5. Afterwards, we can restart from phase (1).

Fig. 4. (a) R_1 hits a particle belonging to P. (b) The triggered shifting process is finished.

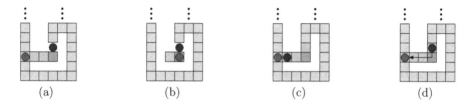

Fig. 5. Traversing a gap by building a bridge

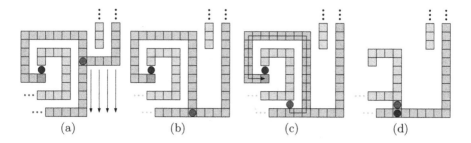

Fig. 6. The second case of finishing the bounding box. (a) An already constructed part of the bounding box is hit. (b) The last boundary side is shifted. (c) R_1 found a suitable new connectivity pixel above the southern side, places a particle and retraces its path to the initial starting position. (d) The unnecessary part of the bounding box is removed and both robots catch up to the new connection.

For phase (3), consider the case when R_1 reaches a particle of the bounding box. If the hit particle is not a corner particle, the current line needs to be shifted outwards until the next corner is reached (see Fig. 6(a)). Then we can search for another suitable connection between P and $bb(P)$, place a particle there, and get to R_2 to remove unnecessary parts of the bounding box (see Fig. 6(b)–(d)). Because $bb(P)$ has only one particle with three adjacent particles left, we can always find the connection between P and $bb(P)$.

Theorem 1. *Given a polyominino P of width w and height h, building a bounding box surrounding P with the need that boundary and P are always connected, can be done with two robots in $O(\max(w, h) \cdot (wh + k \cdot |\partial P|))$ steps, where k is the number of convex corners in P, i.e., a particle t at which we can place a 2×2 square containing t and three empty pixel.*

See our full version [17] for full details.

If we know in advance that the given polyomino contains no holes, then we can build a non-simple bounding box. This requires only one robot, because we can at any moment distinguish the polyomino from the bounding box without having a second robot holding both parts together. Details can be found in our full version [17]. This yields the following corollary.

Corollary 1. *Given a simple polyominino P of width w and height h, building a bounding box surrounding P with the need that boundary and P are always connected, can be done with one robot in $O(\max(w, h) \cdot wh)$ steps.*

4   Scaling Polyominoes

Now we consider scaling a given shape by a positive integer factor c. Note that reducing the size of a polyomino by a factor $\frac{1}{c}$ ("*downscaling*") can then be done in a similar fashion. In the following we assume that the robot R_1 has already built the bounding box and is positioned on one of its particles. See Fig. 7 (a).

The scaling process can be divided into two phases: (1) the preparation phase, and (2) the scaling phase. In phase (1) we fill up the last, i.e., rightmost column within $bb(P)$, add a particle in the second last column above the south side of $bb(P)$, and remove the lowest particle (called *column marker*) and third lowest particle (called *row marker*) on the east side of $bb(P)$ (see Fig. 7(a)). This yields three columns within the bounding box (including $bb(P)$ itself). The first (from west to east) is the current column of P to scale. The second column, which is filled with particles except the topmost row, is used to ensure connectivity and helps to recognize the end of the current column. The third column marks the current overall progress, i.e., we can find the pixel in the correct current column and row that we want to scale next.

In phase (2) we consider four main operations using three variables. b_{COL} denotes whether we scaled the last pixel of the current column, b_{PIXEL} denotes the state of the pixel that we want to scale, and b_{NEW} denotes whether we started scaling up a new column. We initialize phase (2) with $b_{\text{COL}} := 0$, and $b_{\text{NEW}} := 1$.

Find column marker: The robot moves counterclockwise along the boundary until it finds an empty position. This is the column marker. Then we check if we need to *prepare the next column*. Afterwards, we *prepare scaling the next pixel*.

Prepare scaling the next pixel: We start from the column marker and move up until we reach the row marker. We place a particle, move one pixel **up** and try to remove a particle. If there is no particle, then we are about to scale the last pixel in the current column. Let b_{COL} denote whether the pixel was empty or not.

Then the robot moves to the pixel that is scaled next, i.e., the robot moves one pixel **down** and two pixels **left**. The robot stores the state of the pixel in b_{PIXEL}, and places a particle if $b_{\text{PIXEL}} = $ empty. Afterwards, we *scale the pixel*.

Scale the pixel: First we move to the bottom side of the bounding box. Then we move **left** until the next pixel is empty.

If $b_{\text{NEW}} = 1$, we build the $c \times c$-square to the left (with a middle particle missing if $b_{\text{PIXEL}} = $ empty) and we set $b_{\text{NEW}} := 0$.

Else, if $b_{\text{NEW}} = 0$, we move **up** until we step on an empty pixel and build the $c \times c$-square (with a middle particle missing if $b_{\text{PIXEL}} = $ empty).

Afterwards, we return to *find the column marker*.

Prepare next column: If $b_{\text{COL}} = 1$, then we prepare the next column. We move the column marker one pixel **left** and remove the particle two pixels above the column marker, i.e., we place the row marker. In addition, we place a particle one pixel above and one pixel to the left of the column marker. Then we set $b_{\text{NEW}} := 1$.

We iterate through these operations until we scale a column that only contains empty pixels. Afterwards, we start the clean-up phase. We remove all particles from the old bounding box area, proceeding column-wise from right to left. Due to the simple structure, we know that we finished removing this area when the removed column has no empty pixel.

If necessary, all scaled empty particles can also be removed. For each scaled column (e.g. from left to right), we remove empty scaled pixels from top to bottom until we find a scaled occupied pixel t. Then we remove scaled empty pixels from bottom to top until we reach t again. This way, the whole arrangement is always connected.

  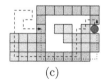 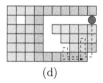

(a)   (b)   (c)   (d)

Fig. 7. Intermediate steps of scaling by factor $c = 3$. Dashed and dotted lines denote the robot's paths. (a) Configuration after the preparation phase showing the column marker (blue circle), row marker (red circle) and the next particle to scale (teal circle). (b)–(d) Cases that appear during the scaling: (b) Scaling an occupied pixel; (c) scaling an empty pixel; (d) reaching the end of a column. The robot prepares the next column. (Color figure online)

Theorem 2. *After building bb(P), scaling a polyomino P of width w and height h by a constant scaling factor c without loss of connectivity can be done with one robot in $O(wh \cdot (c^2 + cw + ch))$ steps.*

Proof. **Correctness:** We scan through the whole bounding box of P and scale every position. This implies that we scale every particle of P. Because we scale columnwise, we ensure that every scaled particle is built at the correct position. Connectivity is guaranteed because we never remove a particle that is necessary to have connectivity.

Time: Each of the $w \cdot h$ pixels within the bounding box of P is scaled. To this end, the robot has to move $O(c(w + h))$ steps to reach the position at which the scaled pixel needs to be constructed. A further $O(c^2)$ steps are needed to construct the particle. Finding the next pixel to scale takes $O(c(w + h))$ steps, including going back, find the correct column and row, and moving the row and column marker. In total we have a runtime of $O(wh(c^2 + cw + ch))$. $\qquad\qquad$ □

5   Scaling Monotone Polyominoes

When the polyomino P is x- or y-monotone, we can scale P using two robots without constructing a bounding box. P is called *x-monotone* (*y-monotone*) if the intersection with any vertical (horizontal) line with P is a connected set. See Fig. 8 for a polyomino and its scaled version. In the following we consider an x-monotone polygon P. We proceed in two phases: (I) scaling the columns of P, (II) scaling the rows of P. Similar to the preceding section, R_1 performs the actual task, whereas R_2 is used to mark particles and to keep everything connected.

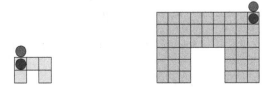

Fig. 8. Left: An x-monotone input polyomino P. Right: P scaled by factor $c = 3$.

5.1   Phase I

During the first phase, we process the polyomino column-wise from left to right to scale the columns of P by the factor c. The marker robot R_2 is placed on the uppermost particle of the current column and R_1 right above. For every particle in that column, R_2 waits for R_1 to communicate the state of the current pixel and moves one step down until the first empty pixel is reached. When R_1 receives a signal for an occupied pixel, it extends the current column on the upper side

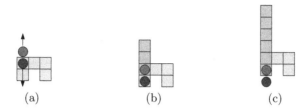

Fig. 9. Intermediate arrangements of scaling a monotone polyomino. Scaled particles are marked gray. (a) Processing one column during the first phase: R_1 extends the column to the upper side and R_2 marks the current progress within that column. (b) The first particle scaled. (c) The first column scaled in y-direction by factor $c = 3$.

by $c - 1$ particles and returns to R_2. When R_2 steps on the first empty pixel, the current column is finished after R_1 returns to R_2; see Fig. 9 (c) for an example.

To scale the next column, we consider three cases. The lowest particle of the next column may have an equal, a higher or a lower y-coordinate than the lowest particle of the current column. Let t_n (t_c, resp.) be the lowest particle of the next (current, resp.) column and y_{t_n} (y_{t_c}, resp.) the y-coordinate of that particle. The three cases are handled as follows.

1. $y_{t_n} = y_{t_c}$: We can simply continue with the next column.
2. $y_{t_n} > y_{t_c}$: Before moving to the next column we have to scale empty pixels. For each empty pixel t_e below t_n with y-coordinate $y_{t_e} \geq y_{t_c}$, we move every column to the right of the current column $c - 1$ units up. This can be done by letting R_2 mark the next empty pixel and by letting R_1 shift the columns up. The shifting process can be done by adding $c - 1$ particles above each column and afterwards removing $c - 1$ particles from the bottom (see Fig. 10).
3. $y_{t_n} < y_{t_c}$: This case is more complex because it is not immediately clear in which direction all remaining columns have to be shifted in order to scale the next column correctly. We perform a scaling of the next column and a shifting of remaining columns at the same time. We proceed as follows. Let t be the particle with y-coordinate $y_t = y_{t_c}$. We scale the column from top to t as described above. For each particle below t starting from the bottom, we add $c - 1$ to the bottom of the column and shift all columns to the right $c - 1$ steps down. Note that this process is completed when R_1 return to R_2 and when R_2 is to the right of t_c. We can now proceed with the next column (see Fig. 11).

5.2   Phase II

When all columns have been scaled, we proceed with phase II to scale the rows. The idea of phase II is as follows. Proceed column-wise; for a column C shift all remaining columns $c - 1$ steps to the right to make space for building $c - 1$ copies of C. Clearly, we cannot simply shift a column $c - 1$ steps to the right, as

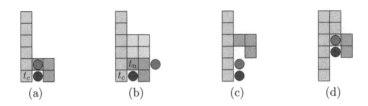

Fig. 10. Example for $y_{t_n} > y_{t_c}$. Scaled tiles are marked gray. (a) Recognizing the case. (b) Two particles placed above every following column. (c) Two particles removed from the bottom end of every column.

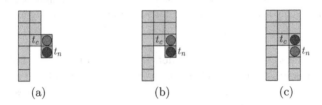

Fig. 11. Recognizing $y_{t_n} < y_{t_c}$. Scaled tiles are marked gray. (a) Recognizing the case. (b) All pixels having a y-coordinate of at least y_{t_c} are scaled upwards. (c) All pixels having a y-coordinate of strictly less than y_{t_c} are scaled downwards.

this would disconnect the shape. Instead, we process the columns from right to left until we reach C and shift the columns in the following way.

For a column C', copy it $c - 1$ times to the right. Then, starting from the bottommost particle of the rightmost copy of C', move c steps **left**. From there, we move **up** until we reach a particle t with y-coordinate y_t. Afterwards, we remove any particle from the next $c - 1$ columns with a y-coordinate strictly larger or smaller than y_t. After this clean-up, the rightmost copy of C' still exists and is connected with its previous column by a bridge. We can now proceed with the column containing t. If this column is C, then we perform the same steps without the clean-up phase (see Fig. 12).

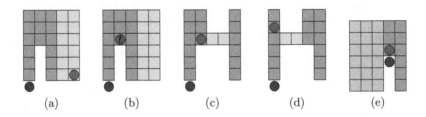

Fig. 12. Intermediate steps of scaling horizontally. Blue particles denote particles that need to be scaled horizontally, light gray particles denote auxiliary structures, dark gray particles denote scaled areas. (a) The rightmost column is copied $c - 1 = 2$ times. (b) R_1 identifies particle t. (c) Bridge is built. (d) Construction after shifting the next column. (e) Construction after scaling the first column. (Color figure online)

Theorem 3. *Scaling an x-monotone polyomino P with N particles, width w, and height h by a constant scaling factor c without losing connectivity can be done with two robots in $O(wc^2N)$ steps.*

Proof. **Correctness phase I:** Scaling the first column is correct, because for each particle we add $c-1$ particles to the top of the column, which results in scaling the column by factor c. Furthermore, the lowest particle t_c of the first column still has the same neighbor t (either an empty pixel or a particle) with the same number of empty and occupied pixels above and below t. We use this fact as an invariant to prove that the remaining columns are also scaled correctly. Now assume we correctly scaled the first k columns. In the first case, when $y_{t_c} = y_{t_n}$, we scale the next column, because it is the first column and all scaled particles have now the correct particles from the k-th column. The invariant still holds for the first $k+1$ columns, because we did not shift any columns.

For the second case ($y_{t_c} < y_{t_n}$), we shift all remaining columns by $c-1$ steps up, such that t_n has the correct neighbor to the left. Note that t_n maintains its right neighbor during the shifting process. Thus, after the shifting process, the invariant holds and we can scale the column.

In the remaining case, we can scale all particles in the next column with y-coordinate at least y_{t_c}, which does not change the invariant for the first $k+1$ columns. When scaling the lower particles, we shift all remaining columns **down**, such that the new bottommost particle has now the neighbor that t_n had. Thus, after scaling this complete column, the invariant holds for the first $k+1$ columns.

By induction, we correctly scale the columns.

Correctness phase II: To prove the correctness of phase II, we show that the shift of columns is performed without losing connectivity. The scaling is done within the shifting process by ignoring the clean-up for the last column. Thus, a repeated shifting phase scales the polyomino.

Consider the rightmost column. After copying this column c times, the whole polyomino is still connected. In the clean-up phase, we keep a bridge between the shifted column and the next column, maintaining connectivity. This bridge can then be used to copy the next column. By induction, we can shift n columns without losing connectivity.

Combining phase I and II, we scale the polyomino by the factor c.

Time phase I: Let n_i denote the number of particles in the ith column in P. Before scaling the ith column, we may need to shift all remaining columns by at most $O(cn_{i-1})$ unit steps in case 2, or $O(cn_i)$ unit steps in case 1. Because there are at most w columns, this lasts $O(wc(n_{i-1}+n_i))$ steps. Scaling each particle in the column takes at most $O(cn_i)$ steps. Summing this up over all columns, we have at most $O(cn_1) + \sum_{i=2}^{w} O(wc(n_{i-1}+n_i)) + O(cn_i) = O(wcN)$.

Time phase II: Consider the ith column of P containing cn_i particles. Shifting all remaining columns $c-1$ unit steps to the right needs $O(c^2N)$ steps. Scaling the ith column needs another $O(c^2n_i)$ steps. Over all columns, phase (2) needs $O(\sum_{i=1}^{w} c^2N + c^2n_i) = O(wc^2N)$ steps in total.   □

6   Adapting Algorithms

As shown in [16], there are algorithms that may not preserve connectivity. An immediate consequence of being able to scale a given shape is that we can simulate any algorithm $\mathcal{A}$ within our model while guaranteeing connectivity: We first scale the polyomino by three and then execute $\mathcal{A}$ by always performing three steps into one direction if $\mathcal{A}$ does one step. If at some point the robot needs to move through empty pixels, then we place a 3×3-square with the middle pixel empty (if a clean-up is desired at the end of $\mathcal{A}$, i.e., removing all scaled empty pixels, we fill up the complete row/column with these squares). This guarantees connectivity during the execution and we obtain the following theorem.

Theorem 4. *If there is an algorithm $\mathcal{A}$ for some problem Π with runtime $\mathcal{T}(\mathcal{A})$, such that the robot moves within a $w' \times h'$ rectangle, then there is an algorithm $\mathcal{A}'$ for Π with runtime $O(wh \cdot (w + h) + \max((w' - w)h', (h' - h)w') + \mathcal{T}(\mathcal{A}))$ guaranteeing connectivity during execution.*

Proof. **Approach:** The first step is to scale the polyomino P of width w and height h by a factor $c = 3$ with the strategy above. We keep any 3×3 square in the clean-up phase of the scaling algorithms. This gives us a $3w \times 3h$ rectangle containing the scaled polyomino and 3×3 segments representing empty pixels from the $w \times h$ area of the initial polyomino.

We adapt the algorithm $\mathcal{A}$ as follows. When the robot places a particle in $\mathcal{A}$, then we place a particle in the middle of the 3×3 square in $\mathcal{A}'$. A removal in $\mathcal{A}$ is represented by removing the middle particle of the 3×3 square in $\mathcal{A}'$.

For each step the robot moves into direction d in $\mathcal{A}$, we move 3 steps into direction d in $\mathcal{A}'$, i.e., the robot effectively moves on a grid scaled up by a factor of three (see Fig. 13(a)). If the robot reaches a position at which no 3×3 square is present (see Fig. 13(b)), then the robot adds such a square representing an empty node and leaves the middle bottom particle missing (see Fig. 13(c)). Then the robot fills up the complete row/column with 3×3 squares and returns to the position at which the middle bottom particle is missing (see Fig. 13(d)). From there we can continue the execution of $\mathcal{A}$.

Analysis: The scaling procedure requires $O(wh \cdot (w + h))$ steps. Due to the described movement adjustment of doing three steps in $\mathcal{A}'$ instead of one step in $\mathcal{A}$, the runtime of $\mathcal{A}$ increases by the constant factor three. Finally, we consider the fill-in procedure to be used in case of stepping on an empty pixel. Depending on the robot's movement area for $\mathcal{A}$, we get $O(max((w' - w)h', (h' - h)w'))$ steps for filling in. This results in an overall runtime of $O(wh \cdot (w + h) + max((w' - w)h', (h' - h)w') + \mathcal{T}(\mathcal{A}))$ steps. $\square$

When the algorithm terminates and there is only one polyomino left in the constructed rectangle area, we can either remove empty cells or downscale the polyomino to its original size.

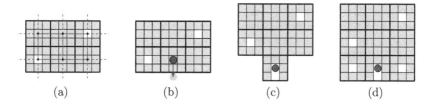

(a)   (b)   (c)   (d)

Fig. 13. (a) A polyomino scaled by a factor of $c = 3$. The robot moves along the red lines when an algorithm is executed. (b) The robot enters an empty pixel when it tries to move south. (c) Marked the first $c \times c$ segment, which the robot hasentered, by removing the bottom-middle particle. (d) The robot hasfilled the row with $c \times c$ segments and moves back to the previously marked segment.

7 Conclusion

We have demonstrated how geometric algorithms for finite automata can be used to enable very simple robots to perform a number of fundamental construction tasks while preserving connectivity. There is a whole range of possible extensions. Is it possible to scale general polyominoes without the preceding bounding box construction? A possible approach is to cut the polyomino into a subset of monotone polyominoes, which could be handled separately. Expanding the existing repertoire of operations to three-dimensional configurations and operations is another logical step. An equally relevant challenge is to develop distributed algorithms with multiple robots that are capable of solving a range of problems with the requirement of connectivity, without having to rely on the preceding scaling procedure that we used in our work. Other questions arise from additional requirements of real-world applications, such as the construction and reconfiguration of space habitats.

References

1. Abdel-Rahman, A., et al.: Space ants: constructing and reconfiguring large-scale structures with finite automata. In: Symposium on Computational Geometry (SoCG), pp. 73:1–73:7 (2020). https://www.ibr.cs.tu-bs.de/users/fekete/Videos/SoCG/2020/Space_final.mp4
2. Bender, M.A., Slonim, D.K.: The power of team exploration: two robots can learn unlabeled directed graphs. In: Symposium on Foundations of Computer Science (FOCS), pp. 75–85 (1994)
3. Blum, M., Kozen, D.: On the power of the compass (or, why mazes are easier to search than graphs). In: Symposium on Foundations of Computer Science (FOCS), pp. 132–142 (1978)
4. Brass, P., Cabrera-Mora, F., Gasparri, A., Xiao, J.: Multirobot tree and graph exploration. IEEE Trans. Robot. **27**(4), 707–717 (2011)
5. Czyzowicz, J., Dobrev, S., Gasieniec, L., Ilcinkas, D., Jansson, J., Klasing, R., Lignos, I., Martin, R., Sadakane, K., Sung, W.-K.: More efficient periodic traversal in anonymous undirected graphs. Theor. Comput. Sci. **444**, 60–76 (2012)

6. D'Angelo, G., D'Emidio, M., Das, S., Navarra, A., Prencipe, G.: Leader election and compaction for asynchronous silent programmable matter. In: Proceedings of the 19th International Conference on Autonomous Agents and MultiAgent Systems, pp. 276–284 (2020)
7. Das, S., Flocchini, P., Kutten, S., Nayak, A., Santoro, N.: Map construction of unknown graphs by multiple agents. Theor. Comput. Sci. **385**(1), 34–48 (2007)
8. Daymude, J.J., Gmyr, R., Richa, A.W., Scheideler, C., Strothmann, T.: Improved leader election for self-organizing programmable matter. In: Fernández Anta, A., Jurdzinski, T., Mosteiro, M.A., Zhang, Y. (eds.) ALGOSENSORS 2017. LNCS, vol. 10718, pp. 127–140. Springer, Cham (2017). https://doi.org/10.1007/978-3-319-72751-6_10
9. Derakhshandeh, Z., Dolev, S., Gmyr, R., Richa, A.W., Scheideler, C., Strothmann, T.: Brief announcement: amoebot - a new model for programmable matter. In: ACM Symposium on Parallelism in Algorithms and Architectures (SPAA), pp. 220–222 (2014)
10. Derakhshandeh, Z., Gmyr, R., Porter, A., Richa, A.W., Scheideler, C., Strothmann, T.: On the runtime of universal coating for programmable matter. In: Rondelez, Y., Woods, D. (eds.) DNA 2016. LNCS, vol. 9818, pp. 148–164. Springer, Cham (2016). https://doi.org/10.1007/978-3-319-43994-5_10
11. Derakhshandeh, Z., Gmyr, R., Richa, A.W., Scheideler, C., Strothmann, T.: An algorithmic framework for shape formation problems in self-organizing particle systems. In: International Conference on Nanoscale Computing and Communication (NANOCOM), pp. 21:1–21:2 (2015)
12. Derakhshandeh, Z., Gmyr, R., Richa, A.W., Scheideler, C., Strothmann, T.: Universal coating for programmable matter. Theor. Comput. Sci. **671**, 56–68 (2017)
13. Derakhshandeh, Z., Gmyr, R., Strothmann, T., Bazzi, R., Richa, A.W., Scheideler, C.: Leader election and shape formation with self-organizing programmable matter. In: International Conference on DNA Computing and Molecular Programming (DNA), pp. 117–132 (2015)
14. Di Luna, G.A., Flocchini, P., Santoro, N., Viglietta, G., Yamauchi, Y.: Shape formation by programmable particles. Distrib. Comput. **33**(1), 69–101 (2019). https://doi.org/10.1007/s00446-019-00350-6
15. Diks, K., Fraigniaud, P., Kranakis, E., Pelc, A.: Tree exploration with little memory. J. Algorithms **51**(1), 38–63 (2004)
16. Fekete, S.P., Gmyr, R., Hugo, S., Keldenich, P., Scheffer, C., Schmidt, A.: CADbots: algorithmic aspects of manipulating programmable matter with finite automata. In: Morales, M., Tapia, L., Sánchez-Ante, G., Hutchinson, S. (eds.) WAFR 2018. SPAR, vol. 14, pp. 727–743. Springer, Cham (2020). https://doi.org/10.1007/978-3-030-44051-0_42
17. Fekete, S.P., Niehs, E., Scheffer, C., Schmidt, A.: Connected assembly and reconfiguration by finite automata. CoRR (2019)
18. Fleischer, R., Trippen, G.: Exploring an unknown graph efficiently. In: Brodal, G.S., Leonardi, S. (eds.) ESA 2005. LNCS, vol. 3669, pp. 11–22. Springer, Heidelberg (2005). https://doi.org/10.1007/11561071_4
19. Fraigniaud, P., Gasieniec, L., Kowalski, D.R., Pelc, A.: Collective tree exploration. Networks **48**(3), 166–177 (2006)
20. Fraigniaud, P., Ilcinkas, D.: Digraphs exploration with little memory. In: Symposium on Theoretical Aspects of Computer Science (STACS), pp. 246–257 (2004)
21. Fraigniaud, P., Ilcinkas, D., Peer, G., Pelc, A., Peleg, D.: Graph exploration by a finite automaton. Theor. Comput. Sci. **345**(2–3), 331–344 (2005)

22. Gasieniec, L., Pelc, A., Radzik, T., Zhang, X.: Tree exploration with logarithmic memory. In: ACM-SIAM Symposium on Discrete Algorithms (SODA), pp. 585–594 (2007)
23. Gąsieniec, L., Radzik, T.: Memory efficient anonymous graph exploration. In: Broersma, H., Erlebach, T., Friedetzky, T., Paulusma, D. (eds.) WG 2008. LNCS, vol. 5344, pp. 14–29. Springer, Heidelberg (2008). https://doi.org/10.1007/978-3-540-92248-3_2
24. Gmyr, R., Hinnenthal, K., Kostitsyna, I., Kuhn, F., Rudolph, D., Scheideler, C.: Shape recognition by a finite automaton robot. In: International Symposium on Mathematical Foundations of Computer Science (MFCS), pp. 52:1–52:15 (2018)
25. Gmyr, R., Hinnenthal, K., Kostitsyna, I., Kuhn, F., Rudolph, D., Scheideler, C., Strothmann, T.: Forming tile shapes with simple robots. In: International Conference on DNA Computing and Molecular Programming (DNA), pp. 122–138 (2018)
26. Gmyr, R., Kostitsyna, I., Kuhn, F., Scheideler, C., Strothmann, T.: Forming tile shapes with a single robot. In: European Workshop on Computational Geometry (EuroCG), pp. 9–12 (2017)
27. Gregg, C.E., Jenett, B., Cheung, K.C.: Assembled, modular hardware architectures - what price reconfigurability? In: IEEE Aerospace Conference, pp. 1–10 (2019)
28. Gregg, C.E., Kim, J.H., Cheung, K.C.: Ultra-light and scalable composite lattice materials. Adv. Eng. Mater. **20**(9), 1800213 (2018)
29. Hurtado, F., Molina, E., Ramaswami, S., Sacristán, V.: Distributed reconfiguration of 2D lattice-based modular robotic systems. Auton. Robots **38**(4), 383–413 (2015). https://doi.org/10.1007/s10514-015-9421-8
30. Jenett, B., Cellucci, D.: A mobile robot for locomotion through a 3D periodic lattice environment. In: IEEE International Conference on Robotics and Automation (ICRA), pp. 5474–5479 (2017)
31. Jenett, B., Cellucci, D., Gregg, C., Cheung, K.: Meso-scale digital materials: modular, reconfigurable, lattice-based structures. In: ASME International Manufacturing Science and Engineering Conference (MSEC) (2016)
32. Jenett, B., Cheung, K.: BILL-E: robotic platform for locomotion and manipulation of lightweight space structures. In: AIAA/AHS Adaptive Structures Conference, p. 1876 (2017)
33. Kosowski, A., Navarra, A.: Graph decomposition for memoryless periodic exploration. Algorithmica **63**(1–2), 26–38 (2012)
34. Niehs, E., et al.: Recognition and reconfiguration of lattice-based cellular structures by simple robots. In: IEEE International Conference on Robotics and Automation (ICRA) (2020, to appear). https://www.ibr.cs.tu-bs.de/users/fekete/hp/publications/PDF/2020-Automata_ICRA.pdf
35. Panaite, P., Pelc, A.: Exploring unknown undirected graphs. J. Algorithms **33**(2), 281–295 (1999)
36. Woods, D., Chen, H.-L., Goodfriend, S., Dabby, N., Winfree, E., Yin, P.: Active self-assembly of algorithmic shapes and patterns in polylogarithmic time. In: 4th Conference on Innovations in Theoretical Computer Science (ITCS), pp. 353–354 (2013)

On Efficient Connectivity-Preserving Transformations in a Grid

Abdullah Almethen$^{(\boxtimes)}$, Othon Michail$^{(\boxtimes)}$, and Igor Potapov$^{(\boxtimes)}$

Department of Computer Science, University of Liverpool, Liverpool, UK
{A.Almethen,Othon.Michail,Potapov}@liverpool.ac.uk

Abstract. We consider a discrete system of n devices lying on a 2-dimensional square grid and forming an initial connected shape S_I. Each device is equipped with a linear-strength mechanism which enables it to move a whole line of consecutive devices in a single time-step. We study the problem of transforming S_I into a given connected target shape S_F of the same number of devices, via a finite sequence of *line moves*. Our focus is on designing *centralised* transformations aiming at *minimising the total number of moves* subject to the constraint of *preserving connectivity* of the shape throughout the course of the transformation. We first give very fast connectivity-preserving transformations for the case in which the *associated graphs* of S_I and S_F are isomorphic to a Hamiltonian line. In particular, our transformations make $O(n \log n)$ moves, which is asymptotically equal to the best known running time of connectivity-breaking transformations. Our most general result is then a connectivity-preserving *universal transformation* that can transform any initial connected shape S_I into any target connected shape S_F, through a sequence of $O(n\sqrt{n})$ moves.

Keywords: Line movement · Discrete transformations · Shape formation · Reconfigurable robotics · Time complexity · Programmable matter

1 Introduction

Over the past few years, many fascinating systems have been developed, leveraging advanced technology in order to deploy large collections of tiny monads. Each monad is typically a highly restricted micro-robotic entity, equipped with a microcontroller and some actuation and sensing capabilities. Through its collaborative complexity, the collection of monads can carry out tasks which are well beyond the capabilities of individual monads. The vision is the development of materials that will be able to algorithmically change their physical properties, such as their shape, colour, conductivity and density, based on transformations executed by an underlying program. These efforts are currently shaping the research area of *programmable matter*, which has attracted much theoretical

The full version of the paper is available at: https://arxiv.org/abs/2005.08351.

and practical interest. The implementation indicates whether the monads are operated centrally or through local decentralised control. In *centralised* systems, there is an external program which globally controls all monads with full knowledge of the entire system. On the other hand, *decentralised* systems provide each individual monad with enough autonomy to communicate with its neighbours and move locally. There are an impressive number of recent developments for collective robotic systems, demonstrating their potential and feasibility, starting from the scale of milli or micro [9,26,29,36] down to nano size of individual monads [20,34].

Recent research has highlighted the need for the development of an algorithmic theory of such systems. Michail and Spirakis [32] and Michail *et al.* [30] emphasised an apparent lack of a formal theoretical study of this prospective, including modelling, possibilities/limitations, algorithms and complexity. The development of a formal theory is a crucial step for further progress in those systems. Consequently, multiple theoretical computer science subfields have appeared, such as metamorphic systems [23,33,37], mobile robotics [11,13,14,18,40], reconfigurable robotics [4,10,15,17,42], passively-mobile systems [6,7,31,32], DNA self-assembly [19,35,38,39], and the latest emerging subarea of "Algorithmic Foundations of Programmable Matter" [25].

Consider a system deployed on a two-dimensional square grid in which a collection of spherical devices are typically connected to each other, forming a shape S_I. By a finite number of valid individual moves, S_I can be transformed into a desired target shape S_F. In this perspective, a number of models are designed and introduced in the literature for such systems. For example, Dumitrescu and Pach [21], Dumitrescu *et al.* [22,23] and Michail *et al.* [30] consider mechanisms where an individual device is capable to move over and turn around its neighbours through empty space. Transformations based on similar moves being assisted by small seeds, have also been considered in [1].

A new linear-strength mechanism was introduced by Almethen *et al.* in [3], where a whole line of consecutive devices can, in a single time-step, move by one position in a given direction. That model comes as a natural generalisation of other existing models of reconfiguration with a particular focus on exploiting the power of parallelism for fast global reconfiguration. Apart from the pure theoretical interest of exploring fast transformations on a grid, this model also provides a practical framework for efficient reconfigurations of real systems. For example, this framework could be applied to reconfigurable robotic systems in which the individual devices are equipped with linear-strength locomotion mechanisms.

Since any two shapes with an equal number of elements can be transformed into each other with line moves [3], the central question remains about understanding the bounds on reachability distances between different shapes (configurations) via line moves. Proving exact reachability bounds can influence the design and analysis of both centralised and distributed algorithms. Our hypothesis is that the reachability distances between any two shapes with n elements can be bounded by $O(n \log n)$, and the bound cannot be improved for a simple pair of shapes such as diagonal and horizontal lines.

In this paper, we embark from the *line-pushing* model of [3], which provided sub-quadratic centralised transformations that may, though, arbitrarily break connectivity of the shape during their course. As our main goal is to investigate the power of the line-pushing model, we focus solely on centralised transformations, as a first step. That is because distributed are model-dependent (e.g., knowledge, communication, etc.), while centralised show what is *in principle* possible. Moreover, some of the ideas in centralised might prove useful for distributed and of course lower bounds also transfer to the distributed case. The only connectivity-preserving transformation in [3] was an $O(n\sqrt{n})$-time transformation for a single pair of shapes of order n, namely from a diagonal into a straight line. All transformations that we provide in the present study preserve connectivity of the shape during the transformation.

We first give very fast connectivity-preserving transformations for the case in which the *associated graphs* of S_I and S_F are isomorphic to a Hamiltonian line. In particular, our transformations make $O(n \log n)$ moves, which is asymptotically equal to the best known running time of connectivity-breaking transformations. Our most general result is then a connectivity-preserving *universal transformation* that can transform any initial connected shape S_I into any target connected shape S_F, through a sequence of $O(n\sqrt{n})$ moves.

1.1   Related Work

For the models of individual moves where only one node moves in a single time-step, [21,30] show universality of transforming any pair of connected shapes (A, B) having the same number of devices (called *nodes* throughout this paper) to each other via sliding and rotation mechanisms. By allowing only rotation, [30] proves that the problem of deciding transformability is in **P**. It can be shown that in all models of constant-distance individual moves, $\Omega(n^2)$ moves are required to transform some pairs of connected shapes, due the inherent distance between them [30]. This motivates the study of alternative types of moves that are reasonable with respect to practical implementations and allow for sub-quadratic reconfiguration time in the worst case.

There are attempts in the literature to provide alternatives for more efficient reconfiguration. The first main approach is to explore parallel transformations, where multiple nodes move together in a single time-step. This is a natural step to tackle such a problem, especially in distributed systems where nodes can make independent decisions and move locally in parallel to other nodes. There are a number of theoretical studies on parallel and distributed transformations [15,16,18,23,30,41] as well as practical implementations [36]. For example, it can be shown that a connected shape can transform into any other connected shape, by performing in the worst case $O(n)$ parallel moves around the perimeter of the shape [30].

The second approach aims to equip nodes in the system with a more powerful mechanism which enables them to reduce the inherent distance by a factor greater than a constant in a single time-step. There are a number of models in the literature in which individual nodes are equipped with strong actuation mechanisms, such as linear-strength mechanisms. Aloupis *et al.* [4,5] provide a node with arms that are capable to extend and contract a neighbour, a subset of the nodes or even the whole shape as a consequence of such an operation. Further, Woods *et al.* [39] proposed an alternative linear-strength mechanism, where a node has the ability to rotate a whole line of consecutive nodes.

Recently, the *line-pushing* model of [3] follows a similar approach in which a single node can move a whole line of consecutive nodes by simultaneously (i.e., in a single time-step) pushing them towards an empty position. The line-pushing model can simulate the rotation and sliding based transformations of [21,30] with at most a 2-factor increase in their worst-case running time. This implies that all transformations established for individual nodes, transfer in the line-pushing model and their universality and reversibility properties still hold true. They achieved sub-quadratic time transformations, including an $O(n \log n)$-time universal transformation which does not preserve connectivity and a connectivity-preserving $O(n\sqrt{n})$-time transformation for the special case of transforming a diagonal into a straight line.

Another relevant line of research has considered a single moving robot that transforms an otherwise static shape by carrying its tiles one at a time [13,24, 27]. Those models are partially centralised as a single robot (usually a finite automaton) controls the transformation, but, in contrast to our perspective, control in that case is local and lacking global information.

1.2   Our Contribution

In this work, we build upon the findings of [3] aiming to design very efficient and general transformations that are additionally able to keep the shape connected throughout their course. We first give an $O(n \log n)$-time transformation, called *Walk-Through-Path*, that works for all pairs of shapes (S_I, S_F) that have the same order and belong to the family of *Hamiltonian shapes*. A *Hamiltonian shape* is any connected shape S whose *associated graph* $G(S)$ is isomorphic to a Hamiltonian path (see also [28]). At the heart of our transformation is a recursive successive doubling technique, which starts from one endpoint of the Hamiltonian path and proceeds in $\log n$ phases (where n denotes the order of the input shape S_I, throughout this paper). In every phase i, it moves a terminal line L_i of length 2^i a distance 2^i higher on the Hamiltonian path through a *LineWalk* operation. This leaves a new terminal sub-path S_i of the Hamiltonian path, of length 2^i. Then the general procedure is recursively called on S_i to transform it into a straight line L'_i of length 2^i. Finally, the two straight lines L_i and L'_i which are perpendicular to each other are combined into a new straight line L_{i+1} of length 2^{i+1} and the next phase begins.

A core technical challenge in making the above transformation work is that Hamiltonian shapes do not necessarily provide free space for the *LineWalk* operation. Thus, moving a line has to take place through the remaining configuration of nodes while at the same time ensuring that it does not break their and its own connectivity, including keeping itself connected to the rest of the shape. We manage to overcome this by revealing a nice property of line moves, according to which a line L can *transparently* walk through *any* configuration S (independently of the latter's density) in a way that: (i) preserves connectivity of both L and S and (ii) as soon as L has gone through it, S has been restored to its original state, that is, all of its nodes are lying in their original positions. This property is formally proved in Proposition 1 (Sect. 2).

Finally, we develop a *universal transformation*, called *UC-Box*, that within $O(n\sqrt{n})$ moves transforms any pair of connected shapes of the same order to each other, while preserving connectivity throughout its course. Starting from the initial shape S_I, we first compute a spanning tree T of S_I. Then we enclose the shape into a square box of size n and divide it into sub-boxes of size $\sqrt{n}$, each of which contains at least one sub-tree of T. By moving lines in a way that does not break connectivity, we compress the nodes in a sub-box into an adjacent sub-box towards a parent sub-tree. By carefully repeating this we manage to arrive at a final configuration which is always a compressed square shape. The latter is a type of a *nice* shape (a family of connected shapes introduced in [3]), which can be transformed into a straight line in linear time. We provide an analysis of this strategy based on the number of *charging phases*, which turns out to be $\sqrt{n}$, each making at most n moves, for a total of $O(n\sqrt{n})$ moves.

Section 2 formally defines the model and the problems under consideration and proves a basic proposition which is a core technical tool in one of our transformations. Section 3 presents our $O(n \log n)$-time transformation for Hamiltonian shapes. Section 4 discusses our universal $O(n\sqrt{n})$-time transformation. Finally, in Sect. 5 we conclude and discuss interesting problems left open by our work.

2 Preliminaries

All transformations in this study operate on a two-dimensional square grid, in which each cell has a unique position of non-negative integer coordinates (x, y), where x represents columns and y denotes rows in the grid. A set of n nodes on the grid forms a shape S (of the order n), where every single node $u \in S$ occupies only one cell, $cell(u) = (u_x, u_y)$. A node u can be indicated at any given time by the coordinates (u_x, u_y) of the unique cell that it occupies at that time. A node $v \in S$ is a *neighbour* of (or *adjacent* to) a node $u \in S$ if and only if their coordinates satisfy $u_x - 1 \le v_x \le u_x + 1$ and $u_y - 1 \le v_y \le u_y + 1$ (i.e., their cells are adjacent vertically, horizontally or diagonally). A graph $G(S) = (V, E)$ is *associated* with a shape S, where $u \in V$ if u is a node of S and $(u, v) \in E$ iff u and v are neighbours in S. A shape S is connected iff $G(S)$ is a connected graph. We denote by $T(S)$ (or just T when clear from context) a spanning tree of $G(S)$. In what follows, n denotes the number of nodes in a shape under consideration, and all logarithms are to base 2.

In this paper, we exploit the linear-strength mechanism of the *line-pushing model* introduced in [3]. A line L is a sequence of nodes occupying consecutive cells in one direction of the grid, that is, either vertically or horizontally but not diagonally. A **line move** is an operation of moving all nodes of L together in a single time-step towards a position adjacent to one of L's endpoints, in a given direction d of the grid, $d \in \{up, down, right, left\}$. A line move may also be referred to as *step*, *move*, or *movement* in this paper. Throughout, the running time of transformations is measured in total number of line moves until completion. A *line move* is formally defined below.

Definition 1 (A Permissible Line Move). *A line $L = (x, y), (x + 1, y), \ldots, (x + k - 1, y)$ of length k, where $1 \le k \le n$, can push all its k nodes rightwards in a single move to positions $(x + 1, y), (x + 2, y), \ldots, (x + k, y)$ iff there exists an empty cell at $(x + k, y)$. The "down", "left", and "up" moves are defined symmetrically, by rotating the whole shape $90°$, $180°$ and $270°$ clockwise, respectively.*

A configuration of the system is defined as a mapping $C \colon \mathbb{Z} \times \mathbb{Z} \to \{0, 1\}$, where $C(x, y) = 0$ if cell(x, y) is empty or $C(x, y) = 1$ if cell(x, y) is occupied by a node. Equivalently, a configuration can be defined as a set $\{(x, y) : x, y \in \mathbb{Z}$ and $C(x, y) = 1\}$. Let C_0 denote the initial configuration of the system. We say that C' is *directly reachable* from C and denoted $C \to C'$, if C can be transformed to C' in one line move. Moreover, C' is reachable from C, denoted $C \to^* C'$, if there is a sequence of configurations $C = C_1, C_2, \ldots, C_t = C'$ such that $C_i \to C_{i+1}$ holds for all $i \in \{1, 2, \ldots, t - 1\}$. We next define a family of shapes that are used in one of our transformations.

Definition 2 (Hamiltonian Shapes). *A shape S is called Hamiltonian iff $G(S) = (V, E)$ is isomorphic to a Hamiltonian path, i.e., a path starting from a node $u \in V$, visiting every node in V exactly once and ending at a node $v \in V$, where $v \ne u$. $\mathcal{H}$ denotes the family of all Hamiltonian shapes, see Fig. 1.*

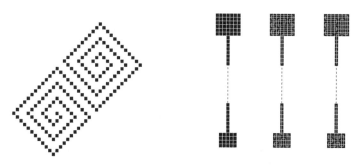

(a) A double-spiral shape.

(b) A shape of two different Hamiltonian paths in yellow (grey in print).

Fig. 1. Examples of Hamiltonian shapes.

We define a *rectangular path* P over the set of cells as $P = [c_1, c_2, c_3, \ldots, c_k]$, where $c_i, c_{i+1} \in \mathbb{Z} \times \mathbb{Z}$ are two cells adjacent to each other either vertically or horizontally, for all $i \in \{1, 2, \ldots, k - 1\}$. Given any *rectangular path* P, let C_P be the configuration of P, which is the subset of C (configuration of the system) restricted to the cells of P. The following proposition proves a basic property of line moves which will be a core technical tool in our transformation for Hamiltonian shapes.

Proposition 1 (Transparency of Line Moves). *Let S be any shape, $L \subseteq S$ any line and P a rectangular path starting from a position adjacent to one of L's endpoints. There is a way to move L along P, while satisfying all the following properties:*

1. No delay: *The number of steps is asymptotically equal to that of an optimum move of L along P in the case of C_P being empty (i.e., if no cells were occupied). That is, L is not delayed, independently of what C_P is.*
2. No effect: *After L's move along P, $C_P' = C_P$, i.e., the cell configuration has remained unchanged. Moreover, no occupied cell in C_P is ever emptied during L's move (but unoccupied cells may be temporarily occupied).*
3. No break: *S remains connected throughout L's move.*

Proof. Whenever L walks through an empty cell (x, y) of P, a node $u \in L$ fills in (x, y). If L pushes the node u of a non-empty cell of P, a node $v \in L$ takes its place. When L leaves a non-empty cell (x, y) that was originally occupied by node v, L restores (x, y) by leaving its endpoint $u \in L$ in (x, y). Finally, Fig. 2 shows how to deal with the case in which L turns at a non-empty corner-cell (x, y) of P, which is only connected diagonally to a non-empty cell of S and is not adjacent to any cell occupied by L.

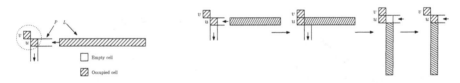

Fig. 2. A line L moving through a path P and arriving at a turning point of P. u occupies a corner cell of P, and v occupies a cell of S and is only connected diagonally to u while not being adjacent to any cell occupied by L. L pushes u one position horizontally and turns all of its nodes vertically. Then u moves back to its original position in P. All other orientations are symmetric and follow by rotating the shape $90°$, $180°$ or $270°$.

We now formally define all problems considered in this work.

HAMILTONIANCONNECTED. Given a pair of connected Hamiltonian shapes (S_I, S_F) of the same order, where S_I is the initial shape and S_F the target shape, transform S_I into S_F while preserving connectivity throughout the transformation.

DIAGONALTOLINECONNECTED. A special case of HAMILTONIANCONNECTED in which S_I is a diagonal and S_F is a straight line.

UNIVERSALCONNECTED. Given *any* pair of connected shapes (S_I, S_F) of the same order, where S_I is the initial shape and S_F the target shape, transform S_I into S_F while preserving connectivity throughout the transformation.

3   An $O(n \log n)$-time Transformation for Hamiltonian Shapes

In this section, we present a strategy for HAMILTONIANCONNECTED, called *Walk-Through-Path*. It transforms any pair of shapes $S_I, S_F \in \mathcal{H}$ of the same order to each other within $O(n \log n)$ moves while preserving connectivity of the shape throughout the transformation. Recall that $\mathcal{H}$ is the family of all Hamiltonian shapes. Our transformation starts from one endpoint of the Hamiltonian path of S_I and applies a recursive successive doubling technique to transform S_I into a straight line S_L in $O(n \log n)$ time. By replacing S_I with S_F in *Walk-Through-Path* and reversing the resulting transformation, one can then go from S_I to S_F in the same asymptotic time. We first demonstrate the core recursive technique of this strategy in a special case which is sufficiently sparse to allow local reconfigurations without the risk of affecting the connectivity of the rest of the shape. In this special case, S_I is a diagonal of any order and observe that $S_I, S_F \in \mathcal{H}$ holds for this case. We then generalise this recursive technique to work for any $S_I \in \mathcal{H}$ and add to it the necessary sub-procedures that can perform local reconfiguration in *any* area (independently of how dense it is), while ensuring that global connectivity is always preserved.

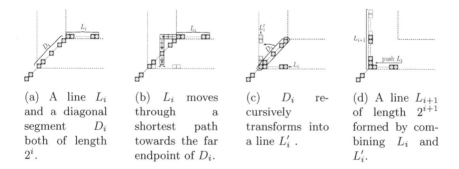

(a) A line L_i and a diagonal segment D_i both of length 2^i.

(b) L_i moves through a shortest path towards the far endpoint of D_i.

(c) D_i recursively transforms into a line L_i'.

(d) A line L_{i+1} of length 2^{i+1} formed by combining L_i and L_i'.

Fig. 3. A snapshot of phase i of *Walk-Through-Path* applied on a diagonal. Light grey cells represent the ending positions of the corresponding moves depicted in each sub-figure.

Let S_I be a diagonal of n nodes $u_n, u_{n-1}, \ldots, u_1$, occupying cells $(x, y), (x + 1, y + 1), \ldots, (x + n - 1, y + n - 1)$, respectively. Assume for simplicity of exposition that n is a power of 2; this can be dropped later. As argued above, it is sufficient to show how S_I can be transformed into a straight line S_L. In phase $i = 0$, the top node u_1 moves one position to align with u_2 and form a line L_1 of length 2. In any phase i, for $1 \leq i \leq \log n$, a line L_i occupies 2^i consecutive cells in a terminal subset of S_I (Fig. 3(a)). L_i moves through a shortest path towards the far endpoint of the next diagonal segment D_i of length 2^i (Fig. 3(b)). Note that for general shapes, this move shall be replaced by a more general *Line-Walk* operation (defined in the sequel). By a recursive call on D_i, D_i transforms into a line L'_i (Fig. 3(c)). Finally, the two perpendicular lines L_i and L'_i are combined in linear time into a straight line L_{i+1} of length 2^{i+1} (Fig. 3(d)). By the end of phase $\log n$, a straight line S_L of order n has been formed.

A core technical challenge in making the above transformation work in the general case, is that Hamiltonian shapes do not necessarily provide free space, thus, moving a line has to take place through the remaining configuration of nodes while at the same time ensuring that it does not break their and its own connectivity. In the more general *LineWalk* operation that we now describe, we manage to overcome this by exploiting *transparency* of line moves, according to which a line L can *transparently* walk through any configuration S (independently of the latter's density); see Proposition 1.

LineWalk. At the beginning of any phase i, there is a terminal straight line L_i of length 2^i containing the nodes $v_1, \ldots, v_{2^i}$, which is connected to an $S_i \subseteq S_I$, such that S_i consists of the 2^i subsequent nodes, that is $v_{2^i+1}, \ldots, v_{2^{i+1}}$. Observe that S_i is the next terminal sub-path of the remaining Hamiltonian path of S_I. We distinguish the following cases: (1) If L_i and S_i are already forming a straight line, then go to phase $i + 1$. (2) If S_i is a line perpendicular to L_i, then combine them into a straight line by pushing L_i to extend S_i and go to phase $i + 1$. Otherwise, (3) check if the (Manhattan) distance between v_{2^i} and v_{2^i+1} is $\delta(v_{2^i}, v_{2^i+1}) \leq 2^i$, then L_i moves from $v_{2^i} = (x, y)$ vertically or horizontally towards either node (x, y') or (x', y) in which L_i turns and keeps moving to $v_{2^i+1} = (x', y')$ on the other side of S_i. If not, (4) L_i must first pass through a middle node of S_i at $v_{2^i+2^{i-1}} = (x'', y'')$, therefore L_i repeats (3) twice, from v_{2^i} to $v_{2^i+2^{i-1}}$ and then towards v_{2^i+1}.

Note that cases (3) and (4) ensure that L_i is not disconnected from the rest of the shape. Moreover, moving L_i must be performed in a way that respects transparency (Proposition 1), so that connectivity of the remaining shape is always preserved and its configuration is restored to its original state. Full details can be found in [2].

Algorithm 1: HAMILTONIANTOLINE(S)

$S = (u_0, u_1, ..., u_{|S|-1})$ is a Hamiltonian shape

Initial conditions: $S \leftarrow S_I$ and $L_0 \leftarrow \{u_0\}$

for $i = 0, \ldots, \log|S|$ **do**
  LineWalk(L_i)
  $S_i \leftarrow$ select(2^i) // select the next terminal subset of 2^i
    consecutive nodes of S
  $L'_i \leftarrow$ HamiltonianToLine(S_i) // recursive call on S_i
  $L_{i+1} \leftarrow$ combine(L_i, L'_i) // combines L_i and L'_i into a new straight
    line L_{i+1}
end

Output: a straight line S_L

Algorithm 1, HAMILTONIANTOLINE, gives a general strategy to transform any Hamiltonian shape $S_I \in \mathcal{H}$ into a straight line in $O(n \log n)$ moves. In every phase i, it moves a terminal line L_i of length 2^i a distance 2^i higher on the Hamiltonian path through a *LineWalk* operation. This leaves a new terminal sub-path S_i of the Hamiltonian path, of length 2^i. Then the general procedure is recursively called on S_i to transform it into a straight line L'_i of length 2^i. Finally, the two straight lines L_i and L'_i which are perpendicular to each other are combined into a new straight line L_{i+1} of length 2^{i+1} and the next phase begins. The output of HAMILTONIANTOLINE is a straight line S_L of order n.

Lemma 1. *Given an initial Hamiltonian shape $S_I \in \mathcal{H}$ of order n, HAMILTO-NIANTOLINE transforms S_I into a straight line S_L in $O(n \log n)$ moves, without breaking connectivity during the transformation.*

Proof. It is not hard to see that the *LineWalk* operation does not break connectivity in cases (1) and (2) in any phase i. For case (3), *LineWalk* moves a line L_i of 2^i nodes, which are enough to fill a path of 2^i empty cells and stay connected. This holds also for case (4) by applying (3) twice. By a careful application of Proposition 1, it can be shown that the argument also holds true for any configuration of the path (and its surrounding cells) along which L_i moves. We now analyse the running time of HAMILTONIANTOLINE. By induction on the number of phases, *Walk-Through-Path* makes a total number of moves bounded by:

$$T = \sum_{i=1}^{\log n} T(i) = \sum_{i=1}^{\log n} 2^{i-1}(i-1) - 2^i = \sum_{i=1}^{\log n-1} (i-2)2^i - 2^{\log n} \leq \sum_{i=1}^{\log n-1} i \cdot 2^i - n$$

$$\leq \sum_{j=1}^{\log n} \sum_{i=j}^{\log n} 2^i - n \leq \sum_{j=1}^{\log n} n - n \leq n \log n - n = O(n \log n).$$

Finally, reversibility of line moves [3] and Lemma 1 together imply that:

Theorem 1. *For any pair of Hamiltonian shapes $S_I, S_F \in \mathcal{H}$ of the same order n, Walk-Through-Path transforms S_I into S_F (and S_F into S_I) in $O(n \log n)$ moves, while preserving connectivity of the shape during its course.*

4   An $O(n\sqrt{n})$-time Universal Transformation

In this section, we develop a transformation that solves the UNIVERSALCON-NECTED problem in $O(n\sqrt{n})$ moves. It is called *UC-Box* and transforms any pair of connected shapes (S_I, S_F) of the same order to each other, while preserving *connectivity* during its course.

Starting from the initial shape S_I of order n with an associated graph $G(S_I)$, compute a spanning tree T of $G(S_I)$. Then enclose the shape into an $n \times n$ square box and divide it into $\sqrt{n} \times \sqrt{n}$ square sub-boxes. Each occupied sub-box contains one or more maximal sub-trees of T. Each such sub-tree corresponds to a sub-shape of S_I, which from now on we call a *component*. Pick a leaf sub-tree T_l, let C_l be the component with which it is associated, and B_l their sub-box. Let also B_p be the sub-box adjacent to B_l containing the unique parent sub-tree T_p of T_l. Then compress all nodes of C_l into B_p through line moves, while keeping the nodes of C_p (the component of T_p) within B_p. Once compression is completed and C_p and C_l have been *combined* into a single component C_p', compute a new sub-tree T_p' spanning $G(C_p')$. Repeat until the whole shape is compressed into a $\sqrt{n} \times \sqrt{n}$ square. The latter belongs to the family of *nice* shapes (a family of connected shapes introduced in [3]) and can, thus, be transformed into a straight line in linear time.

Given that, the main technical challenges in making this strategy work universally is that a connected shape might have many different configurations inside the sub-boxes it occupies, while the shape needs to remain connected during the transformation. In the following, we describe the *compression* operation, which successfully tackles all of these issues by exploiting the linear strength of line moves.

Compress. Let $C_l \subseteq S_I$ be a leaf component containing nodes $v_1, \ldots, v_k$ inside a sub-box B_l of size $\sqrt{n} \times \sqrt{n}$, where $1 \leq k \leq n$, and $C_p \subseteq S_I$ the unique parent component of C_l occupying an adjacent sub-box B_p. If the direction of connectivity between B_l and B_p is vertical or horizontal, push all lines of C_l one move towards B_p sequentially one after the other, starting from the line furthest from B_p. Repeat the same procedure to first align all lines perpendicularly to the boundary between B_l and B_p (Fig. 4(b)) and then to transfer them completely into B_p (e.g., Fig. 4(c)). Hence, C_l and C_p are combined into C_p', and the next round begins. The above steps are performed in a way which ensures that all lines (in C_l or C_p) being pushed by this operation do not exceed the boundary of B_p (e.g., Fig. 4(d)). While C_l compresses vertically or horizontally, it may collide with a component $C_r \subseteq S_I$ inside B_l. In this case C_l stops compressing and combines with C_r into C_r'. Then the next round begins. If C_l compresses diagonally towards C_p (vertically then horizontally or vice versa) via an intermediate adjacent sub-box B_m and collides with $C_m \subseteq S_I$ inside B_m, then C_l

completes compression into B_m and combines with C_m into C'_m. Figure 4 shows how to compress a leaf component into its parent component occupying a diagonal adjacent sub-box.

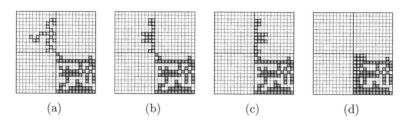

| (a) | (b) | (c) | (d) |

Fig. 4. A leaf component C_l in blue compressing from the top-left sub-box towards its parent component C_p in black inside a diagonal adjacent bottom-right sub-box. C_l compresses first horizontally towards an intermediate top-right sub-box, then vertically into the bottom-right. All other orientations are symmetric and follow by rotating the shape 90°, 180° or 270°.

Algorithm 2, COMPRESS, provides a universal procedure to transform an initial connected shape S_I of any order into a compressed square shape of the same order. It takes two arguments: S_I and the spanning tree T of the *associated graph* $G(S_I)$. In any round: Pick a leaf sub-tree of T_l corresponding to C_l inside a sub-box B_l. Compress C_l into an adjacent sub-box B_p towards its parent component C_p associated with parent sub-tree T_p. If C_l compressed with no collision, perform combine(C_p, C_l) which combines C_l with C_p into one component C'_p. If C_l collides with another component C_r inside B_l, then perform combine(C_r, C_l) into C'_r. If not, as in the diagonal compression in which C_l collides with C_m in an intermediate sub-box B_m, then C_l compresses completely into B_m and performs combine(C_m, C_l) into C'_m. Once compression is completed, update(T) computes a new sub-tree and removes any cycles. The algorithm terminates when T matches a single component of n nodes compressed into a single sub-box.

Algorithm 2: COMPRESS(S)

$S = (u_1, u_2, ..., u_{|S|})$ is a connected shape, T is a spanning tree of $G(S)$ **repeat**

> $C_l \leftarrow$ pick(T_l) // select a leaf component associated with a leaf
> sub-tree
> Compress(C_l) // start compressing the leaf component
> **if** C_l *collides* **then**
> > $C'_r \leftarrow$ combine(C_r, C_l) or $C'_m \leftarrow$ combine(C_m, C_l) // as described
> > in text
>
> **else**
> > $C'_p \leftarrow$ combine(C_p, C_l) // combine C_l with a parent component
>
> **end**
> update(T) // update sub-trees and remove cycles after
> compression

until *the whole shape is compressed into a $\sqrt{n} \times \sqrt{n}$ square*
Output: a square shape S_C

Lemma 2. *Any $\sqrt{n} \times \sqrt{n}$ square box can contain at most $2\sqrt{n}$ components.*

Proof. Observe that any component $C_l \subseteq S_I$ inside a sub-box B_l must be connected via a path to one of the $\sqrt{n}/2$ cells on one of the length-$\sqrt{n}$ boundaries of B_l, resulting in $2\sqrt{n}$ for the four boundaries. Hence, it can contain at most $2\sqrt{n}$ disconnected components inside.

Lemma 3. *Starting from an initial connected shape S_I of order n divided into $\sqrt{n}$ square sub-boxes of size $\sqrt{n} \times \sqrt{n}$, COMPRESS compresses a leaf component $C_l \subseteq S_I$ of $k \geq 1$ nodes, while preserving the global connectivity of the shape.*

The compression cost of this transformation could be very low taking only one move or being very high in some cases up to linear steps. To simplify the analysis, we divide the total cost of *UC-Box* into charging phases. We then manage to upper bound the cost of each charging phase independently of the order of compressions.

Lemma 4. *COMPRESS compresses any connected shape S_I of order n into a $\sqrt{n} \times \sqrt{n}$ square shape, in $O(n\sqrt{n})$ steps without breaking connectivity.*

Hence, by Lemmas 3, 4 and reversibility of nice shapes (from [3]), we have:

Theorem 2. *For any pair of connected shapes (S_I, S_F) of the same order n, UC-Box transforms S_I into S_F (and S_F into S_I) in $O(n\sqrt{n})$ steps, while preserving connectivity during its course.*

5   Conclusions and Open Problems

We have presented efficient transformations for the line-pushing model introduced in [3]. Our first transformation works on the family of all Hamiltonian shapes and matches the running time of the best known $O(n \log n)$-time transformation while additionally managing to preserve connectivity throughout its course. We then gave the first universal connectivity preserving transformation for this model. Its running time is $O(n\sqrt{n})$ and works on any pair of connected shapes of the same order. This work opens a number of interesting problems and research directions. An immediate next goal is whether it is possible to develop an $O(n \log n)$-time universal connectivity-preserving transformation. If true, the existence of lower bound above linear is not known, then a natural question is whether a universal transformation can be achieved in $o(n \log n)$-time (even when connectivity can be broken) or whether there exists a general $\Omega(n \log n)$-time matching lower bound. As a first step, it might be easier to develop lower bounds for the connectivity-preserving case.

We establish $\Omega(n \log n)$ lower bounds for two restricted sets of transformations, which have been shown in our full report [2]. These are the first lower bounds for this model and are matching the best known $O(n \log n)$ upper bounds. For example, it can be shown that any such transformation has a labelled tree representation, and by restricting the consideration to the sub-set of those transformations in which every leaf-to-root path has length at most 2, this captures tranformations in which every node must reach its final destination through at most 1 meeting-hop and at most 2 hops in total. Interestingly, by disregarding the fact that our initial and target instances have specific geometric arrangements, it is known that computing a 2-HOPS MST in the Euclidean 2-dimensional space is a hard optimisation problem and the best known result is a PTAS by Arora *et al.* [8] (cf. also [12]). There are also a number of interesting variants of the present model. One is a centralised parallel version in which more than one line can be moved concurrently in a single time-step. Another, is a distributed version of the parallel model, in which the nodes operate autonomously through local control and under limited information.

References

1. Akitaya, H., et al.: Universal reconfiguration of facet-connected modular robots by pivots: the O(1) musketeers. In: 27th Annual European Symposium on Algorithms, ESA. LIPIcs, vol. 144, pp. 3:1–3:14 (2019)
2. Almethen, A., Michail, O., Potapov, I.: On efficient connectivity-preserving transformations in a grid. CoRR abs/2005.08351 (2020)
3. Almethen, A., Michail, O., Potapov, I.: Pushing lines helps: efficient universal centralised transformations for programmable matter. Theoret. Comput. Sci. **830–831**, 43–59 (2020)
4. Aloupis, G., et al.: Efficient reconfiguration of lattice-based modular robots. Comput. Geom. **46**(8), 917–928 (2013)
5. Aloupis, G., Collette, S., Demaine, E.D., Langerman, S., Sacristán, V., Wuhrer, S.: Reconfiguration of cube-style modular robots using $O(\log n)$ parallel moves. In: Hong, S.-H., Nagamochi, H., Fukunaga, T. (eds.) ISAAC 2008. LNCS, vol. 5369, pp. 342–353. Springer, Heidelberg (2008). https://doi.org/10.1007/978-3-540-92182-0_32
6. Angluin, D., Aspnes, J., Diamadi, Z., Fischer, M., Peralta, R.: Computation in networks of passively mobile finite-state sensors. Distrib. Comput. **18**(4), 235–253 (2006). https://doi.org/10.1007/s00446-005-0138-3
7. Angluin, D., Aspnes, J., Eisenstat, D., Ruppert, E.: The computational power of population protocols. Distrib. Comput. **20**(4), 279–304 (2007). https://doi.org/10.1007/s00446-007-0040-2
8. Arora, S., Raghavan, P., Rao, S.: Approximation schemes for Euclidean k-medians and related problems. In: Proceedings of the Thirtieth Annual ACM Symposium on Theory of computing, pp. 106–113 (1998)
9. Bourgeois, J., Goldstein, S.: Distributed intelligent MEMS: progresses and perspective. IEEE Syst. J. **9**(3), 1057–1068 (2015)
10. Butler, Z., Kotay, K., Rus, D., Tomita, K.: Generic decentralized control for lattice-based self-reconfigurable robots. Int. J. Robot. Res. **23**(9), 919–937 (2004)
11. Cieliebak, M., Flocchini, P., Prencipe, G., Santoro, N.: Distributed computing by mobile robots: gathering. SIAM J. Comput. **41**(4), 829–879 (2012)
12. Clementi, A., Di Ianni, M., Lauria, M., Monti, A., Rossi, G., Silvestri, R.: On the bounded-hop MST problem on random Euclidean instances. Theoret. Comput. Sci. **384**(2–3), 161–167 (2007)
13. Czyzowicz, J., Dereniowski, D., Pelc, A.: Building a nest by an automaton. In: Bender, M.A., Svensson, O., Herman, G. (eds.) 27th Annual European Symposium on Algorithms, ESA (2019)

14. Das, S., Flocchini, P., Santoro, N., Yamashita, M.: Forming sequences of geometric patterns with oblivious mobile robots. Distrib. Comput. **28**(2), 131–145 (2014). https://doi.org/10.1007/s00446-014-0220-9
15. Daymude, J.J., et al.: On the runtime of universal coating for programmable matter. Nat. Comput. **17**(1), 81–96 (2017). https://doi.org/10.1007/s11047-017-9658-6
16. Derakhshandeh, Zahra., Gmyr, Robert., Porter, Alexandra., Richa, Andréa W., Scheideler, Christian, Strothmann, Thim: On the runtime of universal coating for programmable matter. In: Rondelez, Yannick, Woods, Damien (eds.) DNA 2016. LNCS, vol. 9818, pp. 148–164. Springer, Cham (2016). https://doi.org/10.1007/978-3-319-43994-5_10
17. Derakhshandeh, Z., Gmyr, R., Richa, A., Scheideler, C., Strothmann, T.: Universal shape formation for programmable matter. In: Proceedings of the 28th ACM Symposium on Parallelism in Algorithms and Architectures, pp. 289–299. ACM (2016)
18. Di Luna, G.A., Flocchini, P., Santoro, N., Viglietta, G., Yamauchi, Y.: Shape formation by programmable particles. Distrib. Comput. **33**(1), 69–101 (2019). https://doi.org/10.1007/s00446-019-00350-6
19. Doty, D.: Theory of algorithmic self-assembly. Commun. ACM **55**, 78–88 (2012)
20. Douglas, S., Dietz, H., Liedl, T., Högberg, B., Graf, F., Shih, W.: Self-assembly of DNA into nanoscale three-dimensional shapes. Nature **459**(7245), 414 (2009)
21. Dumitrescu, A., Pach, J.: Pushing squares around. In: Proceedings of the Twentieth Annual Symposium on Computational Geometry, pp. 116–123. ACM (2004)
22. Dumitrescu, A., Suzuki, I., Yamashita, M.: Formations for fast locomotion of metamorphic robotic systems. Int. J. Robot. Res. **23**(6), 583–593 (2004)
23. Dumitrescu, A., Suzuki, I., Yamashita, M.: Motion planning for metamorphic systems: feasibility, decidability, and distributed reconfiguration. IEEE Trans. Robot. Autom. **20**(3), 409–418 (2004)
24. Fekete, S., Gmyr, R., Hugo, S., Keldenich, P., Scheffer, C., Schmidt, A.: CADbots: algorithmic aspects of manipulating programmable matter with finite automata. CoRR abs/1810.06360 (2018)
25. Fekete, S., Richa, A., Römer, K., Scheideler, C.: Algorithmic foundations of programmable matter (Dagstuhl Seminar 16271). In: Dagstuhl Reports, vol. 6 (2016). Also in ACM SIGACT News, **48**(2), 87–94 (2017)
26. Gilpin, K., Knaian, A., Rus, D.: Robot pebbles: one centimeter modules for programmable matter through self-disassembly. In: 2010 IEEE International Conference on Robotics and Automation (ICRA), pp. 2485–2492. IEEE (2010)
27. Gmyr, R., et al.: Forming tile shapes with simple robots. Nat. Comput. **19**(2), 375–390 (2019). https://doi.org/10.1007/s11047-019-09774-2
28. Itai, A., Papadimitriou, C., Szwarcfiter, J.: Hamilton paths in grid graphs. SIAM J. Comput. **11**(4), 676–686 (1982)
29. Knaian, A., Cheung, K., Lobovsky, M., Oines, A., Schmidt-Neilsen, P., Gershenfeld, N.: The Milli-Motein: a self-folding chain of programmable matter with a one centimeter module pitch. In: 2012 IEEE/RSJ International Conference on Intelligent Robots and Systems, pp. 1447–1453. IEEE (2012)
30. Michail, O., Skretas, G., Spirakis, P.: On the transformation capability of feasible mechanisms for programmable matter. J. Comput. Syst. Sci. **102**, 18–39 (2019)
31. Michail, O., Spirakis, P.G.: Simple and efficient local codes for distributed stable network construction. Distrib. Comput. **29**(3), 207–237 (2015). https://doi.org/10.1007/s00446-015-0257-4
32. Michail, O., Spirakis, P.: Elements of the theory of dynamic networks. Commun. ACM **61**(2), 72–81 (2018)

33. Nguyen, A., Guibas, L., Yim, M.: Controlled module density helps reconfiguration planning. In: Proceedings of 4th International Workshop on Algorithmic Foundations of Robotics, pp. 23–36 (2000)
34. Rothemund, P.: Folding DNA to create nanoscale shapes and patterns. Nature **440**(7082), 297–302 (2006)
35. Rothemund, P., Winfree, E.: The program-size complexity of self-assembled squares. In: Proceedings of the 32nd annual ACM symposium on Theory of computing (STOC), pp. 459–468. ACM (2000)
36. Rubenstein, M., Cornejo, A., Nagpal, R.: Programmable self-assembly in a thousand-robot swarm. Science **345**(6198), 795–799 (2014)
37. Walter, J., Welch, J., Amato, N.: Distributed reconfiguration of metamorphic robot chains. Distrib. Comput. **17**(2), 171–189 (2004)
38. Winfree, E.: Algorithmic self-assembly of DNA. Ph.D. thesis, California Institute of Technology, June 1998
39. Woods, D., Chen, H., Goodfriend, S., Dabby, N., Winfree, E., Yin, P.: Active self-assembly of algorithmic shapes and patterns in polylogarithmic time. In: Proceedings of the 4th conference on Innovations in Theoretical Computer Science, pp. 353–354. ACM (2013)
40. Yamashita, M., Suzuki, I.: Characterizing geometric patterns formable by oblivious anonymous mobile robots. Theoret. Comput. Sci. **411**(26–28), 2433–2453 (2010)
41. Yamauchi, Y., Uehara, T., Yamashita, M.: Brief announcement: pattern formation problem for synchronous mobile robots in the three dimensional Euclidean space. In: Proceedings of the 2016 ACM Symposium on Principles of Distributed Computing, pp. 447–449. ACM (2016)
42. Yim, M., et al.: Modular self-reconfigurable robot systems [grand challenges of robotics]. IEEE Robot. Autom. Mag. **14**(1), 43–52 (2007)

Live Exploration with Mobile Robots in a Dynamic Ring, Revisited

Subhrangsu Mandal[1]([⊠])(ID), Anisur Rahaman Molla[2](ID), and William K. Moses Jr.[3](ID)

[1] Department of Computer Science and Engineering, Indian Institute of Technology Kharagpur, Kharagpur, India
subhrangsum@cse.iitkgp.ac.in
[2] Computer and Communication Sciences, Indian Statistical Institute, Kolkata, India
molla@isical.ac.in
[3] Faculty of Industrial Engineering and Management, Technion - Israel Institute of Technology, Haifa, Israel
wkmjr3@gmail.com

Abstract. The graph exploration problem requires a group of mobile robots, initially placed arbitrarily on the nodes of a graph, to work collaboratively to explore the graph such that each node is eventually visited by at least one robot. One important requirement of exploration is the *termination* condition, i.e., the robots must know that exploration is completed. The problem of live exploration of a dynamic ring using mobile robots was recently introduced in [Di Luna et al., ICDCS 2016]. In it, they proposed multiple algorithms to solve exploration in fully synchronous and semi-synchronous settings with various guarantees when 2 robots were involved. They also provided guarantees that with certain assumptions, exploration of the ring using two robots was impossible. An important question left open was how the presence of 3 robots would affect the results. In this paper, we try to settle this question in a fully synchronous setting and also show how to extend our results to a semi-synchronous setting.

In particular, we present algorithms for exploration with explicit termination using 3 robots in conjunction with either (i) unique IDs of the robots and edge crossing detection capability (i.e., two robots moving in opposite directions through an edge in the same round can detect each other), or (ii) access to randomness. The time complexity of our deterministic algorithm is asymptotically optimal. We also provide complementary impossibility results showing that there do not exist any explicit termination algorithms for 2 robots even when each robot has a unique ID, edge crossing detection capability, and access to randomness. We also present an algorithm to achieve exploration with partial termination using 3 robots with unique IDs in the semi-synchronous setting.

A. R. Molla was supported, in part, by DST Inspire Faculty research grant DST/INSPIRE/04/2015/002801, Govt. of India. The work of William K. Moses Jr. was supported in part by a Technion fellowship.

C. M. Pinotti et al. (Eds.): ALGOSENSORS 2020, LNCS 12503, pp. 92–107, 2020.
https://doi.org/10.1007/978-3-030-62401-9_7

Keywords: Multi-agent systems · Mobile robots · Exploration · Uniform deployment · Distributed algorithms · Dynamic graph · Ring graph

1 Introduction

The research area of autonomous mobile robots in a graph setting has been well studied over the years. Many fundamental problems have been studied in this area, such as the problem of exploration of a graph using multiple robots. In this problem, multiple robots are placed in nodes in the graph and the goal is to design an algorithm, run by each robot, such that all robots collectively visit each node at least once as quickly as possible. As this fundamental problem has been solved to a large degree in most vanilla settings [2,4,8,11,21], its study has been extended to more exotic, but realistic, settings. One such setting is a dynamic network. In the real world, dynamism is seen fairly regularly in networks. Like most things in real life, the dynamism that appears in the real world is quite complex. In order to work towards a deeper understanding of this complexity, we first start with a simpler model of dynamism, which is a restricted version of *1-interval connectivity* [17] applied to an n node ring in the synchronous setting. This type of dynamism is characterized as follows: in each round, at most one edge of the ring, as chosen by an adversary, may be missing. In this setting, Di Luna et al. [6] were the first to study the problem of graph exploration when robots do not know what the adversary will do next (*live* or *online* dynamism). In [6], Di Luna et al. studied both fully synchronous systems and semi-synchronous systems where nodes are anonymous, i.e. do not have unique IDs.

In the fully synchronous setting, they show that by using just 2 robots without unique IDs, subject to some assumptions, deterministic exploration of a ring in the presence of 1-interval connectivity is possible with explicit termination detection. These assumptions include a mix of the following ideas: (i) robots have knowledge of the value of n, (ii) there exists a *landmark* (a unique node that can be identified by robots as being unique), and (iii) robots have common chirality (a common sense of clockwise/counter-clockwise). They differentiate between *explicit termination* detection where all robots can detect the completion of exploration and subsequently terminate, and *partial termination* detection where at least one of the robots (but not necessarily all of them) detects completion and terminates. They also provide matching impossibility results that deterministic exploration with partial termination is impossible with 2 robots when n is unknown and no landmark is available, even in the presence of robots with unique IDs and common chirality. They also extend the impossibility results to any number of robots, when robots are anonymous.

An important question left unanswered is if exploration with ≥ 3 robots is possible when no knowledge of n is known and no landmark is available but robots may have IDs. In this paper, we settle this question in the fully synchronous setting and provide partial results in the semi-synchronous setting.

Network Model and Assumptions. We consider a 1-interval connected synchronous dynamic ring $\mathcal{R}$ of size n as considered in [5,6]. As $\mathcal{R}$ is a ring, each node in $\mathcal{R}$ has two neighbours connected via two ports. The ring is anonymous, i.e., nodes are indistinguishable. We assume that the nodes are fixed, but the edges of $\mathcal{R}$ may change over time. More precisely, in any round at most one of the edges might be missing from $\mathcal{R}$. An adversary decides which edge, if any, is missing at the beginning of the round. The adversary controls the edge removal using the knowledge of the algorithm and current states and positions of the robots. However, for the randomized algorithms, the random choices made by each robot are not known to the adversary.

There are three robots which explore $\mathcal{R}$. Each robot is equipped with a finite memory, say $O(\log n)$ bits and computational capabilities. Each robot has a unique identifier (ID) and initially a robot only knows its own ID. Furthermore, we assume that the IDs are k-bit strings. Typically $k = O(1)$ suffices to represent 3 distinct IDs. ID of a robot is represented as $b_{k-1}b_{k-2}\cdots b_1 b_0$. Initially robots do not know the size of the ring (not even any bound of it). The robots do not share any common chirality. During movement, at any node a robot can differentiate between the port through which it enters the node and the other port. All the robots execute the same protocol. Multiple robots can reside at a single node at the same time. When multiple robots are on the same node they can exchange information. A robot can *successfully move* in a *fixed* direction if the corresponding adjacent edge is available in the dynamic ring; otherwise, if the edge is missing, the robot does nothing. We assume the *edge crossing detection* capability, i.e., two robots moving in opposite directions on the same edge in the same round can detect that they passed each other in that round and exchange information.

We consider here a synchronous system which progresses in time steps, called as rounds. In a single round, the sequence of operations executed as follows: (i) the robots perform local computation and decide whether to move from the current node and the direction of the movement, (ii) the adversary removes at most one edge from the ring for this round, (iii) the robots execute their movements, if any, as long as the edge they wish to move over is present.

Note that we also consider a semi-synchronous system in Sect. 5. As most of the paper relates to the fully synchronous system as previously described, we postpone the description of the semi-synchronous system to Sect. 5.

Our Contributions. In this paper, we look into exploration of a dynamic ring with 3 robots and show various positive results when certain assumptions are made. We show that deterministic exploration of a dynamic ring of size n with explicit termination detection is indeed possible with 3 robots when n is unknown and no landmark is present. In fact, not only is exploration possible, but the running time of our algorithm (which is linear on the size of the ring) is asymptotically optimal. We require robots to have unique IDs and have the capability of edge crossing detection.

We subsequently remove the need for the edge crossing detection assumption with the help of randomness. We also use randomness to remove the need for robots to have unique IDs. Note that this result when we achieve explicit termination with anonymous 3 robots, no landmark, no knowledge of n, but access to randomness is in sharp contrast to the impossibility result of [6] where even partial termination with any number of robots is impossible without under the same setting but without access to randomness. We also modify our algorithm to achieve partial termination with better runtime. Our positive results are summarized in Table 1.

One may wonder if either the use of edge crossing detection or the use of randomness is sufficient for 2 robots to bypass the impossibility result from [6]. We show that when robots only have access to edge crossing detection, exploration with partial termination of two robots is impossible. We further show that when the use of randomness is also allowed, exploration with explicit termination of two robots is impossible. Thus, only with the use of 3 robots do either of these capabilities provide sufficient power to overcome the impossibility of exploration with explicit termination. Our impossibility results are summarized in Table 2 along with a comparison to the impossibility result from [6].

Finally, we show how to use the ideas we built up throughout the paper in order to achieve partial termination in the semi-synchronous setting when robots do not know an upper bound on the value of n or have access to a landmark.

Table 1. Fully synchronous setting, possibility with 3 robots.

Assumptions	Running time (for explicit termination)
Non-anonymous robots, edge crossing detection	$O(n)$ rounds
Non-anonymous robots, access to randomness	$O(n \log n)$ rounds on expectation[a]
Access to randomness	$O((n + n \cdot 2^l) \log n)$ rounds on expectation[b]

[a] Explicit termination with probability $\geq 1 - 1/n$.
[b] Explicit termination with probability $\geq (1 - O(1/2^l))(1 - 1/n)$, where l is an input to the algorithm.

Table 2. Fully synchronous setting, impossibility results.

Paper	# Robots	Assumptions	Even with assumptions	Which termination impossible
[6]	2	No knowledge of n, no landmark	Non-anonymous robots, chirality	Partial
[6]	Any	No knowledge of n, no landmark, anonymous robots	Chirality	Partial
This paper	2	No knowledge of n, no landmark	Non-anonymous robots, chirality, edge crossing detection	Partial
This paper	2	No knowledge of n, no landmark	Non-anonymous robots, chirality, edge crossing detection, access to randomness	Explicit

Related Work. Exploration of static anonymous graphs using mobile robots has been studied for a very long time. A good survey on the topic is presented in [3,5]. Exploration on anonymous graphs with 1-interval connected dynamism is relatively new and the first paper to study it in the current model is [6]. It should be noted that the way 1-interval connectivity is defined in their paper and also in the current paper is different from the original definition proposed in [16,20]. Specifically, the original definition of 1-interval connectivity allows for permutations of the nodes of the graph, whereas in [6], the nodes remain stationary and the adversary can only choose whether to remove at most one of a fixed set of edges.

There are other works in literature which have addressed the problem of exploration on dynamic graphs. Exploration problem on dynamic ring for T-interval connected case is addressed in [15]. They have extended their work in [13] and addressed the exploration problem on cactus graph when change in the graph topology is known to the robot. There are other works like [9,19] which address the exploration problem for general graphs in centralized environment when the change in the graph topology is already known. There are works [10,14] which address the live or online version of the exploration problem in distributed environment for periodically varying graphs. A very recent work [12], studies exploration in time-varying graphs (including 1-interval connectivity) of arbitrary topology, investigates the number of robots necessary and sufficient to explore such graphs. There have been other papers that look at different problems such as gathering [7] and dispersion [1] on dynamic graphs under 1-interval connectivity.

2   Deterministic Exploration with 3 Robots

In this section, we present a deterministic solution for the exploration problem using three robots. We assume that each robot has a unique ID which is not known to the other robots unless they meet. We further assume that when two robots cross an edge (from opposite directions) in the same round, they *sense* each other and the meeting happens[1]. Note that this edge crossing detection assumption does not help two robots (with unique IDs) to solve the exploration problem (see Sect. 4).

Let us now describe the algorithm. It works in four stages: (Stage 1) first meeting of (any) two robots, (Stage 2) second meeting of two robots, (Stage 3) exploration detection, and (Stage 4) termination.

Stage 1 ensures the first meeting of any two robots at some node or via edge crossing in the ring. For this, we need to make sure that at least two of them move in the opposite directions; otherwise if all the three robots move in the same direction at the same speed, they may never meet even if the adversary never deletes any edge. Thus, we have to break this symmetry deterministically. For this, each robot moves based on the bit string of its ID. Each robot moves in

---

[1] Here by 'sense' we mean the two robots can detect the edge crossing and can exchange information including IDs.

phases and each phase consists of several rounds. More precisely, the number of rounds in the i-th phase is 2^i. Without loss of generality, say that a robot moves in what it considers the clockwise (left) direction in phase i when $b_{i \mod k} = 0$. When $b_{i \mod k} = 1$, the robot moves in the other (right) direction. The first stage ends when at least two robots meet. Let us mark or name the two robots A and B, where the larger ID one is A and the other is B. Note that, the third robot may not know about this meeting and hence is unaware of the end of the first stage. Let us call the third robot as C^2. If these three robots meet at the same time (at some node) then the smallest ID robot gets named C. Notice that if two or three robots are positioned at the same node initially then the algorithm starts from Stage 2.

Then **Stage 2** starts (which is known to at least A and B). The robots A and B start moving in opposite directions from the meeting point (node) from Stage 1 and never change their directions until they terminate the algorithm. A and B each maintain a counter which counts the number of steps the robot successfully moves. Furthermore, each robot stores the ID of the other. Note that a robot cannot move in a particular direction in a round if the corresponding edge is missing (i.e., deleted by the adversary). Each of the robots continues to move until one of them meets the third robot. Stage 2 ends when either of A and B meets the third robot, which subsequently gets named C. Without loss of generality, assume that A and C meet. Then A shares the following stored information with C: ID of B, the direction of B's movement and the number of steps A has successfully moved after Stage 1³. C stores all this information. A and C also store each other's IDs.

Then **Stage 3** starts, which ensures the completion of the ring exploration by at least two robots. This can happen in two ways. (I) if A and B meet (again) then it is guaranteed that exploration of the ring is complete. (II) The adversary can prevent the meeting of A and B by removing an edge between them. Recall that A and B are moving in opposite directions. Eventually these two robots will reach two adjacent nodes and may wait for the (missing) edge to move. In this scenario, exploration is completed but A and B do not know this as n is unknown. If the adversary does not remove the edge in one round, then A and B will meet. Therefore, the adversary will need to remove the edge indefinitely. In this situation, robot C is used to determine the completion of exploration. From the meeting point of A and C in Stage 2, robot C starts moving towards the opposite direction of A (i.e., in the same direction of B) and A continues moving in its fixed direction. Robot B does not know that A and C met in Stage 2, and continues to move in its fixed direction. Robot C moves towards

---

² The third robot gets named C only after it meets either A or B at the end of Stage 2.

³ Note that even if A and C do not have shared chirality, the direction of B can be conveyed as follows. Depending on how A and C meet, C will immediately know the direction A moves in or can take a round or two to understand this based on how A and C both move in their "clockwise" direction and see if they moved to the same node or not. Once C determines the naming mechanism A uses for directions, C can understand exactly which direction B is moving in.

B until it catches B. Subsequently, C changes its direction and move towards A until it catches A. C then repeats this process and moves back to B. Essentially, C performs a zig-zag movement between A and B and checks if the distance (i.e., the hop distance) from A to B, and B to A are the same. For this, the robot C maintains two variables $A\,to\,B$ and $B\,to\,A$. $A\,to\,B$ stores the number of successful steps (moves) towards B, starting from A until it meets B, and $B\,to\,A$ stores a similar number.

When these two distances are equal, i.e., $A\,to\,B\ =\ B\,to\,A$, the algorithm determines that exploration is complete, as this condition implies that A and B lie on two adjacent nodes and the edge between those two nodes has been removed by the adversary. Thus, C has explored the entire graph. Therefore, either A and B meet and detect that exploration is completed, or C deduces the completion of exploration from the hop-distance counts. In the latter case, C would be co-located in a node with either A or B and can thus inform that robot about the completion of exploration. Thus, at least two robots detect the completion of exploration, but the third robot may be unaware of this. Then we begin Stage 4 to ensure that all robots are made aware of the completion of exploration and can terminate.

In **Stage 4**, the two robots which detected the completion of exploration move in order to inform the third robot about this, and all robots terminate (to guarantee the explicit termination). Recall that the robots A and B maintained a counter of their successful moves starting from their meeting in Stage 2. If A and B meet at the same node again, then the sum of their counters is exactly n. If they meet by crossing each other, then the sum of their counters is exactly $n + 1$. If they do not meet but the scenario from Stage 3 plays out, then C and one of the two robots knows the value of $n - 1$. In any case, there are two robots which know that exploration is completed and know the value of n at some node. Then these two robots start moving in opposite directions to each other for at most n rounds. When one of them meets the third robot, it informs the third robot about the completion of exploration and they both terminate. The other robot also terminates after n rounds (if it does not meet the third robot). We show that after n rounds, at least one of the robots (which detects the completion of exploration) meets the third robot and informs it about the completion of exploration.

Correctness and Time Analysis. We first discuss the correctness of the algorithm in the following lemma.

Lemma 1. *The proposed algorithm correctly explores the dynamic ring and guarantees explicit termination.*

Proof. We show that by the end of Stage 3, the ring is explored (by at least two robots). Stage 3 ends when one of the following two cases occurs: (I) robots A and B meet (II) robot C meets A and finds $A\,to\,B = B\,to\,A$ (after zig-zag movement) or C meets B and finds $A\,to\,B = B\,to\,A$.

Case I: Robots A and B meet again after their first meeting in Stage 1. Since they move in opposite directions and never change directions after their first meeting, it is obvious that when they meet again, exploration is completed. The robots can also calculate the value of n when they meet again.

Case II: Robot C meets either of A and B, and learns that $A\,to\,B = B\,to\,A$. This implies that robot C has traversed same number of steps in two consecutive zig-zag movements. This scenario is only possible if both A and B are trying to traverse the same edge from adjacent nodes, since the adversary can remove only one edge at a time. Thus when robot C determines that $A\,to\,B = B\,to\,A$ after two consecutive zig-zag movements, it is guaranteed that C has explored all nodes in the ring and the size of the ring is $A\,to\,B + 1$ or $B\,to\,A + 1$.

Thus, in both cases, at least two robots detect that exploration is completed. Moreover, the robots which detect this also know the size of the ring n at the end of Stage 3. Thus in the termination stage, these two robots, which detected the completion of exploration, start moving in two opposite directions for at most n rounds and terminate. It follows from the proof of Lemma 2 (below) that after n rounds, at least one of them meets the 3rd robot. So the 3rd robot also gets the information about the completion of exploration and terminate. Thus, explicit termination is guaranteed at the end of Stage 4. □

Let us now analyze the time complexity of the exploration algorithm. We calculate the time taken in each stage of the algorithm through several lemmas.

Lemma 2. *If two among the three robots move in opposite directions in a dynamic ring of size n, then at least two of them meet in at most $n - 2$ rounds.*

Proof. If any two among these three robots are initially located at the same node in the ring, then this lemma holds trivially.

We assume that the three robots are initially located on three different nodes in the ring. In this scenario, we prove this lemma by induction on the size of the ring. Recall that a robot always tries to move in some specified direction as long as the corresponding edge is available, i.e. it does not voluntarily remain stationary.

Base Case: Consider the ring of size 3 with each robot initially located on a different node. As the adversary can remove only one edge and at least two robots are moving in opposite directions, at least two of the robots will be on the same node after 1 step (either the two moving in opposite directions meet or if the edge between them is not available then the third one catches one of them). Thus, the base case is true.

Inductive Step: Assume that the claim holds for rings of size up to l. We show that the claim also holds for rings of size $l + 1$. In a ring of size $l + 1$, when all three robots are located at different nodes, the maximum min-distance between two robots is at most $l - 1$. Here, min-distance refers to the distance between two robots on the ring considering their direction of movement. As none of the robots are changing their direction and the adversary can remove only one edge in a round, at least one robot can successfully move one step in one round. Hence, after one round the situation on the ring of size $l + 1$ maps to a situation on the ring of size l (or at least two of them meet). As this lemma holds for a ring of size l or less, at least two robots meet at some node after at most $l - 2$ rounds. Therefore, it takes at most $(l - 2) + 1$, i.e., $l - 1$ rounds, in a ring of size $l + 1$. Hence the lemma holds.   □

Lemma 3. *In Stage 1 of the proposed algorithm, there exists a phase $i \in [0, k-1]$ when at least one robot moves in the direction opposite to the direction followed by other two robots, where k is the length of the ID bit-string of the robots.*

Proof. Recall that in the ith phase a robot moves in some direction for 2^i rounds. It then changes its direction of movement in the next phase if the next bit in its ID is different. Consider the scenario where all robots move in the same direction starting from the first phase (otherwise the lemma is trivially true). There are two scenarios to consider. Either all robots share the same chirality or they do not.

Consider the scenario where all robots share the same chirality. Since the IDs of the robots are different, at least one bit in the ID of each pair of the robots are different. Hence there will be at least two phases in between 0 to $k - 1$ when one of the robots moves in a direction opposite to the direction followed by the other two robots.

Consider the scenario where robots do not share the same chirality. Since chiralities can be different, two robots with different chiralities can have IDs that are complementary (e.g., 000 and 111) and thus move in the same direction in all phases. However, since all IDs are different, the third robot's ID will be such that there will exist at least one phase where one of the robots moves in a different direction from the other two.   □

Lemma 4. *Stage 1 of the proposed algorithm finishes in at most $n + n \cdot 2^k$ rounds, where k is the length of the ID bit-string of the robots.*

Proof. We show that there exists a phase $i \in [0, j(k-1)]$ when at least two robots meet in Stage 1, where k is the length of the IDs of the robots and j is some positive integer. It follows from Lemma 3 that there exists a phase $i \in [0, k - 1]$ when at least two robots move in the opposite directions to each other. The number of rounds in that phase is 2^i. If $2^i \geq n - 2$ then it follows from Lemma 2 that any two robots meet. However, it might be the case that $2^i < n - 2$ for that i in $[0, k - 1]$. Then according to our algorithm (see Stage 1), these two robots (again) move in the opposite directions in each of the phases $j(k - 1) + i$ for $j = 1, 2, \ldots$, and hence Stage 1 finishes when $2^{j(k-1)} \leq n-3$ and $2^{j(k-1)+i} \geq n-2$ for some positive integer j. Thus, Stage 1 takes at most $\sum_{t=0}^{j(k-1)+i} 2^t$ rounds. The sum is bounded above by $(n + n \cdot 2^i)$, since $2^{j(k-1)} \leq n - 3$. Therefore, Stage 1 of the proposed algorithm finishes in at most $n + n \cdot 2^k$ rounds, since $i < k$. □

Further, it follows from the algorithm that Stage 2, Stage 3 and Stage 4 finishes in $O(n)$ rounds. Thus we get the following result.

Theorem 1. *The proposed algorithm correctly explores a 1-interval connected dynamic (anonymous) ring of size n in $O(n + n \cdot 2^k)$ rounds with 3 robots such* that each robot has unique ID of length k bits and the robots have no knowledge of n and no common chirality.

Corollary 1. *There exists an algorithm which explores a 1-interval connected dynamic (anonymous) ring of size n in $O(n)$ rounds with 3 robots having unique IDs of length $O(1)$ bits and without the knowledge of n and without common chirality.*

3   Exploration with Randomness

We can remove the need for edge crossing detection through the creative use of randomness, resulting in an algorithm that is both Las Vegas and Monte Carlo in nature. We bound the algorithm's expected running time and success probability in this section. Subsequently, we show how to further use randomness to remove the requirement of having unique IDs initially assigned to each robot.

Removing Edge Crossing Detection. In this section, we first discuss the changes to the algorithm proposed in Sect. 2, that are required to make it work. We then subsequently provide bounds for the running time and correctness.

Notice that edge crossing detection is used when two robots are located at adjacent nodes and must move in opposite directions along the same edge in the same round. A simple way to get the robots to meet is to force one to be stationary while the other moves. This can easily be achieved by having each robot flip a fair coin to decide if it should move or not. If the result of the coin toss is heads, then the robot performs the movement it initially planned to do. If the result is tails, then the robot does not move. Call this subroutine as RANDOM-MOVEMENT.

RANDOM-MOVEMENT can be run as a subroutine by every robot in every round, after deciding to move (and where to) but before the actual movement. We now describe how to further modify the algorithm proposed in Sect. 2, in addition to using the subroutine, so that we may remove the need for edge crossing detection.

In Stage 1, notice that if the algorithm required a robot to move for s steps in r rounds, then directly using RANDOM-MOVEMENT in the algorithm may cause that robot to move for less than s steps in r rounds, even when the adversary does not block any movement of the robot. This is slightly problematic as we require that there exists a phase in which robots can move for at least n steps, and we do not want to drastically increase the running time. An easy fix is to extend the number of rounds of each phase i by a constant factor, say 8, in order to ensure that on expectation and with high probability, the number of steps a robot moves through is at least 2^i when $2^i \geq n^4$.

For Stage 2 to occur, we need two robots to come into contact with each other and be marked A and B. Since the probability that two robots that were

---

[4] The expectation is easy to see. The high probability bound can be seen by applying a simple Chernoff bound.

supposed to move through the same edge meet instead is $1/2$, on expectation, at least one such meeting occurs within 2 phases of the first phase i where $2^i \geq n$. Thus, on expectation after $O(n)$ rounds are complete, Stage 1 is over and Stage 2 begins.

Now, in Stage 2, we require either A or B to come into contact with the third robot. Notice that this third robot is not constrained to only move in one direction, but may move in both directions. Thus, it may only come into contact with either A or B as a result of crossing an edge. Again, through the use of RANDOM-MOVEMENT, it takes 2 such attempts on expectation at edge crossing between the third robot and either A or B before contact is made and the third robot gets marked as C. Then the algorithm moves to Stage 3. Notice that before the third robot becomes marked, it is possible that A and B meet again, thus sending the algorithm directly into Stage 4 (since A or B may miss to meet C as there is no edge crossing detection).

If the algorithm is in Stage 3, then the third robot has been marked C. Now, either A and B meet again or the adversary blocks A and B at adjacent nodes and C moves back and forth between them. In the latter case, it takes $O(n)$ rounds with high probability[5] to move to Stage 4 and C, and one of A and B will know the exact value of n[6]. In the former case, after some cn rounds, where c is a positive constant, A and B will meet on expectation. Thus, A and B will know an upper bound cn of n.

In Stage 4, let us assume that without loss of generality, two of the robots A and B learn an upper bound N on the value of n, i.e., $N = cn$ for some constant c. Now, either the third robot is marked or it is not. Either way, our goal in this stage is to inform this third robot that exploration is complete. It is possible that every interaction of A or B with the third robot is a situation where edge crossing would normally occur. In the event of one such interaction, the probability of the third robot being informed is $1/2$. After $2 \log N$ such interactions, the probability of the third robot being informed is at least $1 - 1/n$. Recall that in this stage, robots A and B use a counter and will stop after N rounds. If we change the counter to end at $16N \log N$ instead, then the third robot has $2N \log N$ opportunities with high probability to interact with either robot. Thus, with probability at least $1 - 1/n$ the third robot will interact with at least one of the robots and terminate, eventually resulting in explicit termination.

Construct the new algorithm MODIFIED-EXPLORE-DYNAMIC-RING-3-ROBOTS using the above mentioned modifications to the stages and the use of RANDOM-MOVEMENT. Thus we get the following result (see proof in [18]).

---

[5] The high probability is a result of the use of RANDOM-MOVEMENT.

[6] It is possible that A and B may have crossed each other several times before the adversary blocks them at adjacent nodes and the latter case occurs. In this case, C and the robot it finally interacts with will know an upper bound on n. Note that if A and B cross each other at least twice, then on expectation they will meet, leading to the former case.

Theorem 2. *When the robots run* MODIFIED-EXPLORE-DYNAMIC-RING-3-ROBOTS, *exploration of the ring with explicit termination occurs with probability at least* $1 - 1/n$ *in* $O(n \log n)$ *rounds on expectation.*

Remark 1. If we relax our termination condition to partial termination, we can eliminate Stage 4 of MODIFIED-EXPLORE-DYNAMIC-RING-3-ROBOTS entirely and simply have robots terminate instead of moving to Stage 4. Then the exploration of the ring with partial termination occurs with high probability in $O(n)$ rounds on expectation.

Assigning Unique IDs. Throughout this paper, we made the assumption that each robot was initially assigned a unique ID from the range $[1, 2^k]$ prior to the start of the algorithm, where k is the length of the ID bits. This assumption can be removed by having each robot pick an ID uniformly at random from a range of numbers $[1, 2^l]$, where l is a parameter to the algorithm[7]. It is easy to see that the probability that all robots have unique IDs is $(1 - 1/2^l)(1 - 2/2^l) = 1 - O(1/2^l)$. It should be noted that although l can be made arbitrarily large to improve the probability that each robot has a different ID, a larger value of l possibly results in a longer runtime of the algorithm (refer to Lemma 4).

Theorem 3. *When robots run* MODIFIED-EXPLORE-DYNAMIC-RING-3-ROBOTS *and choose IDs uniformly at random from the range* $[1, 2^l]$, *exploration of the ring with explicit termination occurs with probability at least* $(1 - 1/n)(1 - O(1/2^l))$ *in* $O((n + n \cdot 2^l) \log n)$ *rounds on expectation.*

4   Impossibility of Exploration with 2 Robots

In this section, we extend the impossibility results from [6] to the scenario where robots also have the edge crossing detection capability and access to randomness. Due to space constraints, the proofs of theorems can be found in the full version of the paper [18]. First, we make a similar observation to Observation 2 from [6].

Observation 1. *The adversary can prevent two robots starting at different locations from meeting each other even if they have unlimited memory, common chirality, distinct known IDs, the edge crossing detection capability, and access to randomness when* $n \geq 5$. *When robots do not have access to randomness, then it is only required that* $n \geq 3$.

This observation is clear to see by considering the following adversary strategy. If the two robots are on adjacent nodes (or on nodes at distance 2), then the adversary removes the edge between those two nodes (or one of the two edges between the three nodes). When robots do not have access to randomness, it suffices for the adversary to only remove an edge if not doing so results in both

---

[7] Since the number of robots 3 is given to the robots, they can use it to set a value for l, e.g., $l = 2^3 + 12 = 20$.

robots landing on the same node. Now, using this observation, we are able to prove the following impossibility result, which is a more general version of that seen in [6].

Theorem 4. *There does not exist any exploration algorithm with partial termination of anonymous rings of unknown size by two robots, even when robots have distinct IDs, common chirality, the edge crossing detection capability, and when the scheduler is fully synchronous.*

We now provide a similar impossibility result when robots have access to randomness. Note that for this result, we are showing the impossibility of explicit termination and not partial termination.

Theorem 5. *There does not exist any exploration algorithm with explicit termination of anonymous rings of unknown size (≥ 5) by two robots, even when robots have distinct IDs, common chirality, the edge crossing detection capability, access to randomness, and when the scheduler is fully synchronous.*

5   Exploration in Semi-Synchronous Setting (SSYNC)

In this section, we extend our ideas to the passive transport semi-synchronous model proposed in [6] in order to achieve exploration with partial termination using 3 robots even in the absence of a landmark or the knowledge of n.

We now describe the model. In the semi-synchronous setting, in every round, a subset of the robots are put to sleep by the adversary with the restriction that the number of rounds any robot remains asleep is finite. In this setting, passive transport relates to how the robot moves given the following setup. Suppose a robot is awake and wants to travel along an edge e in a round i and the adversary removed that edge in that round. Now, suppose the adversary subsequently puts the robot to sleep from round $i + 1$ until some round j. If e is present again for the first time in some round $k : i + 1 \leq k \leq j$, then the robot moves along the edge in round k even though it is asleep.

In this setting, Di Luna et al. [6] showed that with 3 robots and either the knowledge of an upper bound on n or the presence of a landmark, they were able to achieve exploration with partial termination. We show that it is possible for 3 robots to achieve exploration with partial termination without either of the above two requirements, so long as the robots have access to randomness and the ability of edge crossing detection. We assume that robots have unique IDs, but that requirement can be removed through the use of randomness as described in Sect. 3.

We consider the four stage algorithm presented in Sect. 2 and show how to modify it to achieve exploration with partial termination in this passive transport semi-synchronous model. We first replace Stage 1 with the following zero round protocol. Each robot flips a coin and chooses which direction to move (until Stage 2 is reached) based on the result of the coin toss. With probability 3/4, two robots will move in one direction while the third moves in the other direction.

Stage 2 proceeds as described in the original algorithm. Stage 3 is modified as follows. Robot C will check for an additional condition before determining that the ring has been explored. If A to $B = B$ to A, and A and B were both trying to move on an edge removed by the adversary, then C determines that the ring has been explored. We explain below how C can detect that A and B were trying to move on an edge. Note that it is not necessary that A and B were awake when C visited, but merely that they were attempting to move.

The reasoning behind the above changes is that Stage 1 and Stage 4 require robots to rely on counting the number of rounds. While the simple trick of flipping coins to choose directions solves the Stage 1 problem, there is no immediate fix to the problems present in Stage 4. For Stage 3, we require the above change in order to protect against the adversary simply putting A and B to sleep while C moves back and forth between them. The condition ensures that C has to see them both wanting to move (but not necessarily awake) and prevented to by the adversary before deciding to terminate. Since the adversary can only keep a robot asleep for a finite number of rounds and only remove at most one edge from the graph, eventually, one of the robots will make progress on the ring until either the condition is met or A and B meet.

There is the following subtlety to take into account. Suppose that two robots cross the same edge in the same round (or end up co-located at the same node) and at least one of them is asleep. We need both of them to detect that such an edge crossing (or meeting) occurred and furthermore, be able to swap data with one another. This data should include information about whether one of the robots tried to move along an edge while awake but was subsequently put to sleep before the move could be completed.

With the above modifications, we achieve the following theorem.

Theorem 6. *There exists an algorithm that correctly explores a 1-interval connected dynamic (anonymous) ring of size n with probability $3/4$ in $O(fn)$ steps, where f is the largest interval of time between two consecutive activations of any robot, using 3 robots with unique IDs that neither have common chirality, nor knowledge of an upper bound on n, nor access to a landmark.*

Note that we measure number of steps moved and not running time. Furthermore, note that the number of steps is $O(fn)$ and not $O(n)$. This is due to the fact that the adversary can put A and B to sleep for an arbitrarily long time in Stage 3, but not an infinitely long time.

6   Conclusion

In this paper, we looked into the problem of exploration of a dynamic ring in the presence of 1-interval connectivity. We first showed that exploration with explicit termination subject to some constraints with just two robots equipped with unique IDs even with access to edge crossing detection and randomness is impossible. Subsequently, we presented a deterministic algorithm where three uniquely identifiable robots with edge crossing detection capability explore any 1-interval connected dynamic ring in optimal time. We also showed how to remove the requirement of this capability and allow the robots to be anonymous while still achieving explicit termination with high success probability through the use of randomness. We finally extended our results to the semi-synchronous setting.

There is an interesting line of future research. Our algorithms intimately used advance knowledge of the number of robots present in the system. If that knowledge is unknown and ≥ 3 robots are present, is there an algorithm to solve exploration with explicit termination?

References

1. Agarwalla, A., Augustine, J., Moses Jr., W.K., Sankar, K.M., Sridhar, A.K.: Deterministic dispersion of mobile robots in dynamic rings. In: International Conference on Distributed Computing and Networking, ICDCN, pp. 19:1–19:4. ACM (2018)
2. Albers, S., Henzinger, M.R.: Exploring unknown environments. SIAM J. Comput. **29**(4), 1164–1188 (2000)
3. Das, S.: Graph explorations with mobile agents. In: Flocchini, P., Prencipe, G., Santoro, N. (eds.) Distributed Computing by Mobile Entities. Lecture Notes in Computer Science, vol. 11340, pp. 403–422. Springer, Cham (2019). https://doi.org/10.1007/978-3-030-11072-7_16
4. Deng, X., Papadimitriou, C.H.: Exploring an unknown graph. J. Graph Theory **32**(3), 265–297 (1999)
5. Di Luna, G.A.: Mobile agents on dynamic graphs. In: Flocchini, P., Prencipe, G., Santoro, N. (eds.) Distributed Computing by Mobile Entities. Lecture Notes in Computer Science, vol. 11340, pp. 549–584. Springer, Cham (2019). https://doi.org/10.1007/978-3-030-11072-7_20
6. Di Luna, G.A., Dobrev, S., Flocchini, P., Santoro, N.: Live exploration of dynamic rings. In: International Conference on Distributed Computing Systems, ICDCS, pp. 570–579. IEEE (2016)
7. Di Luna, G.A., Flocchini, P., Pagli, L., Prencipe, G., Santoro, N., Viglietta, G.: Gathering in dynamic rings. Theoret. Comput. Sci. **811**, 79–98 (2020)
8. Dieudonné, Y., Pelc, A.: Deterministic network exploration by anonymous silent agents with local traffic reports. ACM Trans. Algorithms **11**(2), 10:1–10:29 (2014)
9. Erlebach, T., Hoffmann, M., Kammer, F.: On temporal graph exploration. In: Halldórsson, M., Iwama, K., Kobayashi, N., Speckmann, B. (eds.) Automata, Languages, and Programming. ICALP 2015. Lecture Notes in Computer Science, vol. 9134, pp. 444–455. Springer, Heidelberg (2015) . https://doi.org/10.1007/978-3-662-47672-7_36
10. Flocchini, P., Mans, B., Santoro, N.: On the exploration of time-varying networks. Theoret. Comput. Sci. **469**, 53–68 (2013)
11. Fraigniaud, P., Ilcinkas, D., Peer, G., Pelc, A., Peleg, D.: Graph exploration by a finite automaton. Theoret. Comput. Sci. **345**(2–3), 331–344 (2005)
12. Gotoh, T., Flocchini, P., Masuzawa, T., Santoro, N.: Tight bounds on distributed exploration of temporal graphs. In: International Conference on Principles of Distributed Systems, OPODIS (2019)
13. Ilcinkas, D., Klasing, R., Wade, A.M.: Exploration of constantly connected dynamic graphs based on cactuses. In: Halldórsson, M.M. (ed.) SIROCCO 2014. LNCS, vol. 8576, pp. 250–262. Springer, Cham (2014). https://doi.org/10.1007/978-3-319-09620-9_20

14. Ilcinkas, D., Wade, A.M.: On the power of waiting when exploring public transportation systems. In: Fernàndez Anta, A., Lipari, G., Roy, M. (eds.) OPODIS 2011. LNCS, vol. 7109, pp. 451–464. Springer, Heidelberg (2011). https://doi.org/10.1007/978-3-642-25873-2_31

15. Ilcinkas, D., Wade, A.M.: Exploration of the T-interval-connected dynamic graphs: the case of the ring. In: Moscibroda, T., Rescigno, A.A. (eds.) SIROCCO 2013. LNCS, vol. 8179, pp. 13–23. Springer, Cham (2013). https://doi.org/10.1007/978-3-319-03578-9_2

16. Kuhn, F., Lynch, N., Oshman, R.: Distributed computation in dynamic networks. In: ACM symposium on Theory of computing, STOC, pp. 513–522. ACM (2010)

17. Kuhn, F., Oshman, R.: Dynamic networks: models and algorithms. SIGACT News 42(1), 82–96 (2011)

18. Mandal, S., Molla, A.R., Moses Jr., W.K.: Live exploration with mobile robots in a dynamic ring, revisited. arXiv preprint arXiv:2001.04525 (2020)

19. Michail, O., Spirakis, P.G.: Traveling salesman problems in temporal graphs. Theoret. Comput. Sci. 634, 1–23 (2016)

20. O'Dell, R., Wattenhofer, R.: Information dissemination in highly dynamic graphs. In: Joint Workshop on Foundations of Mobile Computing, DIALM-POMC, pp. 104–110. ACM (2005)

21. Panaite, P., Pelc, A.: Exploring unknown undirected graphs. J. Algorithms 33(2), 281–295 (1999)

Asynchronous Filling by Myopic Luminous Robots

Attila Hideg[1] and Tamás Lukovszki[2(✉)]

[1] Department of Automation and Applied Informatics,
Budapest University of Technology and Economics, Budapest, Hungary
Attila.Hideg@aut.bme.hu
[2] Faculty of Informatics, Eötvös Loránd University, Budapest, Hungary
lukovszki@inf.elte.hu

Abstract. We consider the problem of filling an unknown area represented by an arbitrary connected graph of n vertices by mobile luminous robots. In this problem, the robots enter the graph one-by-one through a specific vertex, called the Door, and they eventually have to cover all vertices of the graph while avoiding collisions. The robots are anonymous and make decisions driven by the same local rule of behavior. They have limited persistent memory and limited visibility range. We investigate the Filling problem in the asynchronous model.

We assume that the robots know an upper bound Δ on the maximum degree of the graph before entering. We present an algorithm solving the asynchronous Filling problem with robots having 1 hop visibility range, $O(\log \Delta)$ bits of persistent storage, and $\Delta + 4$ colors, including the color when the light is off. We analyze the algorithm in terms of asynchronous rounds, where a round means the smallest time interval in which each robot, which has not yet finished the algorithm, has been activated at least once. We show that this algorithm needs $O(n^2)$ asynchronous rounds. Our analysis provides the first asymptotic upper bound on the running time in terms of asynchronous rounds.

Then we show how the number of colors can be reduced to $O(1)$ at the cost of the running time. The algorithm with 1 hop visibility range, $O(\log \Delta)$ bits of persistent memory, and $O(1)$ colors needs $O(n^2 \log \Delta)$ rounds. We show how the running time can be improved by robots with a visibility range of 2 hops, $O(\log \Delta)$ bits of persistent memory, and $\Delta + 4$ colors (including the color when the light is off). We show that the algorithm needs $O(n)$ asynchronous rounds. Finally, we show how to extend our solution to the k-Door case, $k \geq 2$, by using $\Delta + k + 4$ colors, including the color when the light is off.

1 Introduction

In swarm robotics, a large number of autonomous mobile robots cooperate to achieve a complex goal. The robots of the swarm are simple, cheap, and

The research has been partially supported by the European Union, co-financed by the European Social Fund (EFOP-3.6.3-VEKOP-16-2017-00002).

C. M. Pinotti et al. (Eds.): ALGOSENSORS 2020, LNCS 12503, pp. 108–123, 2020.
https://doi.org/10.1007/978-3-030-62401-9_8

computationally limited. They act according to local rules of behavior. Robot swarms can achieve high scalability, fault tolerance, and cost-efficiency.

The robots can cooperatively solve different problems, as gathering, flocking, pattern formation, dispersing, filling, coverage, and exploration (e.g. [1,3–6,9, 12,19,21].

The Filling (or, Uniform Dispersal) problem was introduced by Hsiang et al. [19], where the robots enter an a priori unknown but connected area and have to disperse. The area is subdivided into pixels, and at the end of the dispersion, each pixel has to be occupied by exactly one robot.

Model: We consider the Filling problem, where the area is represented by a connected graph, which is unknown for the robots. The robots enter the graph one-by-one through a specific vertex, which is called the *Door* and have to disperse to cover all vertices of the graph while avoiding collision, i.e. two or more robots can not be at the same vertex. At the end of the dispersion, each vertex of the graph has to be occupied by exactly one robot. When the Door vertex becomes empty, a new robot is placed there immediately. We assume that the robots know an upper bound Δ on the maximum degree of the graph.

For simplicity, we assume that the degree of the Door vertex is 1. Otherwise, we introduce an auxiliary vertex of degree 1 connected only to the Door, which takes the role of the original Door (this models the two sides of a doorstep). We assume that, for each vertex v, the adjacent vertices are arranged in a fixed cyclic order. This cyclic order is only visible for robots at v, and it does not change during the dispersion. When a robot r arrives at vertex v from a vertex u, then the cyclic order of neighbors is used by r as a linear order of $\deg(v) - 1$ neighbors by cutting and removing u.

The robots act according to the Look-Compute-Move (LCM) model. In this model, their actions are decomposed into three phases: In the *Look* phase, a robot takes a snapshot of its surroundings, i.e. the vertices and the robots within its visibility range. In the *Compute* phase, it performs calculations based on the surrounding and determines a neighboring vertex as target vertex, or decide to stay at place. In the *Move* phase, if necessary, it moves to the target vertex. The next LCM cycle starts when the target is reached.

Based on the activation times of the robots, there are three main synchronization models studied in the literature: the fully synchronous (FSYNC), the semi-synchronous (SSYNC), and the asynchronous (ASYNC). In the FSYNC model, all robots are activated at the same time, and they perform their Look, Compute, and Move phases synchronously at the same time, which is ensured by a global clock. In the SSYNC model, some robots might skip an LCM cycle and stay inactive. In the ASYNC model, there is no common notion of time available: the robots activate independently after a finite but arbitrary long time, and perform their LCM cycles. Moreover, their LCM cycle length is not fixed; it also can be arbitrarily long.

The robots are *autonomous*, i.e. no central coordination is present, *homogeneous*, i.e. all the robots have the same capabilities and behaviors, *anonymous*, i.e. they cannot distinguish each other, *myopic*, i.e. they have limited visibility range, and *silent*, i.e. they have no communication capabilities and cannot directly talk to one another. However, *luminous* robots can communicate indirectly by using a light. Such robots have a light attached to them, which is externally visible by every robot in their visibility range. They can use a finite set of colors (including the color when the light is off) representing the value of a state variable. The robots are allowed to change these colors in their Compute phase. We denote by X^i the model $X \in \{$ASYNC, SSYNC, FSYNC$\}$ when every robot is enhanced by a light with $i > 1$ colors. In the ASYNC$^{O(1)}$ model, the robots use a constant number of colors (see, e.g. [10]).

Related Work: The Filling (or, Uniform Dispersal) problem was introduced by Hsiang et al. [19], where the robots enter an unknown but connected orthogonal area and have to disperse. The area is subdivided into pixels, and at the end of the dispersion, each pixel has to be occupied by exactly one robot. Hsiang et al. [19] considered this problem in the FSYNC model. They assumed that robots have a limited ability to communicate with nearby robots. They proposed two solutions, BFLF and DFLF, both modeling generally known algorithms: BFS and DFS. DFLF required a visibility range of 2 hops. It was assumed that the robots are able to detect the orientation of each other. Barrameda et al. [5,6] investigated the asynchronous case. In [5] the authors assumed common top-down and left-right directions for the robots and showed that robots with visibility range of 1 hop and 2 bits of persistent memory could solve the problem in an orthogonal area if the area does not contain holes, without using explicit communication in finite time. In [6] Barrameda et al. presented two methods for filling an unknown orthogonal area in presence of obstacles (holes) in the ASYNC model. Their first method, called TALK, requires a visibility range of 2 hops[1] if the robots have explicit communication. The other method, called MUTE, does not use explicit communication between the robots, but it requires a visibility range of 6. Both methods need $O(1)$ bits of persistent memory and terminate in finite time.

In [16,18] the Filling problem has been investigated in the FSYNC model. In [16] the authors gave a solution for the orthogonal Filling problem by using robots with 1 hop visibility range and $O(1)$ bits of persistent memory for both the Single and Multiple Door cases. In [18] a method for a general Filling problem has been presented, where the area is represented by an arbitrary connected graph. The robots require 1 hop visibility range and $O(\Delta)$ bits of persistent memory, where Δ is the degree of the graph. For the k-Door case, the memory requirement is $O(\Delta \cdot \log k)$. The general method is called the Virtual Chain Method (VCM), which is a leader-follower method. In the VCM, the robots form a chain and fill the area mimicking a DFS-like traversal of the graph. The algorithms presented in [16] and [18] are intensively utilizing the synchronous nature of the model to avoid collisions and backtracking.

---

[1] In [6] it is assumed that the robot sees all eight sourrounding cells and able to communicate with robots at that eight cells. Assuming orthogonal movements, a cell sharing only one corner with the current cell of the robot are reachable in two hops.

The model of luminous robots was introduced by Peleg [24]. Subsequently, significant amount of research has been carried for a plenty of problems using this model (e.g. [2,7,8,14,15,20,22,23,25–27]). Das et al. [10,11] considered the model, where the robots can move in the continuous Euclidean plane, and they proved that the asynchronous model with a constant number of colors $\text{ASYNC}^{O(1)}$ is strictly more powerful than the semi-synchronous model SSYNC, i.e. $\text{ASYNC}^{O(1)} > \text{SSYNC}$. Das et al. [11] also prove that there are problems that robots cannot solve without lights, even if they are fully synchronous, but can be solved by asynchronous luminous robots with $O(1)$ colors.

D'Emidio et al. [13] have shown that on graphs one task can be solved in the fully synchronous model FSYNC but not in the asynchronous lights-enhanced model, while for other tasks, the converse holds. In this work, we show that the Filling problem can be solved in both models by robots with 1 hop visibility range and $O(1)$ bits of persistent memory.

Our Contribution: In this work, we present solutions for the Filling problem by luminous robots on graphs in the $\text{ASYNC}^{O(1)}$ model.

First, we describe a method, called PACK, which solves the problem by robots with 1 hop visibility range, $O(\log \Delta)$ bits of persistent memory, and $\Delta + 4$ colors for the single Door case, including the color when the light is off. We analyze the algorithm in terms of asynchronous rounds, where a round means the smallest time interval in which each robot, which has not yet finished the algorithm, has been activated at least once. We show that this algorithm needs $O(n^2)$ asynchronous rounds. Regarding asynchronous algorithms for the Filling problem, former works only guarantee termination within finite time. Our analysis provides the first asymptotic upper bound on the running time in terms of asynchronous rounds.

Then we show how the number of colors can be reduced to $O(1)$ at the cost of running time. The algorithm with 1 hop visibility range, $O(\log \Delta)$ bits of persistent memory, and $O(1)$ colors needs $O(n^2 \log \Delta)$ rounds.

After this, we show how the running time can be significantly improved by robots with a visibility range of 2 hops, with no communication, $O(\log \Delta)$ bits of persistent memory, and $\Delta + 4$ colors, by presenting the algorithm called BLOCK. This algorithm needs $O(n)$ rounds.

Then we extend the BLOCK algorithm for solving the k-Door Filling problem, $k \geq 2$, by using $O(\log \Delta)$ bits of memory and $\Delta + k + 4$ colors, including the color when the light is off. The visibility range of 2 hops is optimal for the k-Door case (a counterexample when this problem cannot be solved in the ASYNC model with a visibility range of 1 hop was presented in [5], also holds for the $\text{ASYNC}^{O(1)}$ model).

2   PACK Algorithm

Now we describe the PACK algorithm to solve the Filling problem for an area represented by a connected graph of n vertices. PACK is based on the Virtual

Chain Method described in [18], in which the robots filled the area in a DFS-like dispersion.

The robots are allowed to be in one of the following states: None, Follower, Leader, Finished. They are initialized with None state when placed at the Door. The first robot becomes the Leader and moves to a vertex that has never been occupied before (these vertices are called *unvisited* vertices). The rest of the robots will become Followers and follow the Leader, until the Leader becomes stuck (i.e. no unvisited neighbors available). Then the robot behind the Leader, called the *successor* robot, becomes a new Leader and moves if possible. The previous Leader switches to Finished state. The algorithm terminates when each robot is in Finished state.

The name Virtual Chain comes from the fact that all active robots (i.e. the Leader and the Followers) are on the path traversed by the current Leader from the Door. This path is called the chain. The chain contains only visited vertices, which can be occupied by the Followers. Each Follower follows its *predecessor*, which is the previously placed robot.

The difficulty is to select the next target vertex for the Leader with a visibility range of 1 hop by ensuring that no other robot can move to that vertex because the Leader can not see all adjacent vertices of the target and robots on those vertices do not see the Leader.

We define the state *Packed* for the chain. The chain is in Packed state, when each Follower is immediately behind its predecessor, i.e. each vertex on the path traversed by the current Leader from the Door is occupied by a Follower robot. In this state none of the robots can move except the Leader. Therefore, only the Leader has to know this state.

The Concept: The Leader moves to unvisited vertices until there is no such neighboring vertex. Before each movement, the Leader waits for Packed state; thus, it cannot collide with other robots, and the Leader can decide which vertex is unvisited. When the Leader has no neighboring unvisited vertex, it switches to Finished state and does not move anymore. Its successor then becomes the Leader and the new Leader moves to other unvisited vertices. The robots use $\Delta + 4$ colors, including the color, when the light is off. The first Δ colors show the direction of the target vertex (for each vertex, the adjacent vertices are arranged in a fixed cyclic order), we refer to them as *DIR* colors. Furthermore, we use two colors, denoted by *CONF* and *CONF2* colors, for confirming that a robot has seen a DIR color of the predecessor, which allows the predecessor to move. For this purpose, the CONF color is sufficient, when the predecessor is a Follower robot. However, when the predecessor robot is the Leader, and it must change the target vertex after the Packed state is reached (details are provided later) or the predecessor becomes the Leader and it chooses an unvisited target vertex, it indicates the new direction with a new DIR color. Then the CONF2 color is needed for ensuring that the successor has seen the lastly shown DIR color. Furthermore, we use an additional color, called *MOV* color to indicate that a robot is on the way to its target vertex.

Now we describe the rules followed by the robots in different states.

Leader: Can only move to an unvisited vertex. When it wants to move, it shows the direction it wants to go to by setting the corresponding DIR color, and then it waits until its successor gives a confirmation that it can move by setting its CONF color. During the movement, the Leader shows the MOV color. When its successor sets its CONF color, the chain is in Packed state. This means each not occupied vertex is also an unvisited vertex (as each vertex in the path of the Leader is occupied by a robot). If the Leader is still on the Door vertex, therefore, it does not have a successor, it can move without waiting for the CONF color.

Follower: Follows its predecessor. The Follower robot r sets the CONF color if and only if i) the predecessor of r is showing its direction, and ii) the successor of r – if exists – have set its CONF color (i.e. the successor knows in which direction r will move). This allows the predecessor r' of r to move to its destination knowing: i) all the robots behind r' have set CONF color, and ii) the robots behind r' will not move until the predecessor of r moved. When r' is the Leader, the chain is in Packed state.

None: The robots are initialized with None state when they are placed at the Door. If the robot r in None state has no neighboring robot, then r changes its state to Leader, chooses the unique neighboring vertex as target vertex, sets the MOV color, and starts moving there. Otherwise, if the robot r in None state has one neighboring robot, then r becomes a Follower and sets the neighbor to its predecessor.

There are three special situations where we need the following additional rules:

Leader target change: It might happen that the Leader r chooses a target vertex v, which is unoccupied at the moment when r performs its Look operation, however, when the successor of r sets the CONF color and r could start to move to v, another robot already moved to v. In such case, the Leader r has to choose a new target, and the successor of r has to know about this choice. Assume first that r has an unvisited neighboring vertex. Then r sets the corresponding DIR color and waits until its successor sets the CONF2 color. Finally, the Leader moves to the target.

Note that the chain is in Packed state when the successor of the Leader r sets the CONF color. If the Leader changes the target, no other robot can move until r sets the CONF2 color, and the Leader moves to the target. Consequently, the Leader can change the target vertex only once between two movements.

If r does not have any unvisited neighboring vertex after r sees the CONF color of the successor, then r can not move anymore and the successor must take the leadership (see the rule below). The robot r sets the Δ direction color, which has special meaning. The successor r' confirms this by setting the CONF2 color. Then r turn off its light r' becomes the Leader. (Note that it would be possible to omit the Leader target change rule by introducing a new color for signaling the Packed state. Then the Leader would only show its direction once the Packed state is achieved, which could be acknowledged with the CONF color.)

Taking the leadership: When the Leader r cannot move anymore, its successor has to become the new Leader. The Leader r indicates that it does not have any unvisited neighboring vertex by setting its direction color to Δ. i.e. this color has a special meaning: it indicates that the Leader cannot move anymore and wants to switch to Finished state, and the leadership must be taken by its successor. When this is detected by the successor r', it sets its CONF color, waits for the previous Leader to turn off its light, then r' becomes the Leader. Afterwards, r' tries to move to an unvisited vertex.

Setting movement color: Before performing the movement, the robots have to set their color to MOV. Keeping the old color could lead to an error. E.g., consider the following situation. 1. The Leader sets a DIR color. 2: The Follower confirms it by the CONF color. 3: The Leader moves by keeping the DIR color. 4: The Follower shows the corresponding DIR color, receives a CONF, and follows the Leader. 5: The Follower reaches its target, sees the old DIR color of the Leader and sets the CONF color, before the Leader chooses the new target. In order to prevent such situations, the moving robots set their color to MOV and keep this color until the target is reached, and a new target is determined. After the movement, the robot sets the previous position as its *Entry* vertex.

Pseudocode of the PACK algorithm is provided in the full version of this article [17].

2.1   Analysis

The proofs of Lemmata 1–4 are available in the full version of the article [17].

Lemma 1. *Leader only moves to unvisited vertices.*

Lemma 2. *There can be at most one Leader at any time.*

Lemma 3. *Robots cannot collide.*

Lemma 4. *PACK fills the area represented by a connected graph.*

Theorem 1. *Algorithm PACK fills an area represented by a connected graph in the ASYNC model by robots having a visibility range of 1 hop, $O(\log \Delta)$ bits of persistent storage, and $\Delta + 4$ colors, including the color when the light is off.*

Proof. As the area is filled (by Lemma 4), and collisions are not possible (by Lemma 3), the area will be filled without collisions. The robots require $O(\log \Delta)$ bits of memory to store the following: *State* (4 states: 2 bits), *Target* (direction of the target vertex: $\lceil \log \Delta \rceil$ bits), *NextTarget* (direction of the vertex, where the robot needs to move after the vertex *Target* is reached: $\lceil \log \Delta \rceil$ bits). Regarding the number of colors, the robots use Δ colors to show the direction where the target of the robot is. There are two additional colors (CONF and CONF2) for confirming the robot saw the signaled direction of the predecessor and one color (MOV) during the movement.

Now we analyze the running time of the algorithm in terms of asynchronous rounds. An asynchronous round means the shortest time in which each robot, which is not in Finished state yet, has been activated at least once and performed an LCM cycle.

Theorem 2. *The algorithm PACK runs in $O(n^2)$ asynchronous rounds.*

Proof. Assume a chain containing $r_1, r_2, \ldots, r_i$ (where r_1 is the active Leader, and $r_2, \ldots, r_i$ are on the path from the Leader to the Door), and assume that the chain is in Packed state.

Assume first that the Leader r_1 has an unoccupied neighboring vertex. Denote by T the time between two consecutive movements of the Leader. We divide T into three time intervals: $T = T_1 + T_2 + T_3$. T_1 starts with the movement of the Leader, it includes the time, when all robots in the chain, making one step forwards. T_2 starts with placing a new robot at the Door. In T_2 the robots, starting from the Door, set their CONF color one by one. This CONF color is 'propagated' to the Leader, meaning that the Packed state is reached. T_3 starts when the Leader recognizes the CONF color of the successor, i.e. after achieving the Packed state. Then the Leader might find its target occupied by another robot. In this case, the *Leader target change* rule will be used.

Let t be the first asynchronous round of T_1, i.e. in round t the Leader r_1 moves to its target and sets its direction color. At the latest in round $t + 1$ the robot r_2 detects that r_1 left its previous vertex v and in that round r_2 moves to v and sets its direction color. This argument can be repeated to all robots until the last one r_i moves at the latest in round $t + i - 1$. Therefore, $T_1 \leq i$.

Now the second phase T_2 starts with the placing of a new robot r_{i+1} at the latest in the round $t + i$. In that round, the new robot r_{i+1} sets its color to CONF. The robot r_i sees this color at the latest in the next round t_{i+1} and sets its color to CONF in that round. Repeating this argument for $r_{i-1}, \ldots, r_2$, we obtain that r_2 sets the CONF color at the latest in round t_{2i-1}. Therefore, $T_2 \leq i$.

Now T_3 starts. The Leader r_1 recognizes the CONF color of its successor at the latest in round t_{2i}. Then Leader knows that the chain is in Packed state. If the target vertex v of the Leader is unoccupied, the Leader can move immediately, since in Packed state each unoccupied vertex is unvisited. Otherwise, if v is occupied, the *Leader target change* protocol is performed, i.e. 1: the Leader chooses a new unoccupied neighboring vertex and shows the corresponding DIR color (in round t_{2i} at the latest), 2: then its successor sets its color to CONF2 (in round t_{2i+1} at the latest). At the latest in the round t_{2i+2} the Leader recognizes this and can move. Then $T = T_1 + T_2 + T_3 \leq 2i + 2 \leq 2n$ rounds.

Assume now that the Leader r_1 has no unoccupied neighboring vertex. If r_1 is at the Door, then it turns the light off and switches to Finished state; the graph is filled. Otherwise, r_i sees the CONF color of r_2 and recognizes the Packed state in the round t_{2i} at the latest. Then r_1 sets its Δ color in that round. The robot r_2 recognizes it in round t_{2i+1} at the latest and sets its CONF color. The robot r_1 sees the CONF color in round t_{2i+2} at the latest, r_1 turns its light off and switches to Finished state. The robot r_2 sees it in round t_{2i+3} at the latest, r_2 becomes the new Leader in that round, and checks if there is an unoccupied neighboring vertex. If so, r_2 sets the corresponding DIR color in the same round and waits for the CONF2 color from the successor. The successor sets the CONF2 color in round t_{2i+4} at the latest, and r_2 sees the CONF2 color at the latest in round t_{2i+5}. Since the chain is already in Packed state, the robot r_2 can move in the same round (in round t_{2i+5} at the latest). Otherwise, if r_2 has no unoccupied neighboring vertex, then the leadership has to be taken by its successor when the successor exists, i.e. r_2 is not at the Door. If r_2 is at the Door, then r_2 turns the light off and switches to Finished state; the graph is filled.

When a Leader can move, it occupies an unvisited vertex within $2n$ asynchronous rounds. Otherwise, its successor takes the leadership and performs a target change. Taking the leadership and the target change need at most 5 rounds. Since the leadership is taken at most once by each robot during the whole algorithm, and there are n robots in the filled graph, at most $5n$ time is used for all leadership taking with target change altogether. Therefore, after at most $2n^2 + 5n = O(n^2)$ rounds all vertices of the graph become filled.

Remark: In the ASYNC model, a robot can be inactive between two LCM cycles. Since the inactive phase allowed to be finite but arbitrarily long, an asynchronous round and the runtime of the algorithm can also be arbitrarily long. In the case where we do not allow inactive intervals between the LCM cycles and every LCM cycle of every robot takes at most t_{max} time then we can upper bound the time of an asynchronous round by $2 \cdot t_{max}$.

Corollary 1. *(i) Assume that every LCM cycle of every robot takes at most t_{max} time and there are no inactive intervals between the LCM cycles. Then the running time of the PACK algorithm is $O(n^2 t_{max})$. (ii) In the FSYNC model the PACK algorithm needs $O(n^2)$ LCM cycles.*

2.2   Filling of Graphs Using Constant Number of Colors

The PACK algorithm uses $\Delta + 4$ colors (including the color when the light is off). We can reduce the number of colors to $O(1)$ at the cost of the running time, as follows. We encode the $L = \Delta + 4$ colors by a sequence of $\lceil \log L \rceil$ bits and transmit this sequence by emulating the Alternating Bit Protocol (ABP), also referred to as Stop-and-wait ARQ (see, e.g. [28]). This protocol uses a sequence number from $\{0, 1\}$ alternately to transmit the bits. The sender has four states corresponding to the transmitted bit $b \in \{0, 1\}$ and the sequence number. The receiver has two states that represent which sequence number is awaited. The data bits are accepted with alternating sequence numbers. This protocol ensures the correct transmission of the bit sequence without duplicates.

We emulate the ABP by using six different colors, one for each of the four states of the sender and one for each of the two states of the receiver. Seeing the current color of the sender, the receiver can decode the sequence number and the data bit. When a color corresponding to the correct sequence number is seen, the receiver sets its color, indicating that it waits for the next bit. When the sender sees the changed color of the receiver, it sets its color corresponding to the next data bit and the next sequence number. Therefore, encoding an original color in a sequence of $\lceil \log L \rceil = O(\log \Delta)$ bits and transmitting this sequence takes $O(\log \Delta)$ rounds. This leads to the following Theorem.

Theorem 3. *The modified Algorithm PACK fills an area represented by a connected graph in the ASYNC model by robots having a visibility range of 1, $O(\log \Delta)$ bits of persistent storage and $O(1)$ colors. The algorithm needs $O(n^2 \log \Delta)$ asynchronous rounds.*

3   BLOCK Algorithm

The PACK algorithm solves the Filling problem in arbitrary connected graphs by robots with a visibility range of 1 hop. An important property of the PACK algorithm is that the Leader can only move when the chain has reached the Packed state. Now we consider robots with a visibility range of 2 hops. Then the robots see each robot, that potentially could choose the same target vertex. The idea is that the Leader only chooses a vertex v as the target, if the 1 hop neighborhood of v does not contain any other robot with the light turned on, except when the light showing direction Δ (i.e. the robot will not move anymore, it wants to switch to Finished state, and waiting for the confirmation of the successor). A vertex neighboring to a robot with its light on (except the color Δ) is considered as *blocked* vertex for the Leader.

We introduce the following additional rules for the robots:

Leader: The Leader must not choose a blocked vertex as the target. As the visibility range of the robots is 2 hops, the Leader can identify the blocked neighbors. When only blocked or occupied vertices surround the Leader, it chooses to terminate its actions (sets the color Δ and after the confirmation of the successor it switches to Finished state), and the leadership will be taken by its successor.

Follower: Follower robots 'block' all their unoccupied neighboring vertices. As a result, all unoccupied vertices that are part of the chain are blocked: Before a Follower r would move from a vertex v, it sets the DIR color corresponding to the target and blocks all of its unoccupied neighboring vertices. In particular, it blocks the target vertex. Thus the Leader cannot choose the same target. Then r waits until the successor r' sets its CONF color and r moves from v. During the movement, the MOV color is set, which keeps the same unoccupied vertices blocked. When r leaves v, the vertex v is blocked by r'.

These rules ensure that each vertex on the chain is either occupied or blocked. Consequently, the Leader only moves to unvisited vertices. The pseudocode of the BLOCK algorithm is provided in the full version of the article [17].

3.1   Analysis

The proofs of Lemmata 5–8 are available in the full version of the article [17].

Lemma 5. *Leader only moves to unvisited vertices.*

Lemma 6. *There can be at most one Leader at a time.*

Lemma 7. *Robots cannot collide.*

Lemma 8. *BLOCK fills the area represented by a connected graph.*

Theorem 4. *Algorithm BLOCK fills the area represented by a connected graph in the ASYNC model by robots having a visibility range of 2 hops, $O(\log \Delta)$ bits of persistent storage, and using $\Delta + 4$ colors, including the color when the light is off.*

Proof. We can use the arguments of the proof of Theorem 1 as the area is filled (by Lemma 8), and collisions are not possible (by Lemma 7), the area will be filled without collisions. The robots store the same data in their persistent storage as in Theorem 1 and use the same set of colors.

Theorem 5. *In the ASYNC model, the BLOCK algorithm fills the area represented by a connected graph in $O(n)$ asynchronous rounds.*

Proof. Assume that the chain contains the robots $r_1, r_2, \ldots, r_j$, where r_1 is the current Leader and $r_2, \ldots, r_j$ are on the path from the Leader to the Door, and assume that the Leader r_1 occupied its position and its successor r_2 has arrived at the previous position of r_1. When the first robot r_1 is placed at the Door (i.e. $j = 1$), it detects in the first asynchronous round, whether it is a Leader or a Follower. If the only neighbor is unoccupied, it becomes a Leader and moves in the first round. The first round ends. After r_1 left the Door, the next robot is placed there.

   Assume now that $j \geq 2$. Let r_i, $i < j$ be a robot (r_i is either a Leader or a Follower) and assume that its successor r_{i+1} at its previous vertex. Let t be the current asynchronous round. If r_i is Leader, i.e. $i = 1$, we additionally assume that it has an unblocked and unoccupied neighboring vertex v. Otherwise, if r_i is not the Leader, assume that the target vertex of v of r_i is unoccupied, i.e. the predecessor r_{i-1} left v already. Then r_i sets the corresponding DIR color in round t. At the latest in round $t + 1$ the robot r_{i+1} sees the DIR color and sets its color to the CONF, allowing r_i to move. At the latest in round $t+2$ the robot r_i detects this and moves to its target v and at the end of that round r_i and r_{i-1} become neighbors again. Then, at the latest in round $t + 3$ the robot r_{i+1} detects that r_i left the neighboring vertex v'. If r_{i+1} is at the Door it moves at the latest in round $t + 3$. Otherwise, if r_{i+1} is not at the Door, and therefore, a successor robot r_{i+2} exists, r_{i+1} has to wait for the confirmation of r_{i+2} before the movement. We will show that r_{i+2} must be at the neighbor vertex behind r_{i+1} in round $t + 4$ at the latest. At the latest in round $t + 4$ the robot r_{i+2} sets its CONF color. Therefore, r_{i+1} can move to v' at the latest in round $t + 5$ and at the end of that round r_{i+1} and r_i become neighbors again. At the latest in round $t+6$ we have the same situation regarding r_i and r_i+1 as in round t, i.e. r_{i-1} shows its DIR color and r_i confirms it.

It remains to show that in round $t+4$ at the latest r_{i+2} must be on the neighbor vertex of r_{i+1}. If r_{i+2} is at the Door, then it appeared there after r_{i+1} left the Door, i.e. before round t and r_{i+1} did not move; therefore they must be neighbors in round $t+4$. Otherwise, let t' be the latest round before t, where r_{i+1} and r_{i+2} were neighbors and the robot r_{i+1} detects that its predecessor r_i moved from the neighboring vertex and r_{i+1} sets the DIR color. Then we can repeat the arguments with robots r_{i+1}, r_{i+2}, and round t' described above, and we obtain that (i) r_{i+1} moves in round $t'' \leq t'+2$ and at the end of round $t'+2$ the robots r_i and r_{i+1} become neighbors again, and (ii) r_{i+2} can move again at the latest in round $t''+3$ and in round $t''+4$ at the latest r_{i+2} and r_{i+1} must be neighbors. Since $t'' \leq t$, in round $t+4$ at the latest r_{i+2} and r_{i+1} must be neighbors.

Summarizing the above description, the robot r_i moves at the latest in every 6th round if r_i is a Follower or it is a Leader with an unblocked and unoccupied neighbor.

Assume now that r_i is Leader, its successor r_{i+1} is at its previous vertex, and all neighboring vertices of r_i are blocked or occupied in round t. Then r_i sets its Δ color to show the successor that it has to switch to Finished state. The successor r_{i+1} confirms it at the latest in round $t+1$. At the latest in round $t+2$ the robot r_i becomes Finished and turns the light off. At the latest in round $t+3$ the robot r_{i+1} becomes the new Leader. Therefore, the leadership is taken within 4 rounds. At the latest in round $t+3$ the new Leader r_{i+1} shows its new target if there is an unblocked and unoccupied neighboring vertex, or it sets the Δ to show the successor that it has to switch to Finished state.

When a Leader can move, it occupies an unvisited unblocked vertex in every 6th round. Otherwise, its successor takes the leadership. Since the leadership is taken at most once by each robot during the whole algorithm, and there are n robots in the filled graph, at most $4n$ rounds used for all 'leadership taking'. Therefore, after $6n + 4n = 10n$ rounds, all vertices of the graph become filled.

4   Multiple Doors

We now consider the case in which there are $k \geq 2$ Doors. For the k-Door Filling, there is a situation that cannot be solved by the above methods: Let v be an unvisited vertex, which is neighboring to (at least) two Leaders r_1 and r_2. In order to fill the graph, exactly one of the Leaders, r_1 or r_2, has to move to vertex v. If one of the robots, say r_1, has been activated earlier, then r_1 sets the direction color corresponding to v, and it prevents r_2 to move to v (r_1 blocks v from r_2). However, if the activation times of r_1 and r_2 are exactly the same, then they would set the direction color at the same time, meaning they mutually block each other from moving to v. If r_1 or r_2 has no other unvisited vertex in their neighborhood, then none of them could move, and particularly, none of them would occupy v.

We use the concept from [5] and assume that robots entering from different doors have distinct colors. We propose a protocol, which uses a strict priority order between the Leaders originating from different Doors.

Priority Protocol: The robots have k additional different colors corresponding to the Door they used for entering the area, where k is the number of Doors. We define a strict total order between these colors, called priority order. We call these k colors priority colors. After showing the direction to the successor and after the successor has confirmed it, the Leader sets its color to the corresponding priority color (instead of the MOV color) and starts its movement. It arrives to its target showing its priority color. We modify the blocking rule for the Leader in the following way: If there is a robot with a direction color (except the special color Δ), or confirmation color, or MOV color, or priority color with higher priority than r, then its neighbors are considered as blocked. Since there is a strict total order between the priority colors, in such a situation exactly one of them is allowed to move there.

We slightly change the rule *taking the leadership*: when the successor robot r notices that the Leader is switching to Finished state (by setting the direction color to Δ), r confirms it by setting its color to the priority color of the old Leader.

The proofs of Lemmata 9 and 10 are available in the full version of the article [17].

Lemma 9. *Priority protocol does not allow collisions.*

Lemma 10. *The BLOCK algorithm extended with the Priority protocol fills the connected graph.*

Theorem 6. *Algorithm BLOCK extended with the Priority protocol solves the k-Door Filling problem, $k \geq 2$, in the ASYNC model in finite time, with 2 hops of visibility, $O(\log \Delta)$ bits of memory and using $\Delta + k + 4$ colors including the color when the light is off.*

Proof. We can use the arguments of the proof of Theorem 1 as the area is filled (by Lemma 10), and collisions are not possible (by Lemma 9), the area will be filled without collisions. The robots store the same data in their persistent storage as in Theorem 1 and use $\Delta + k + 4$ colors. □

5   Summary

In this work, we have presented solutions for the Filling problem by luminous robots in the $\text{ASYNC}^{O(1)}$ model. We have presented a method, called PACK, which solves the problem by robots with 1 hop visibility range, $O(\log \Delta)$ bits of persistent memory, and $\Delta + 4$ colors for the single Door case, including the color when the light is off. We have shown that this algorithm needs $O(n^2)$ asynchronous rounds. Regarding asynchronous algorithms for the Filling problem, former works only guarantee termination within finite time. Our analysis provides the first asymptotic upper bound on the running time in terms of asynchronous rounds.

Then we have shown how the number of colors can be reduced to $O(1)$ at the cost of running time. The algorithm with 1 hop visibility range, $O(\log \Delta)$ bits of persistent memory, and $O(1)$ colors needs $O(n^2 \log \Delta)$ rounds.

After this, we have shown how the running time can be significantly improved by robots with a visibility range of 2 hops, with no communication, $O(\log \Delta)$ bits of persistent memory, and $\Delta + 4$ colors, by presenting the algorithm called BLOCK. This algorithm needs $O(n)$ rounds.

Then we have extended the BLOCK algorithm for solving the k-Door Filling problem, $k \geq 2$, by using $O(\log \Delta)$ bits of memory, and $\Delta + k + 4$ colors, including the color when the light is off. The visibility range of 2 hops is optimal for the k-Door case (a counterexample when this problem cannot be solved in the ASYNC model with a visibility range of 1 hop was presented in [5], also holds for the $\text{ASYNC}^{O(1)}$ model).

References

1. Albers, S., Henzinger, M.R.: Exploring unknown environments. SIAM J. Comput. **29**(4), 1164–1188 (2000)
2. Aljohani, A., Poudel, P., Sharma, G.: Complete visitability for autonomous robots on graphs. IPDPS 2018, pp. 733–742 (2018)
3. Amir, M., Bruckstein, A.M.: Minimizing travel in the uniform dispersal problem for robotic sensors. In: AAMAS 2019, pp. 113–121 (2019)
4. Augustine, J., Moses Jr., W.K.: Dispersion of mobile robots: a study of memory-time trade-offs. In: ICDCN 2018, pp. 1:1–1:10 (2018)
5. Barrameda, E.M., Das, S., Santoro, N.: Deployment of asynchronous robotic sensors in unknown orthogonal environments. In: Fekete, S.P. (ed.) ALGOSENSORS 2008. LNCS, vol. 5389, pp. 125–140. Springer, Heidelberg (2008). https://doi.org/10.1007/978-3-540-92862-1_11
6. Barrameda, E.M., Das, S., Santoro, N.: Uniform dispersal of asynchronous finite-state mobile robots in presence of holes. In: Flocchini, P., Gao, J., Kranakis, E., Meyer auf der Heide, F. (eds.) ALGOSENSORS 2013. LNCS, vol. 8243, pp. 228–243. Springer, Heidelberg (2014). https://doi.org/10.1007/978-3-642-45346-5_17
7. Bhagat, S., Mukhopadhyaya, K.: Optimum algorithm for mutual visibility among asynchronous robots with lights. In: Spirakis, P., Tsigas, P. (eds.) SSS 2017. LNCS, vol. 10616, pp. 341–355. Springer, Cham (2017). https://doi.org/10.1007/978-3-319-69084-1_24
8. Bose, K., Kundu, M.K., Adhikary, R., Sau, B.: Arbitrary pattern formation by asynchronous opaque robots with lights. In: Censor-Hillel, K., Flammini, M. (eds.) SIROCCO 2019. LNCS, vol. 11639, pp. 109–123. Springer, Cham (2019). https://doi.org/10.1007/978-3-030-24922-9_8
9. Cohen, R., Peleg, D.: Convergence properties of the gravitational algorithm in asynchronous robot systems. SIAM J. Comput. **34**(6), 1516–1528 (2005)
10. Das, S., Flocchini, P., Prencipe, G., Santoro, N., Yamashita, M.: The power of lights: synchronizing asynchronous robots using visible bits. In: ICDCS 2012, pp. 506–515 (2012)

11. Das, S., Flocchini, P., Prencipe, G., Santoro, N., Yamashita, M.: Autonomous mobile robots with lights. Theor. Comput. Sci. **609**, 171–184 (2016)
12. Daymude, J.J., Hinnenthal, K., Richa, A.W., Scheideler, C.: Computing by programmable particles. In: Flocchini, P., Prencipe, G., Santoro, N. (eds.) Distributed Computing by Mobile Entities. LNCS, vol. 11340, pp. 615–681. Springer, Cham (2019). https://doi.org/10.1007/978-3-030-11072-7_22
13. D'Emidio, M., Frigioni, D., Navarra, A.: Synchronous robots vs asynchronous lights-enhanced robots on graphs. Electron. Notes Theor. Comput. Sci. **322**, 169–180 (2016)
14. Feletti, C., Mereghetti, C., Palano, B.: Uniform circle formation for swarms of opaque robots with lights. In: Izumi, T., Kuznetsov, P. (eds.) SSS 2018. LNCS, vol. 11201, pp. 317–332. Springer, Cham (2018). https://doi.org/10.1007/978-3-030-03232-6_21
15. Flocchini, P., Santoro, N., Wada, K.: On memory, communication, and synchronous schedulers when moving and computing. In: OPODIS 2019, pp. 25:1–25:17 (2019)
16. Hideg, A., Lukovszki, T.: Uniform dispersal of robots with minimum visibility range. In: Fernández Anta, A., Jurdzinski, T., Mosteiro, M.A., Zhang, Y. (eds.) ALGOSENSORS 2017. LNCS, vol. 10718, pp. 155–167. Springer, Cham (2017). https://doi.org/10.1007/978-3-319-72751-6_12
17. Hideg, A., Lukovszki, T.: Asynchronous filling by myopic luminous robots. CoRR abs/1909.06895 (2019). http://arxiv.org/abs/1909.06895
18. Hideg, A., Lukovszki, T., Forstner, B.: Filling arbitrary connected areas by silent robots with minimum visibility range. In: Gilbert, S., Hughes, D., Krishnamachari, B. (eds.) ALGOSENSORS 2018. LNCS, vol. 11410, pp. 193–205. Springer, Cham (2019). https://doi.org/10.1007/978-3-030-14094-6_13
19. Hsiang, T.-R., Arkin, E.M., Bender, M.A., Fekete, S.P., Mitchell, J.S.B.: Algorithms for rapidly dispersing robot swarms in unknown environments. In: Boissonnat, J.-D., Burdick, J., Goldberg, K., Hutchinson, S. (eds.) Algorithmic Foundations of Robotics V. STAR, vol. 7, pp. 77–93. Springer, Heidelberg (2004). https://doi.org/10.1007/978-3-540-45058-0_6
20. Kamei, S., Lamani, A., Ooshita, F., Tixeuil, S., Wada, K.: Gathering on rings for myopic asynchronous robots with lights. In: OPODIS 2019, pp. 27:1–27:17 (2019)
21. Lukovszki, T., Meyer auf der Heide, F.: Fast collisionless pattern formation by anonymous, position-aware robots. In: Aguilera, M.K., Querzoni, L., Shapiro, M. (eds.) OPODIS 2014. LNCS, vol. 8878, pp. 248–262. Springer, Cham (2014). https://doi.org/10.1007/978-3-319-14472-6_17
22. Luna, G.D., Flocchini, P., Chaudhuri, S.G., Poloni, F., Santoro, N., Viglietta, G.: Mutual visibility by luminous robots without collisions. Inf. Comput. **254**(3), 392–418 (2017)
23. Ooshita, F., Tixeuil, S.: Ring exploration with myopic luminous robots. In: Izumi, T., Kuznetsov, P. (eds.) SSS 2018. LNCS, vol. 11201, pp. 301–316. Springer, Cham (2018). https://doi.org/10.1007/978-3-030-03232-6_20
24. Peleg, D.: Distributed coordination algorithms for mobile robot swarms: new directions and challenges. In: Pal, A., Kshemkalyani, A.D., Kumar, R., Gupta, A. (eds.) IWDC 2005. LNCS, vol. 3741, pp. 1–12. Springer, Heidelberg (2005). https://doi.org/10.1007/11603771_1
25. Sharma, G., Vaidyanathan, R., Trahan, J.L.: Constant-time complete visibility for asynchronous robots with lights. In: Spirakis, P., Tsigas, P. (eds.) SSS 2017. LNCS, vol. 10616, pp. 265–281. Springer, Cham (2017). https://doi.org/10.1007/978-3-319-69084-1_18

26. Sharma, G., Vaidyanathan, R., Trahan, J.L., Busch, C., Rai, S.: Complete visibility for robots with lights in $O(1)$ time. In: Bonakdarpour, B., Petit, F. (eds.) SSS 2016. LNCS, vol. 10083, pp. 327–345. Springer, Cham (2016). https://doi.org/10.1007/978-3-319-49259-9_26

27. Sharma, G., Vaidyanathan, R., Trahan, J.L., Busch, C., Rai, S.: O(log N)-time complete visibility for asynchronous robots with lights. In: IPDPS 2017, pp. 513–522 (2017)

28. Tanenbaum, A.S., Wetherall, D.J.: Computer Networks, 5th edn. Prentice Hall Press, London (2010)

Weighted Group Search on a Line

Konstantinos Georgiou$^{(\boxtimes)}$ and Jesse Lucier

Department of Mathematics, Ryerson University, Toronto, Canada
konstantinos@ryerson.ca

Abstract. We introduce and study a new search-type problem on the line with 2 searchers. As in so-called *evacuation* search problems with multiple searchers, we require that all searchers reach a hidden item (the exit), placed in an unknown location on a line. The novelty of our problem, *weighted group search on a line*, pertains to the cost function of a search trajectory, which is defined as the weighted average (1 for the light searcher and $w \geq 1$ for the heavy searcher) of the times that each searcher reaches the exit and stays there indefinitely. For that problem, and for every $w \geq 1$, we design searchers' trajectories (algorithms) that aim to perform well under the lens of (worst case) competitive analysis.

Keywords: Linear/group search · Online algorithms · Competitive analysis

1 Introduction

Searching for a hidden item with mobile agents has been the subject of study since the early 60's, see for example the early works of Bellman [9] and Beck [8]. In a typical setting of the optimization problem, a unit speed mobile agent (robot or searcher), starts from a designated point (the origin) of a known search-domain. An item (exit), is placed at an unknown location ℓ, $d(\ell)$ away from the origin. The item is not visible from distance, neither is the value of $d(\ell)$ known. The objective of the problem is to specify a trajectory of the mobile agent so as to minimize the worst case time untill the robot passes over location ℓ, relative to $d(\ell)$, for the first time, where the worst case is over all possible placements of ℓ. In the literature of online algorithms (i.e. algorithms that run with partial information about the input), this measure of algorithmic efficiency is known as the competitive ratio of the trajectory. Quite interestingly, constant competitive ratio trajectories are known for a number of search problem variants. For some of them, optimal trajectories are also known, with the proof of optimality usually being technical.

K. Georgiou—Research supported in part by NSERC Discovery grant.
J. Lucier—Research was part of an undergraduate thesis at Ryerson University, Dept. of Mathematics.

Two of the most celebrated results in the area pertain to the problems of searching with 1 and 2 robots, where in particular the termination time $d(\ell)$ is the first time that the last (hence all) robot(s) reach location ℓ, see [7] and [16], respectively. In particular, it is known that with 1 robot, the optimal competitive ratio is 9. For 2 robots, when they operate under the so-called face-to-face communication model, where no distant information exchange is possible, the competitive ratio of 9 is not improvable. When robots operate in the wireless model, where distant information exchange is instantaneous, the optimal competitive ratio is 3. A number of studies have emerged for search problems where the termination time depends either on the time that the first, or the last, or a distinguished robot reaches the location of the exit (see related work for more extensive discussion).

In this work we consider a search problem on a line with 2 mobile agents. We deviate from all previous works and, to the best of our knowledge, we study for the first time a notion of termination cost that is the weighted average, 1 for the light robot and w for the heavy robot, of the first time that each robot reaches the exit and stays there indefinitely. The main questions we address for the two communication models are:

1. (Wireless Model): Is it possible to beat competitive ratio of 3, for any weight w, even when $w \to \infty$?
2. (Face-to-Face Model): Is it possible to beat competitive ratio of 9, for any weight w, even when $w \to \infty$?

We address the questions above in various information settings. In our main contribution, we propose and analyze algorithms that know the identities of the robots and the value of w. Maybe surprisingly, we establish competitive ratios which are less than 2.414 and 6.829, for the two communication models, respectively (and for all values of $w \geq 1$). Moreover, we prove that our wireless algorithm is optimal. As a series of complementary, but very simple, results we also present and analyze algorithms that are oblivious to the value of w and/or the identity of the heavy robot, in the two communication models (see Sect. 2 for an exposition of our results, and Table 1 for a brief summary). Our results give also, as immediate corollaries, upper bounds for searching the line with 2 robots in the so-called priority evacuation search problem (previously considered only on the disk) in which the termination cost is determined by the time a distinguished searcher reaches the exit.

1.1   Related Work

Search theory has been a subject of systematic study in Theoretical Computer Science for at least five decades, resulting in a number of book-type expositions of related problems, see for example [1,3,4,30,40], and survey [20] for an overview of more recent results. Even though search-type problems are interesting in their own right from a mathematical perspective, applications can be found in foraging, data structures and primarily in mobile agent computing, see [2, 15, 34, 36, 39] for some examples.

The first known reported treatment of a problem similar to what we study here (one searcher looking for a hidden item on a line, under a Bayesian lens) can be found in the seminal works of Beck [8] and Bellman [9]. Some of these first results were later rediscovered by the Computer Science community, for example in [6, 35], where also many more variations of search-type problems were studied. Since then, the list of closely related problems keeps growing. Below we provide just a high level overview of some representative results, giving emphasis to the most recent ones.

Search-type problems admit a number of classifications depending, among others, on the search domain, the number of searchers, the searchers' communication model (if more than one), moving specifications, termination objective function, known input information, algorithmic analysis (e.g. worst-case or average case), etc. The most primitive search domain is one dimensional [6] where a hidden item is located on a line. A natural generalization of the problem is to find a hidden line on the plane [28, 33]. Other settings have been studied as well, for example searching on circle [37] for a point, or on polygons [25], graphs [5], grids [14], d-dimensional grids [18], m-rays [13], to name just a few. While the traditional termination criterion has been the time by which the last searcher reaches the hidden item, other criteria have been studied as well. Some examples include the time that a distinguished searcher reaches the exit [23], or the time that an immobile item is fetched to the exit [31]. For two or more searchers, search-type problems are defined for various communication models, such as the wireless and the face-to-face [19] models. Apart form the time that robots need to reach the exit, a notion of energy [22] has also been considered. Worst-case average-case tradeoffs have been considered in [17]. Numerous more variations of search-type problems have been proposed, pertaining to turning [27] and revisiting [11] costs, to the knowledge of the input [12], to speed restrictions [26], to faulty searchers [32], to probabilistically faulty searchers [10], to Bayesian searchers in discrete spaces [29] and to special memory specs [38]), to name a few.

Past results which are the closest related to our work are [6, 16, 21], in chronological order (at least for our main contributions pertaining to the face-to-face communication model). Baeza-Yates et al. studied in [6] the problem of searching with one searcher on a line for a hidden item. The corresponding seminal result is that a zig-zag type trajectory of the searcher, expanding in each step the searched space by a factor of 2 in each direction, and alternating, is optimal, and never more than 9 times more costly than the distance of the hidden item to the placement of the searcher (and so in standard terminology, 9 is the optimal competitive ratio). Then, Chrobak et al. addressed in [16] the problem on the same search space, but with many searchers, all of which having to reach the hidden item (hence the problem is usually referred to as evacuation). The termination cost was defined as the (worst case) time that the last searcher reaches the hidden item. Even though searchers can simulate the previous strategy resulting in competitive ratio 9, somehow surprisingly this value is optimal. Nevertheless, a number of different strategies achieve the same performance, with the majority of them having searchers reach the hidden item simultaneously.

Our work studies an evacuation problem, i.e. all searchers need to reach the hidden item. At the same time, our work deviates from the previous results in that the termination cost with two searchers is defined as the (worst case) weighted average time that each searcher (finds and) stays at the hidden item indefinitely. In light of the negative results of [16], all algorithms that have both searchers reach the hidden item simultaneously are bound to have competitive ratio at 9. A search strategy presented in [16] that is different, is the one in which two searchers perform symmetrically the zig-zag search strategy of [6]. Searchers have a number of scheduled meetings at the origin, and when a meeting is not realized, the searcher at the origin deduces the direction of the hidden item and moves toward it. In a strong sense, our algorithms for the weighted group search problem on a line are generalizations of this latter approach. More specifically, our two searchers determine an infinite sequence of carefully chosen meeting points, not at the origin, that allow them to deduce the direction of a hidden item if a meeting is not realized.

Our search trajectories also resemble the algorithms of Czyzowicz et al. [21]. In the latter, searchers move along semi-symmetric zig-zag trajectories, each searcher is assigned a different direction of the line, and meeting points may occur away from the origin. Finally, a notable implication of our results gives an upper bound also for the so-called priority evacuation problem, as per [23,24], in which only a distinguished searcher needs to reach the hidden item. In that direction, and somehow surprisingly, we prove among others that a competitive ratio of much better than 9 is possible in the face-to-face model.

2   Problem Definition and Main Results

We study a variant of linear-search in which two robots move on the infinite line trying to locate a hidden object. The object, sometimes also referred to as the *exit* or the *treasure*, can only be detected when any of the robots walks over it. The underlying assumptions in the definitions below is that synchronous speed-1 robots can move at any speed at most 1, and they can adjust their speeds or even change directions at no additional cost. Moreover, in the *wireless communication model*, robots can exchange information pertaining to their findings from any distance and instantaneously. In contrast, robots cannot exchange messages from distance if they operate under the *face-to-face (f2f) model*. In any case, robots are fully aware of all their trajectories, and can perform any actions, e.g. change of movements, synchronously, i.e. using the same clock. Robots will be denoted by R_1, R_2. For any $t \geq 0$, $R_i(t) \in \mathbb{R}$ will denote the location of robot i at time t, $i = 1, 2$. Moreover $\{R_1(t), R_2(t)\}_{t \geq 0}$ will be referred to as an *evacuation trajectory* or algorithm.

Definition 1. *In the weighted w-Group-Search problem GS_w^c, two speed-1 robots R_1, R_2 start from a point (we call the origin) of an infinite line and they perform under communication model $c \in \{f2f, wireless\}$. For a fixed evacuation trajectory, let $I \in \mathbb{R}$ be the unknown location of the hidden exit. The evacuation time $t_i(I)$ of robot R_i is the smallest time τ such that $R_i(t) = I$ for all $t \geq \tau$, $i = 1, 2$. The competitive ratio of the trajectory is defined as*

$$\sup_{|I| \geq 1} \frac{t_1(I) + w \cdot t_2(I)}{(1+w)|I|}. \tag{1}$$

In the full information setting, algorithms know the identities of the robots, hence *heavy* robot R_2 of weight w is distinguished from *light* robot R_1. Moreover, the value of w is known. In the partial information setting, the identities of the robots and/or the value of w are unknown.

Weighted w-Group-Search is classified under the so-called evacuation problems in which all searchers need to eventually reach the hidden object (for any possible placement). Termination cost is a function of the trajectories of both robots, as in all evacuation problems. In particular, in all previous evacuation problems the cost of an algorithm was defined as $\sup_{|I| \geq 1} \max\{t_1(I), t_2(I)\}$. We deviate from previous approaches, and we introduce weight $w \geq 1$ in order to distinguish R_2 as at least as expensive as R_1 that has weight 1. We consider the cost of an algorithm to be determined by the weighted sum of the evacuation times of robots (not the times that they reach the exit for the first time, rather the first time that each stays there indefinitely). Note that if the exit was placed at location $I \in \mathbb{R}$, then every algorithm (even if the input was known) would incur cost at least $(1+w)|I|$. Therefore, as also in traditional competitive analysis, we consider the competitive ratio as the worst case ratio between the cost of the (online) algorithm and the cost of the optimal (offline) solution. In other words, the competitive ratio can also be thought as the worst case relative evacuation time of the evacuation trajectory, over all possible placements of the exit.

When $w = 1$, the termination cost is the average evacuation time of the two robots (similarly, weighted average for any $w \geq 1$). It may be tempting to believe that as $w \to \infty$ the objective of GS_w^c tends to $\sup_{|I| \geq 1} \max\{t_1(I), t_2(I)\}/|I|$. Counter-intuitively, we show that for every $w \geq 1$, problem GS_w^c admits solutions which are strictly better than in the traditional group search (evacuation), in both communication models. More specifically, our main contributions pertain to algorithms for $GS_w^{wireless}$ and GS_w^{f2f}, that depend both on the knowledge of the identities of the robots, as well as the value of w. The competitive ratios in the two models, range between 2 and $1 + \sqrt{2}$ (Sect. 3), and 6.60258 and 6.82843 (Sect. 4), respectively, for all $w \geq 1$. Note that these values are bounded away from 3 and 9, which are provably the best ratios one can achieve had the objective been to minimize $\sup_{|I| \geq 1} \max\{t_1(I), t_2(I)\}/|I|$. We also complement our main results by showing that the performance we achieve in the wireless model is optimal (Sect. 3). Finally, as an easy observation, we also design algorithms (see Sect. 5) that are oblivious to the identity of the heavy robot and/or the value of w. All our upper bounds are summarized in Table 1.

Table 1. Summary of results.

	Wireless	Face-to-Face
Known Identities & known w	$\sqrt{\frac{2w}{1+w}}+1$ (Theorem 2)	Between 6.603 and 6.83 (Theorems 7, 8 and 9)
Known w (only)	$\frac{2w}{w+1}+1$ (Theorem 10)	$\frac{2w+4\sqrt{w(w+1)}}{w+1}+3$ (Theorem 11ii)
Identities & w both unknown	$\frac{2w}{w+1}+1$ (Theorem 10)	$\frac{4w}{w+1}+5$ (Theorem 11i)

All results of Table 1 give also upper bounds for the priority evacuation problem on the line (introduced in [23,24] when searching the circle), which, to the best of our knowledge, has not been considered before for searching the line. Indeed as per Definition 1, $\sup_{|I|\geq 1}\frac{t_2(I)}{|I|} = \lim_{w\to\infty}\frac{w}{1+w}\sup_{|I|\geq 1}\frac{t_2(I)}{|I|} \leq \lim_{w\to\infty}\sup_{|I|\geq 1}\frac{t_1(I)+w\cdot t_2(I)}{(1+w)|I|}$. The left hand-side of the previous expression is the termination cost of the priority evacuation problem, where the cost is determined by the time that distinguished searcher #2 reaches the hidden item, while the right hand-side expression is the competitive ratio of the weighted group search problem we introduce in this work. Some notable implications, when the identity of the distinguished searcher is known, are that competitive ratios of at most 6.60258 and $1+\sqrt{2}$ are possible, in the face-to-face model and wireless models, respectively. The reader should contrast these numbers with 9 and 3, i.e. the best possible competitive ratio when the cost is the time that the last searcher reaches the exit, in the face-to-face and wireless model respectively.

Apart from our tight lower bounds in the wireless model, our main technical contributions pertain to the design and analysis of our search algorithms, in particular in the face-to-face model. More specifically, most of our technical work is devoted in proving i) that trajectories are well-defined even when $w \to \infty$ (which, in fact, allows us to generalize our results for the priority evacuation setting) and ii) that for (worst case) competitive analysis one needs to only consider exits placed arbitrarily away from the origin. For the latter, we utilize the standard practice in similar problems in which the exit is assumed, by definition, to be placed bounded away from the origin, where this arbitrary bound is set to 1 (otherwise the problem is degenerate). Due to space limitations, any omitted proofs will become available in the full version of the paper.

3   Weighted Group Search in the Wireless Model

In this section we prove the following theorem.

Theorem 1. *The optimal competitive ratio for $GS_w^{wireless}$ is $\sqrt{\frac{2w}{1+w}}+1$.*

In order to prove Theorem 1, first we present an algorithm that achieves the promised bound. Then, we prove that no algorithm can perform better. In order to simplify notation, in the remaining of the section we introduce abbreviation

$s_0(w) := \sqrt{2 + \frac{2}{w}} - 1$, and note that $\sqrt{2} - 1 \le s_0(w) \le 1$, for all $w \ge 1$. Whenever w is clear from the context, we will write s_0 instead of $s_0(w)$.

Next we propose an algorithm whose performance is as in the statement of Theorem 1. Note that since searchers perform under the wireless communication model, it is enough to describe the trajectories with the assumption that no exit is found. Whoever finds the exit first stays put. Since the other robot is notified instantaneously, it can move at full speed 1 towards the exit and evacuate.

Theorem 2. *For every $w \ge 1$, the evacuation trajectory $\{R_1(t), R_2(t)\}_{t \ge 0}$ for $GS_w^{wireless}$ defined as $R_1(t) = t$, $R_2(t) = -s_0 t$ induces competitive ratio equal to*
$$\sqrt{\frac{2w}{w+1}} + 1.$$

Note that when $w = 1$ the achieved competitive ratio equals 2. The competitive ratio is strictly increasing in w, and in the limit it equals $1 + \sqrt{2}$.

Next we prove that every algorithm for $GS_w^{wireless}$ has competitive ratio at least $\sqrt{\frac{2w}{1+w}} + 1$. First we make a useful observation that will be used repeatedly in the next lemmata.

Observation 3. *Fix an evacuation trajectory $\{R_1(t), R_2(t)\}_{t \ge 0}$ for $GS_w^{wireless}$, and suppose that for some $\tau \ge 1$ we have that $R_1(\tau) = x\tau$ and $R_2(\tau) = y\tau$. If for some $z > 0$ and for arbitrary small $\epsilon > 0$, any of the locations $\pm(z\tau + \epsilon)$ has not been visited by any robot, then the algorithm's competitive ratio is at least $1 + \frac{1}{1+w} \frac{1 \mp x + w(1 \mp y)}{z}$, respectively.*

Next we show that in any efficient algorithm, R_2 stays relatively close to the origin.

Lemma 1. *Consider an evacuation trajectory $\{R_1(t), R_2(t)\}_{t \ge 0}$ for $GS_w^{wireless}$. Unless $|R_2(t)| \le s_0 t$, for all $t \ge 1$, the competitive ratio is at least $\sqrt{\frac{2w}{1+w}} + 1$.*

Assuming Lemma 1, the next lemma shows that in every efficient algorithm, R_1 searches only one side of the line.

Lemma 2. *Consider trajectory $\{R_1(t), R_2(t)\}_{t \ge 0}$ for $GS_w^{wireless}$. Unless $R_1(t)$ preserves sign for all $t \ge 0$, the competitive ratio is at least $\sqrt{\frac{2w}{1+w}} + 1$.*

Theorem 4. *Every algorithm for $GS_w^{wireless}$ has competitive ratio at least*
$$\sqrt{\frac{2w}{1+w}} + 1.$$

Proof. Fix an evacuation trajectory $\{R_1(t), R_2(t)\}_{t \ge 0}$. By Lemma 1, we may assume that $|R_2(t)| \le s_0 t$, for all $t \ge 0$, as otherwise the competitive ratio is at least the aimed bound. By Lemma 2, we may also assume that $R_1(t)$ preserves sign, for all $t \ge 0$, as otherwise the competitive ratio is again at least the aimed bound. By symmetry, we may assume, without loss of generality, that $R_1(t) \ge 0$, for all $t \ge 0$.

Now consider some time $\tau \geq 1$, and observe that neither of the locations $-s_0\tau - \epsilon$ and $\tau + \epsilon$ have been explored by any of the searchers, for any $\epsilon > 0$. Observation 3 then implies that the competitive ratio is at least $1 + \frac{1}{1+w}$ max $\left\{ \frac{1+x+w(1+y)}{s_0}, 1 - x + w(1 - y) \right\}$. The last expression is minimized when the two arguments of max become equal, which occurs when $x = \frac{(s_0-1)(w+1)}{s_0+1} - wy$. Substituting back this value of x shows that competitive ratio is at least $1 + \frac{2}{1+s_0} = 1 + \sqrt{\frac{2w}{1+w}}$. $\qquad\square$

4 Weighted Group Search in the Face-to-Face Model

In this section we design and analyze an algorithm for GS_w^{f2f} that has competitive ratio bounded away from (and strictly less than) 9, for every $w \geq 1$. Our main contribution, at a high level is the following.

Theorem 5. *For every $w \geq 1$, problem GS_w^{f2f} admits a search strategy with competitive ratio strictly decreasing in w, and ranging in value between 6.82843 and 6.60258.*

4.1 Algorithm F2F-Search for the Face-to-Face Model

Our algorithm is determined by two infinite and strictly increasing sequences $\{x_i, y_i\}_{i\geq 1}$ (that we will call turning points), each of which we allow to depend on w. The underlying assumption will be that $x_i \geq y_i$, for every $i \geq 1$. In order to present our algorithm, and for each $i \geq 1$, we introduce the following notation $m_i := x_i - y_i$, $M_i := \sum_{j=0}^{i-1} m_j$, with the understanding that $m_{-1} = m_0 := 0$ (hence $M_0 := M_1 := 0$). Since $x_i \geq y_i$, it follows that $M_i \geq 0$, for all $i \geq 1$. Robot R_1 (with weight 1) will be exploring the positive (right) side of the line, while R_2 (with weight w) will be exploring the negative (left side). A location $z > 0$ will refer to the point that is z away from the origin on the right side. Location $z < 0$ will be the one that is $|z|$ away from the origin to the left.

Both robots in our algorithm follow a full-speed zig-zag-type trajectory that is described by Algorithm 1 Unbounded-Search (note that this is not our final algorithm).

Algorithm 1. Unbounded-Search

1: Searcher R_1:	1: Searcher R_2:
2: **for** $i = 1, 2, \ldots$ **do**	2: **for** $i = 1, 2, \ldots$ **do**
3: Move to the right for time M_i.	3: Move to the left for time M_i.
4: Move to the right for time x_i.	4: Move to the left for time y_i.
5: Move to the left to location M_{i+1}.	5: Move to the right to location M_{i+1}.
6: **end for**	6: **end for**

Lemma 3. *Robots following Unbounded Search with turning points $\{(x_i, y_i)\}_{i\geq 1}$ meet at locations M_i.*

Motivated by Lemma 3, we refer to location M_i as the i-th (scheduled) meeting location of the robots. We are now ready to present our algorithm for GS_w^{f2f}.

Definition 2 (Algorithm F2F-Search). *F2F-Search with turning points $\{x_i, y_i\}_{i \geq 1}$ is the following algorithm for GS_w^{f2f}. As long as no exit is found, each of the robots executes Unbounded-Search with the same turning points. If the exit is found, the finder robot stays at the exit (indefinitely). Also, if at any meeting location the meeting is not realized between the two robots, then (instead of changing direction) the robot that arrived at the meeting location continues moving in the same direction untill exit is found.*

F2F-Search will be invoked in this paper with turning points $x_i := s \cdot b^i, y_i := b^i$, for some constants (s, b). In the remaining of the paper, this algorithm will be denoted as (s, b)-*F2F-Search*.

Lemma 4. *Let both x_i, y_i be positive, strictly increasing and tend to infinity. Then, F2F-Search with these turning points terminates (i.e. both robots reach the exit in finite time) for any placement of the exit.*

Note that by the proof of Lemma 4, after the k-th meeting is realized (for some $k \geq 0$), robot R_1 traverses the newly explored interval $\mathcal{R}_k := (2M_{k-1} + x_k, 2M_k + x_{k+1}]$, while robot R_2 traverses the newly explored interval $\mathcal{L}_k := [-y_{k+1}, -y_k)$, just before a new meeting is attempted at location M_{k+1}. Moreover, for every $i \geq 1$, the time between the $(i-1)$'st and i-th scheduled meetings (as a function of each robot's perspective) are $2(M_{i-1} + x_i) - m_i$, for R_1 and $2(M_{i-1} + y_i) + m_i$, for R_2, which are also equal by the previous observations.

4.2   Competitive Analysis for Algorithm F2F-Search

The following definition will be critical for the analysis of our algorithm.

Definition 3. *Triplet (w, s, b) is called effective if $w \geq 1$, $2 \leq b \leq 3$, $1 \leq s \leq 2$, and $s = 1$ only when $w = 1$.*

The following is a technical lemma that shows that, under some critical assumptions, if the exit is found by the light robot (to the right of the origin), then the worst placement of the exit is arbitrarily away from the origin.

Lemma 5. *Let (w, s, b) be an effective triplet. Assuming that the exit is located in the interval $\mathcal{R}_k$, for some $k \geq 60$, the competitive ratio of (s, b)-F2F-Search, for problem GS_w^{f2f}, is strictly increasing in k, and in the limit it equals*

$$\frac{b}{(b-1)(w+1)} \frac{\left(b^2 + ((b-2)b + 3)s - 3\right)(bw + 1)}{((b-1)b + 2)s - 2} + 1 \qquad (2)$$

Similarly, the next lemma describes the worst case placement of the exit, if it is found by the heavy robot (to the left of the origin).

Lemma 6. *Let (w, s, b) be an effective triplet. Assuming that the exit is located in the interval $\mathcal{L}_k$, for some $k \geq 1$, the competitive ratio of (s, b)-F2F-Search, for problem GS_w^{f2f}, is strictly increasing in k, and in the limit it equals*

$$\frac{(b(bs + b - 2) + s - 1)(b + w)}{(b - 1)^2 (w + 1)} + 1 \tag{3}$$

Next we attempt to make the competitive ratio independent of the location of the exit. To this end and for each $w \geq 1$ and $b \in [2, 3]$, we consider polynomial

$$p(s) := \alpha_2 s^2 + \alpha_1 s + \alpha_0 \tag{4}$$

with $\alpha_i = \alpha_i(b, w)$ defined as

$$\alpha_0 := 2w - b \left(b \left(b^2 + (b((b - 1)b - 3) + 5)w + b - 7 \right) - 4w + 1 \right)$$
$$\alpha_1 := b(b(b(-(b - 4)b(w - 1) - 8w + 4) + 4(w - 2)) - 3w - 1) - 4w$$
$$\alpha_2 := ((b - 1)b + 2) \left(b^2 + 1 \right) (b + w).$$

In the special case $w = 1$, the values simplify to $\alpha_0 = -(b - 2)(b + 1)^2 \left(b^2 + 1 \right)$, $\alpha_1 = -4(b + 1) \left(b^2 + 1 \right)$, $\alpha_2 = b^5 + 2b^3 + 2b^2 + b + 2$.

The discriminant of $p(s)$ is equal to $b^2(b - 1)^2 q(b, w)$, where $q(b, w) := \beta_2 w^2 + \beta_1 w + \beta_0$ and

$$\beta_0 := b(b(b(b(b((b - 2)b + 19) - 28) + 43) - 26) + 9$$
$$\beta_1 := -14 + 2b(30 + b(-37 + b(36 + b(-13 + b(6 + b)))))$$
$$\beta_2 := b(b(b(b((b - 2)b + 19) - 28) + 43) - 26) + 9,$$

where in particular $q(b, 1) = \beta_0 + \beta_1 + \beta_2 = 4(1 + b + b^2 + b^3)^2$. It is easy to see that for all $b \in [2, 3]$ we have that $\beta_0, \beta_1, \beta_2 > 0$, and hence the discriminant of $p(s)$ is strictly positive, for all $w \geq 1$. This motivates the following definition. For each $w \geq 1$ and $b \in [2, 3]$, we define the (w, b)-*equalizer* $\bar{s}$ as the largest root of $p(s)$, that is

$$\bar{s}(w, b) := \frac{-\alpha_1 + b(b - 1)\sqrt{\beta_2 w^2 + \beta_1 w + \beta_0}}{2\alpha_2}. \tag{5}$$

Notably, $\bar{s}(1, b)$ is 1 for all $b \geq 1$ (using the aforementioned values of α_1, α_2, $\beta_0, \beta_1, \beta_2$, when $w = 1$). This suggests that when our instance to GS_w^{f2f} is symmetric (both robots have the same weight), then the search strategy is symmetric too.

The next lemma establishes the competitive ratio of an F2F-Search that uses the notion of equalizers in order to diminish the power of an adversary to place strategically the exit. The proof of the lemma relies on that the exit is not placed arbitrarily close to the origin, as well as on that the parameters of F2F-Search do not explode, even when $w \to \infty$.

Lemma 7. *For each $w \geq 1$ and $b \in [2,3]$, let $\bar{s}$ be the (w, b)-equalizer, and suppose that triplet $(w, \bar{s}, b)$ is effective. Let also $x_i := \frac{1}{3^{62}} \bar{s} \cdot b^i, y_i := \frac{1}{3^{62}} b^i$. Then the competitive ratio of F2F-Search with turning points $\{x_i, y_i\}_{i \geq 1}$, for problem GS_w^{f2f}, equals*

$$R(w, b) := \frac{(b(b\bar{s} + b - 2) + \bar{s} - 1)(b + w)}{(b - 1)^2(w + 1)} + 1. \tag{6}$$

All our positive results in the next section will be obtained as a corollary of Lemma 7. Note that the algorithm achieving the promised bounds is an (s, b)-F2F-Search algorithm where the turning points are scaled by $\frac{1}{3^{62}}$. For notational convenience, we will refer to such an algorithm as *modified (s, b)-F2F-Search.*

4.3 Parametric Choices for Algorithm F2F-Search and Quantitative Results

The next lemma shows that as long as expansion factor b remains appropriately bounded for all $w \geq 1$, then the (w, b)-equalizer $\bar{s}$ induces well behaving trajectories $(\bar{s}, b)$-F2F-Search, even when $w \to \infty$.

Lemma 8. *For every $w \geq 1$ and $b \in [2, 2.9]$, let $\bar{s}$ be the (w, b)-equalizer. Then, triplet $(w, \bar{s}, b)$ is effective, and $R(w, b)$ (see (6)) is decreasing in w.*

We can now obtain our first guarantees for GS_w^{f2f} for special values of w.

Theorem 6. *For $w \in \{1, \infty\}$, let $\bar{b} = \bar{b}(w)$ be the corresponding minimizer of $R(w, b)$, and $\bar{s}$ the corresponding $(w, \bar{b})$-equalizer. Then the competitive ratio of the modified $(\bar{s}, \bar{b})$-F2F-Search equals 6.82843 and 6.60258, for $w = 1$ and $w \to \infty$, respectively.*

The following lemma is the analog of Lemma 8 for non-constant values of b and is obtained numerically. Its conclusions pertain to the best possible competitive ratio we can achieve for GS_w^{f2f}, for every $w \geq 1$, modulo that correctness is shown numerically (the extreme values of w are provably treated in Theorem 6). Later we provably obtain upper bounds, which are very close to these best guarantees known.

Lemma 9. *For every $w \geq 1$, let $\bar{b} = \bar{b}(w)$ be the minimizer of $R(w, b)$ subject to $b \geq 2$, and let $\bar{s}$ denote the corresponding $(w, \bar{b})$-equalizer. Then, triplet $(w, \bar{s}, \bar{b})$ is effective, and $R(w, \bar{b})$ is decreasing in w. Moreover, the value of $R(w, \bar{b})$ for $w = 1$ and $w \to \infty$ become 6.82843 and 6.60258, respectively.*

The following theorem (proven numerically) follows immediately from Lemma 9 together with Lemma 7.

Theorem 7. *For every $w \geq 1$, let $\bar{b} = \bar{b}(w)$ be the minimizer of $R(w, b)$ subject to $b \geq 2$, and let $\bar{s}$ denote the corresponding $(w, \bar{b})$-equalizer. Then, $R(w, \bar{b})$ is the competitive ratio of the modified $(\bar{s}, \bar{b})$-F2F-Search algorithm. Moreover, the competitive ratio is decreasing in w with extreme values 6.82843 and 6.60258, for $w = 1$ and $w \to \infty$, respectively.*

We conclude this section by using our findings to determine heuristic values of b that induce nearly optimal (under the family F2F-search algorithms) performances, which however allow for provable performance guarantees (non-numerical).

The following theorem is motivated by the observation that, for each $w \geq 1$, the optimal values of $\bar{b}$, as of Theorem 6 and Lemma 9 are between $b_1 = 2.41421$ and $b_\infty = 2.55869$, and $\bar{b}$ is increasing in w. By Lemma 8, for every $w \geq 1$, for every constant $b_0 \in [b_1, b_\infty]$, and for the corresponding (w, b_0)-equalizer $\bar{s}$, triplet $(w, \bar{s}, b)$ is effective. Hence $R(w, b_0)$ is the competitive ratio of the modified $(\bar{s}, b_0)$-F2F-Search algorithm. The constant value of b_0 that induces the best performance relative to the one described in Theorem 7 (multiplicatively off[1] only by at most 0.0485%) is reported next. The value of b_0 was chosen so as to satisfy $R(1, b_0) = \lim_{w \to \infty} R(w, b_0)$.

Theorem 8. *Let $b_0 = 2.48417$. For every $w \geq 1$, let $\bar{s}$ denote the corresponding (w, b_0)-equalizer. Then, $R(w, \bar{b}_0)$ is the competitive ratio of the modified $(\bar{s}, b_0)$-F2F-Search algorithm. Moreover, the competitive ratio is decreasing in w with extreme values 6.82843 and 6.60258, for $w = 1$ and $w \to \infty$, respectively.*

Even though the guarantee of Theorem 8 is very close to the best one we (numerically) reported in Theorem 7, we can further improve the competitive ratio by choosing non-constant values of b. Motivated by the performance of the optimizers $\bar{b}(w)$ of Lemma 9, we choose the following heuristic function of b; $b_h(w) := b_\infty + \frac{b_1 - b_\infty}{\sqrt{w}} \approx 2.55869 - 0.14447/\sqrt{w}$. Clearly, for every $w \geq 1$ we have $b_h \in [b_1, b_\infty]$. It is easy to show that for the corresponding (w, b_h)-equalizer $\bar{s}$, triplet $(w, \bar{s}, b_h)$ is effective. So, by Lemma 7 we know the competitive ratio of the modified $(\bar{s}, b_h)$-F2F-Search algorithm, which turns out to be only 0.01% multiplicatively off from the performance described in Theorem 7. The claim is summarized in the next theorem.

Theorem 9. *For every $w \geq 1$, and $b_h = b_h(w)$, let $\bar{s}$ denote the corresponding (w, b_h)-equalizer. Then, $R(w, b_h)$ is the competitive ratio of the modified $(\bar{s}, b_h)$-F2F-Search algorithm. Moreover, the competitive ratio is decreasing in w with extreme values 6.82843 and 6.60258, for $w = 1$ and $w \to \infty$, respectively.*

5 Partial Information Algorithms in the Wireless and Face-to-Face Models

Our main contributions pertaining to $GS_w^{wireless}, GS_w^{f2f}$ are the design and analysis of search algorithms whose competitive ratios, for every $w \geq 1$, are bounded away from 3 and 9, respectively. The latter constant values quantify the best performance possible in the traditional group search problem where the termination time is determined by the robot that reaches the hidden exit last. Our

---

[1] This is referring to the relative multiplicative error, that is *(heuristic-optimal)/ optimal.*

algorithms rely on the knowledge of the identity of the heavy robot, as well as of the value w. Indeed, both in $GS_w^{wireless}$ and GS_w^{f2f} the w-heavy robot expands her searched space slower than the other robot (for $w > 1$). A natural question to ask is whether one can achieve bounds better than 3 and 9, in the two communication models, when the identity of the heavy robot and/or the value of w are/is unknown). We answer this in the affirmative for bounded values of w, i.e. unless w tends to infinity, both for the wireless and face-to-face models. All our observations are obtained almost immediately from the previous sections. In all cases, the algorithms we describe are symmetric, therefore they apply also to the case where the identities of the robots are not known. When robots trajectories do not depend on w, algorithms are also applicable to the case of unknown w.

The proof of the next theorem follows immediately from the calculations of Theorem 2 (taking $s_0 = 1$), since in the worst case the exit is found by the lighter robot. The statement refers to the wireless model, when neither the identities of the robots, nor the value of w are known (interestingly, we do not know how to use only the value of w, without robots' identities, to induce improved performance in the wireless model).

Theorem 10. *For every $w \geq 1$, the evacuation trajectory $\{R_1(t), R_2(t)\}_{t \geq 0}$ for problem $GS_w^{wireless}$ defined as $R_1(t) = t$, $R_2(t) = -t$, induces competitive ratio equal to $\frac{2w}{1+w} + 1$.*

For the face-to-face model, we present two algorithms, depending on whether either only robots' identities or both robots' identities and weight w are unknown, gradually compromising on the performance.

Theorem 11. *For every $w \geq 1$, the $(1,b)$-F2F-Search algorithm, for problem GS_w^{f2f}, defined as*
(i) $b = 2$, induces competitive ratio equal to $\frac{4w}{w+1} + 5$.
(ii) $b = \sqrt{\frac{1}{w} + 1} + 1$, induces competitive ratio equal to $\frac{2w+4\sqrt{w(w+1)}}{w+1} + 3$.

6   Discussion and Open Problems

We introduced and studied weighted group search on the line with 2 searchers, and established bounds for both the wireless and the face-to-face model. Our results are proved to be optimal only in the wireless model. Lower bounds for the face-to-face model remain open, as well as generalization to more robots. Two interesting questions arising from our work are the following. First, the competitive ratio (upper bound) guarantees for the two communication models exhibit different monotonicity in the value w. We have no explanation of this phenomenon, i.e. why the larger the value of w is, the more difficult or easier the problem becomes in the wireless and the face-to-face models, respectively. Second, in the auxiliary results pertaining to partial information algorithms, we show how in the face-to-face model we can utilize the value of w even when we do not know who is the heavy robot. In the wireless model, we do not know how to use the same information so as to have advantage over the case of unknown weight and unknown searchers' identities.

References

1. Ahlswede, R., Wegener, I.: Search Problems. Wiley-Interscience (1987)
2. Albers, S., Henzinger, M.R.: Exploring unknown environments. SIAM J. Comput. **29**(4), 1164–1188 (2000)
3. Alpern, S., Gal, S.: The Theory of Search Games and Rendezvous. Springer, Heidelberg (2003). https://doi.org/10.1007/b100809
4. Alpern, S., Fokkink, R., Gasieniec, L.A., Lindelauf, R., Subrahmanian, V.S. (eds.): Search Theory: A Game Theoretic Perspective, pp. 223–230. Springer, New York (2013). https://doi.org/10.1007/978-1-4614-6825-7
5. Angelopoulos, S., Dürr, C., Lidbetter, T.: The expanding search ratio of a graph. Discrete Appl. Math. **260**, 51–65 (2019)
6. Baeza Yates, R., Culberson, J., Rawlins, G.: Searching in the plane. Inf. Comput. **106**(2), 234–252 (1993)
7. Baeza-Yates, R.A., Culberson, J.C., Rawlins, G.J.E.: Searching with uncertainty extended abstract. In: Karlsson, R., Lingas, A. (eds.) SWAT 1988. LNCS, vol. 318, pp. 176–189. Springer, Heidelberg (1988). https://doi.org/10.1007/3-540-19487-8_20
8. Beck, A.: On the linear search problem. Israel J. Math. **2**(4), 221–228 (1964)
9. Bellman, R.: An optimal search. SIAM Rev. **5**(3), 274–274 (1963)
10. Bonato, A., Georgiou, K., MacRury, C., Prałat, P.: Probabilistically faulty searching on a half-line. In 14th Latin American Theoretical Informatics Symposium (LATIN 2020). Lecture Notes in Computer Science (2020, to appear)
11. Bose, P., De Carufel, J.-L.: A general framework for searching on a line. Theoret. Comput. Sci. **703**, 1–17 (2017)
12. Bose, P., De Carufel, J.-L., Durocher, S.: Searching on a line: a complete characterization of the optimal solution. Theoret. Comput. Sci. **569**, 24–42 (2015)
13. Brandt, S., Foerster, K.-T., Richner, B., Wattenhofer, R.: Wireless evacuation on m rays with k searchers. In: Das, S., Tixeuil, S. (eds.) SIROCCO 2017. LNCS, vol. 10641, pp. 140–157. Springer, Cham (2017). https://doi.org/10.1007/978-3-319-72050-0_9
14. Brandt, S., Uitto, J., Wattenhofer, R.: A tight lower bound for semi-synchronous collaborative grid exploration. In: DISC, pp. 13:1–13:17 (2018)
15. Burgard, W., Moors, M., Stachniss, C., Schneider, F.E.: Coordinated multi-robot exploration. IEEE Trans. Robot. **21**(3), 376–386 (2005)
16. Chrobak, M., Gasieniec, L., Gorry, T., Martin, R.: Group search on the line. In: Italiano, G.F., Margaria-Steffen, T., Pokorný, J., Quisquater, J.-J., Wattenhofer, R. (eds.) SOFSEM 2015. LNCS, vol. 8939, pp. 164–176. Springer, Heidelberg (2015). https://doi.org/10.1007/978-3-662-46078-8_14
17. Chuangpishit, H., Georgiou, K., Sharma, P.: Average case - worst case tradeoffs for evacuating 2 robots from the disk in the face-to-face model. In: Gilbert, S., Hughes, D., Krishnamachari, B. (eds.) ALGOSENSORS 2018. LNCS, vol. 11410, pp. 62–82. Springer, Cham (2019). https://doi.org/10.1007/978-3-030-14094-6_5
18. Cohen, L., Emek, Y., Louidor, O., Uitto, J.: Exploring an infinite space with finite memory scouts. In: Proceedings of the Twenty-Eighth Annual ACM-SIAM Symposium on Discrete Algorithms, pp. 207–224. SIAM (2017)

19. Czyzowicz, J., Gąsieniec, L., Gorry, T., Kranakis, E., Martin, R., Pajak, D.: Evacuating robots via unknown exit in a disk. In: Kuhn, F. (ed.) DISC 2014. LNCS, vol. 8784, pp. 122–136. Springer, Heidelberg (2014). https://doi.org/10.1007/978-3-662-45174-8_9

20. Czyzowicz, J., Georgiou, K., Kranakis, E.: Group search and Evacuation. In: Flocchini, P., Prencipe, G., Santoro, N. (eds.) Distributed Computing by Mobile Entities, Current Research in Moving and Computing. LNCS, vol. 11340, pp. 335–370. Springer, Heidelberg (2019). https://doi.org/10.1007/978-3-030-11072-7_14

21. Czyzowicz, J., et al.: Energy consumption of group search on a line. In: 46th International Colloquium on Automata, Languages, and Programming, ICALP 2019, 9–12 July 2019, Patras, Greece, vol. 132. LIPIcs, pp. 137:1–137:15. Schloss Dagstuhl - Leibniz-Zentrum fuer Informatik (2019)

22. Czyzowicz, J.., et al.: Time-energy tradeoffs for evacuation by two robots in the wireless model. In: Censor-Hillel, K., Flammini, M. (eds.) SIROCCO 2019. LNCS, vol. 11639, pp. 185–199. Springer, Cham (2019). https://doi.org/10.1007/978-3-030-24922-9_13

23. Czyzowicz, J., et al.: Priority evacuation from a disk: the case of n = 1, 2, 3. Theoret. Comput. Sci. **806**, 595–616 (2020)

24. Czyzowicz, J., et al.: Priority evacuation from a disk using mobile robots. In: Lotker, Z., Patt-Shamir, B. (eds.) SIROCCO 2018. LNCS, vol. 11085, pp. 392–407. Springer, Cham (2018). https://doi.org/10.1007/978-3-030-01325-7_32

25. Czyzowicz, J., Kranakis, E., Krizanc, D., Narayanan, L., Opatrny, J., Shende, S.: Wireless autonomous robot evacuation from equilateral triangles and squares. In: Papavassiliou, S., Ruehrup, S. (eds.) ADHOC-NOW 2015. LNCS, vol. 9143, pp. 181–194. Springer, Cham (2015). https://doi.org/10.1007/978-3-319-19662-6_13

26. Czyzowicz, J., Kranakis, E., Krizanc, D., Narayanan, L., Opatrny, J., Shende, S.: Linear search with terrain-dependent speeds. In: Fotakis, D., Pagourtzis, A., Paschos, V.T. (eds.) CIAC 2017. LNCS, vol. 10236, pp. 430–441. Springer, Cham (2017). https://doi.org/10.1007/978-3-319-57586-5_36

27. Demaine, E.D., Fekete, S.P., Gal, S.: Online searching with turn cost. Theoret. Comput. Sci. **361**(2), 342–355 (2006)

28. Feinerman, O., Korman, A., Lotker, Z., Sereni, J.-S.: Collaborative search on the plane without communication. In: Proceedings of the 2012 ACM Symposium on Principles of Distributed Computing, pp. 77–86 (2012)

29. Fraigniaud, P., Korman, A., Rodeh, Y.: Parallel Bayesian search with no coordination. J. ACM (JACM) **66**(3), 1–28 (2019)

30. Gal, S.: Search Games. Wiley Encyclopedia for Operations Research and Management Science (2011)

31. Georgiou, K., Karakostas, G., Kranakis, E.: Search-and-fetch with 2 robots on a disk: wireless and face-to-face communication models. Discrete Math. Theoret. Comput. Sci. **21**(3) (2019)

32. Georgiou, K., Kranakis, E., Leonardos, N., Pagourtzis, A., Papaioannou, I.: Optimal circle search despite the presence of faulty robots. In: Dressler, F., Scheideler, C. (eds.) ALGOSENSORS 2019. LNCS, vol. 11931, pp. 192–205. Springer, Cham (2019). https://doi.org/10.1007/978-3-030-34405-4_11

33. Jeż, A., Łopuszański, J.: On the two-dimensional cow search problem. Inf. Process. Lett. **109**(11), 543–547 (2009)

34. Kagan, E., Ben-Gal, I.: Search and Foraging: Individual Motion and Swarm Dynamics. CRC Press (2015)

35. Kao, M.-Y., Reif, J.H., Tate, S.R.: Searching in an unknown environment: an optimal randomized algorithm for the cow-path problem. Inf. Comput. **131**(1), 63–79 (1996)
36. Koutsoupias, E., Papadimitriou, C., Yannakakis, M.: Searching a fixed graph. In: Meyer, F., Monien, B. (eds.) ICALP 1996. LNCS, vol. 1099, pp. 280–289. Springer, Heidelberg (1996). https://doi.org/10.1007/3-540-61440-0_135
37. Pattanayak, D., Ramesh, H., Mandal, P.S., Schmid, S.: Evacuating two robots from two unknown exits on the perimeter of a disk with wireless communication. In: ICDCN, pp. 20:1–20:4 (2018)
38. Reingold. O.: Undirected st-connectivity in log-space. In: STOC, pp. 376–385 (2005)
39. Schwefel, H.-P.P.: Evolution and Optimum Seeking: The Sixth Generation. Wiley, Hoboken (1993)
40. Stone, L.: Theory of Optimal Search. Academic Press, New York (1975)

Fast Byzantine Gathering with Visibility in Graphs

Avery Miller[✉][iD] and Ullash Saha

University of Manitoba, Winnipeg, Canada
{amiller,sahau}@cs.umanitoba.ca

Abstract. We consider the gathering task by a team of m synchronous mobile robots in a graph of n nodes. Each robot has an identifier (ID) and runs its own deterministic algorithm, i.e., there is no centralized coordinator. We consider a particularly challenging scenario: there are f Byzantine robots in the team that can behave arbitrarily, and even have the ability to change their IDs to any value at any time. There is no way to distinguish these robots from non-faulty robots, other than perhaps observing strange or unexpected behaviour. The goal of the gathering task is to eventually have all non-faulty robots located at the same node in the same round. It is known that no algorithm can solve this task unless there at least $f + 1$ non-faulty robots in the team. In this paper, we design an algorithm that runs in polynomial time with respect to n and m that matches this bound, i.e., it works in a team that has exactly $f + 1$ non-faulty robots. In our model, we have equipped the robots with sensors that enable each robot to see the subgraph (including robots) within some distance H of its current node. We prove that the gathering task is solvable if this visibility range H is at least the radius of the graph, and not solvable if H is any fixed constant.

Keywords: Robot gathering · Byzantine faults · Visibility · Graphs · Distributed algorithms

1 Introduction

Mobile robots play a vital role in real-life applications such as military surveillance, search-and-rescue, environmental monitoring, transportation, mining, infrastructure protection, and autonomous vehicles. In networks, the robots/agents move from one location to another to collectively complete a task, and might all need to meet at one location in order to share information or start their next task. Therefore, gathering becomes a fundamental problem for mobile robots in networks.

Gathering is hard to accomplish even in a fault-free system, as the robots may not have any planned location where to meet, nor any initial information about the topology of the network. Moreover, in a distributed system, each robot runs its own deterministic algorithm to make decisions, i.e., there is no centralized

© Springer Nature Switzerland AG 2020
C. M. Pinotti et al. (Eds.): ALGOSENSORS 2020, LNCS 12503, pp. 140–153, 2020.
https://doi.org/10.1007/978-3-030-62401-9_10

coordinator. We want a deterministic algorithm that can be run by each robot, and eventually, they will gather at a single node which is not fixed in advance. Additionally, we consider a particularly challenging scenario in which some of the robots are Byzantine: such robots do not follow our installed algorithm and can behave arbitrarily. We can think of these robots as malicious robots in our system, i.e., they have been compromised by outsiders/hackers, and, knowing the algorithm we intend to run, they can behave in ways that attempt to mislead the non-faulty robots into making incorrect decisions. Moreover, non-faulty robots do not know which of the robots (or even how many of the robots) are Byzantine, because all robots look identical. We might face this type of scenario in real-world applications when attackers try to disrupt the normal behavior of systems, so algorithms that are resilient to such attacks are very useful.

The relative number of non-faulty robots versus Byzantine robots is an essential factor in solving this problem. If there are many Byzantine robots compared to the number of non-faulty robots, then the behaviour of the Byzantine robots can be very influential. As shown in previous work [10], a team that contains f Byzantine robots cannot solve gathering if the number of non-faulty robots is less than $f + 1$. The challenge, and the goal of our work, is to provide an efficient gathering algorithm that works when this bound is met, i.e., when the number of non-faulty robots is exactly $f + 1$. We provide such an algorithm in a model in which each robot is endowed with sensors that allow them to see all nodes and robots within a fixed distance H of its current location, where H is at least the radius of the network. We also prove an impossibility result which shows that no algorithm can solve gathering in this model if H is any fixed constant (i.e., independent of any graph parameter). It's important to note that this impossibility result does not contradict previous results [4,5,10,19] that provide gathering algorithms with no visibility, as those algorithms make assumptions about additional information known to the robots (such as bounds on the network size, or on the number of Byzantine robots) or make assumptions about additional features such as authenticated whiteboards at the nodes.

1.1 Model and Definitions

We consider a team of m robots that are initially placed at arbitrary nodes of an undirected connected graph $G = (V, E)$. We denote by n the number of nodes in the graph, i.e., $n = |V|$. The nodes have no labels. At each node v, the incident edges are labeled with port numbers $0, \ldots, deg(v) - 1$ in an arbitrary way, where $deg(v)$ represents the degree of node v. The two endpoints of an edge need not be labeled with the same port number.

For any two nodes v, w, the *distance between v and w*, denoted by $d(v, w)$, is defined as the length of a shortest path between v and w. The *eccentricity of a node v*, denoted by $ecc(v)$, is the maximum distance from v to any other node, i.e., $ecc(v) = \max_{w \in V}\{d(v, w)\}$. The *radius* of a graph, denoted by R, is defined as the minimum eccentricity taken over all nodes, i.e., $R = \min_{v \in V}\{ecc(v)\}$.

The team of m robots contains f Byzantine robots and $m - f$ non-faulty robots. Each robot α has a distinct identifier (ID) l_α, and it knows its own

ID. The Byzantine and non-faulty robots look identical, i.e., there is no way to distinguish them other than perhaps noticing strange or unexpected behaviour. All robots have unbounded memory, i.e., they can remember all information that they have previously gained during their algorithm's execution. We describe the differences between the two types of robots below.

Properties of Non-faulty Robots. The non-faulty robots have no initial information about the size or topology of the graph, and they have no information about the number of Byzantine robots. A non-negative integer parameter H defines the *visibility range* of each robot, which we describe in Partial Snapshot below. Each non-faulty robot executes a synchronous deterministic algorithm: in each round, each robot performs one Look-Compute-Move sequence, i.e., it performs the following three operations in the presented order.

1. **The Look operation:** A non-faulty robot α located at a node v at the start of round t gains information from two types of view.
   - *Local View:* Robot α can see the degree of node v and the port numbers of its incident edges. It can also see any other robots located at v at the start of round t, along with their ID numbers.
   - *Partial Snapshot View:* Robot α sees the subgraph consisting of all nodes, edges, and port numbers that belong to paths of length at most H that have v as one endpoint. Also, for each node w in this subgraph, robot α sees the list of all IDs of the robots occupying w at the start of round t.
2. **The Compute operation:** Using the information gained during all previous Look operations, a robot α located at a node v deterministically chooses a value from the set $\{null, 0, \ldots, deg(v) - 1\}$. In particular, it chooses *null* if it decides that it will stay at its current node v, and it chooses a value $p \in \{0, \ldots, deg(v) - 1\}$ if it decides to move to the neighbour of node v that is the other endpoint of the incident edge labeled with port number p.
3. **The Move operation:** A robot α located at a node v performs the action that it chose during the Compute operation. In particular, it does nothing if it chose value *null*, and otherwise, it moves towards a neighbour w of v along the incident edge labeled with the chosen port number p, and it arrives at w at the start of the next round. It sees the port number that it uses to enter node w. There is no restriction of how robots move along an edge, i.e., multiple robots may traverse an edge simultaneously, in either direction.

All non-faulty robots wake up at the same time and perform their Look-Compute-Move sequences synchronously in every round.

Properties of the Byzantine Robots. We assume that a centralized adversary controls all of the Byzantine robots. This adversary has complete knowledge of the algorithm being executed by the non-faulty robots, and can see the entire network and the positions of all robots at all times. In each round, the adversary can make each Byzantine robot move to an arbitrary neighbouring node. Further, we assume that the faulty robots are *strongly Byzantine*, which means that the adversary can change the ID of any Byzantine robot at any time (in contrast, a *weakly Byzantine* robot would have a fixed ID during the entire execution).

Problem Statement. Assume that m robots are initially placed at nodes of a network, where f of the robots are strongly Byzantine. The robots synchronously execute a deterministic distributed algorithm. Eventually, all non-faulty robots must terminate their algorithm in the same round, and at termination, all non-faulty robots must be located at the same node.

1.2 Related Work

The study of algorithms for mobile robots is extensive, as evidenced by a recent survey [13]. The Gathering problem has been investigated thoroughly under a wide variety of model assumptions, as summarized in [3,9,12] for continuous models and in [8,18] for discrete models. Of particular interest to our current work are discrete models where the robots are located in a network, have some amount of visibility beyond its own position [1,2,7,11,15], and where faults may occur [6,16,17].

Most relevant to our current work are the results about Gathering in networks when some of the robots can be Byzantine [4,5,10,14,19]. In [19], the authors consider weakly Byzantine agents and add authenticated whiteboards to the model. Additionally, each robot has the ability to write "signed" messages that authenticate the ID of the writer and whether the message was originally written at the current node. The authors provide an algorithm such that all correct robots gather at a single node in $O(f \cdot |E|)$ rounds, where f is an upper bound on the number of Byzantine robots and $|E|$ is the number of edges in the network.

For the model we consider in our work (but with visibility range 0), the Gathering problem was first considered in [10]. The authors explored the gathering problem under four variants of the model: (i) known size of the graph, weakly Byzantine robots, (ii) known size of the graph, strongly Byzantine robots, (iii) unknown size of the graph, weakly Byzantine robots, and (iv) unknown size of the graph, strongly Byzantine robots. In all cases, the authors assume that the upper bound f on the number of Byzantine robots is known to all non-faulty robots. The authors provided a deterministic polynomial-time algorithms for the two models with weakly Byzantine robots. In the model when the size of the graph is known, their algorithm works for any number of non-faulty robots in the team. Recently, the authors of [14] provided a significantly faster algorithm under the assumption that the number of non-faulty robots in the team is at least $4f^2 + 8f + 4$. In [10], assuming that the size of the graph is unknown and f robots are weakly Byzantine, the authors provide an algorithm that works when the number of non-faulty robots in the team is $f + 2$. They prove a matching lower bound in this scenario: no algorithm can solve Gathering if the number of non-faulty robots in the team is less than $f + 2$. For the model with strongly Byzantine robots and known graph size, the authors provided a randomized algorithm that guarantees that the agents gather in a finite number of rounds, and with high probability terminates in n^{cf} rounds for some constant $c > 0$. They also provided a deterministic algorithm whose running time is exponential in n and the largest ID belonging to a non-faulty agent. In both cases, the number of non-faulty robots in the team is assumed to be at least $2f + 1$. The authors also proved a lower bound for this model: no algorithm can solve Gathering if the number of non-faulty robots in the team is less than $f + 1$. Finally, for the model with strongly Byzantine robots and unknown graph size, they provided a deterministic algorithm that works when the number of non-faulty robots in the team is at least $4f + 2$. The running time is exponential in n and the largest ID belonging to a non-faulty agent. They also proved a lower bound in this model: no algorithm can solve Gathering if the number of non-faulty robots in the team is less than $f + 2$. Subsequent work focused on the case of strongly Byzantine robots and attempted to close the gaps between the known upper and lower bounds on the number of non-faulty robots in the team. This was achieved in [4], as the authors provided algorithms that work when the number of non-faulty robots in the team are $f + 1$ and $f + 2$ for the cases of known and unknown graph size, respectively. However, the running times of these algorithms were also exponential in n and the largest ID belonging to a non-faulty agent.

More recently, the authors of [5] considered a version of the above model that does not assume knowledge of the graph size nor the upper bound f on the number of strongly Byzantine agents. Instead, they considered the amount of initial knowledge as a resource to be quantitatively measured as part of an algorithm's analysis. In this model, they designed an algorithm whose running time is polynomial in n and the number of bits in the smallest ID belonging to a non-faulty agent, where $O(\log \log \log n)$ bits of initial information is provided to all robots. The initial information they provide is the value of $\log \log n$, which the algorithm uses as a rough estimate of the graph size. Their algorithm works as long as the number of non-faulty robots in the team is at least $5f^2 + 6f + 2$. They also proved a lower bound on the amount of initial knowledge: for any deterministic polynomial Gathering algorithm that works when the number of non-faulty robots in the team is at least $5f^2 + 6f + 2$ and whose running time is polynomial in n and the number of bits in the smallest ID, the amount of initial information provided to all robots must be at least $\Omega(\log \log \log n)$ bits.

1.3   Our Results

We consider a graph-based model in which each robot has no initial information other than its own ID and has some visibility range H. We prove that no algorithm can solve Gathering in the presence of Byzantine robots if H is any fixed constant. We also design an algorithm that solves Gathering in any graph with n nodes containing m robots, f of which are strongly Byzantine, and where each non-faulty robot has visibility range H equal to the radius of the graph (or larger). Our algorithm has the following desirable properties: (1) the number of rounds is polynomial with respect to n and m, in contrast to several previous algorithms whose running times are exponential in n and the largest robot ID; (2) it works when the number of non-faulty robots in the team is $f + 1$

(or larger), which is optimal due to an impossibility result from [10] that also holds in our model, and significantly improves on the best previous polynomial-time algorithm, which requires at least $5f^2 + 6f + 2$ non-faulty robots; (3) it does not assume any initial global knowledge, in contrast to previous algorithms that assume a known bound on the graph size or on the number of Byzantine robots. Such assumptions might be unrealistic in many applications. Several proofs have been omitted and will appear in the full version of the paper.

2   The Algorithm

First, we define some notation that will be used in the algorithm's description and analysis. For any graph G, the *center of graph G* is the set of all nodes that have minimum eccentricity, i.e., all nodes $v \in V(G)$ such that $ecc(v) = R$, and the *center graph of a graph G*, denoted by $C(G)$, is defined as the subgraph induced by the center nodes. The following terminology will be used to refer to what a robot α can observe in the Look operation of any round t during the execution of an algorithm. The *local view at a node v for round t* is denoted by $Lview(v, t)$, and refers to all of the following information: the degree of v, the port numbers of its incident edges, and a list of the IDs of all other robots located at node v at the start of round t. The *snapshot view at a node v for round t* is denoted by $Sview(v, t)$, and refers to all of the following information: the subgraph consisting of all nodes, edges, and port numbers that belong to paths of length at most H that have v as one endpoint, and, for each node w in this subgraph, the list of IDs of all robots occupying w at the start of round t. For any graph G, an ID l is called a *singleton ID* if the total number of times that l appears as a robot ID at the nodes of G is exactly 1.

2.1   Algorithm Description

In what follows, we assume that the visibility range of a non-faulty robot is at least equal to the radius of the graph, i.e., $H \geq R$. We also assume that the number of non-faulty robots is at least $f + 1$.

The algorithm's progress can be divided into three parts. The first part makes each non-faulty robot move to a node v_{max} such that the robot's snapshot view from v_{max} contains all the nodes of the network G. This is the purpose of our **Find-Lookout** subroutine, which we now describe. Each robot α produces a list of potential nodes in its initial snapshot view where it thinks it might be located, and it does this by comparing its local view with the degree and robot list of each node in its initial snapshot. It cannot be sure of its initial position within its snapshot view since Byzantine robots can forge α's ID and position themselves at other nodes that have the same degree as α's current node. From each guessed initial position, α computes a port sequence of a depth-first traversal of its snapshot view and tries following it in the real network. Since one of the guessed initial positions must be correct, at least one of the depth-first traversals will successfully visit all nodes contained in α's initial snapshot view. Since the visibility range is at least the radius of the network, the robot's initial snapshot view must contain a node in the center of the network G, so at least one step of at least one of the traversals will visit a node in the center of G. When located at such a node, the robot will see all nodes in the network. So, by counting how many nodes it sees at every traversal step, and keeping track of where it saw the maximum, it can correctly remember and eventually go back to a node v_{max} from which it saw all nodes in the network. See Algorithm 1 for the pseudocode of Find-Lookout. After returning to v_{max} at the end of Find-Lookout, each robot α constructs a set P_α consisting of nodes in its snapshot view that match its local view. These can be thought of as 'candidate' locations where α thinks it might actually be located within its snapshot view.

Algorithm 1. Find-Lookout, executed by α starting at a node v in round 0

1: Store the initial snapshot $Sview(v, 0)$ in its memory as S_0
2: Determine which nodes in S_0 might be its starting location, i.e., compute a set X of nodes $w \in S_0$ where the degree of w and the list of robot ID's at w is the same as v's local view in round 0.
3: **for** each $w \in X$ **do**
4:     Compute a port sequence τ corresponding to a depth-first traversal of S_0 starting at w, and attempt to follow this port sequence in the actual network
5:     In every round of the attempted traversal, take note of the number of nodes seen in the snapshot view, and remember the maximum such number n_{max}, a node v_{max} where this maximum was witnessed, the number m_{max} of robots seen in the snapshot when located at v_{max}, and the sequence of ports τ_{max} used to reach v_{max} from the starting location
6:     Return to the starting node by reversing the steps taken during the attempt
7: **end for**
8: For the largest n_{max} seen in any of the traversal attempts, go to the corresponding node v_{max} using the sequence τ_{max}

The second part of the algorithm ensures that, eventually, there is a robot with a singleton ID that is located in the center of the network G. This is the purpose of our **March-to-Center** subroutine, which depends highly on the fact that each robot starts this part of the algorithm at a node v_{max} from which it can see every node in the network. If a robot starts March-to-Center knowing where in its snapshot view it is located (i.e., $|P_\alpha| = 1$), then the robot moves directly to the center of G: it computes the center of its snapshot, and moves to one of the nodes in the center of this snapshot, which is also the center of the entire network G. If all robots do this, then the center of the network will contain a singleton ID, since there are more non-faulty robots than Byzantine robots, and all non-faulty robots have distinct ID's. The difficult case is when a robot α is not sure where in its snapshot it is located at the start of March-to-Center (i.e., $|P_\alpha| > 1$). This is because the Byzantine robots can forge α's ID and position themselves at other nodes with the same degree as α's current node. In this case, α will not move during March-to-Center, and simply watch to see if it can spot any inconsistencies between its local view and its possible starting locations in its snapshot. The key observation, which we will prove, is that at least one of the following must happen in each execution of March-to-Center: there is a robot with a singleton ID located at a node in the center of the network, or, at least one robot sees an inconsistency and narrows down its list of possible starting locations. So, after enough repetitions of March-to-Center, we can guarantee that there will be a robot with a singleton ID that is located in the center of the network. The location of the robot with the smallest such singleton ID is chosen as v_{target} by all non-faulty robots, and this is the place where the robots will eventually gather. See Algorithm 2 for the pseudocode of March-to-Center.

Algorithm 2. March-to-Center(P_α), run by α starting at a node v in round t

---

1: **if** $|P_\alpha| = 1$ **then**
2:     Use current snapshot $Sview(v,t)$ to compute a shortest path π starting at the node $v_0 \in P_\alpha$ and ending at a node $v_{closest}$ in the center graph $C(Sview(v,t))$ that minimizes the distance $d(v_0, v_{closest})$
3:     Move along the port sequence in π and then wait $H - |\pi|$ rounds at $v_{closest}$
4: **else**
5:     Wait at current node v for H rounds, and observe every node $v_j \in P_\alpha$ in every snapshot view during the waiting period
6:     If, in any round of the waiting period, there is some v_j that does not have any robot with ID l_α, then remove v_j from P_α (as we're not currently located at v_j)
7: **end if**
8: In both cases, at the end of the waiting period, check if there is a singleton ID in the center graph $C(Sview(v, t + H))$. If there is such a singleton ID, set v_{target} as the node that contains a robot with the smallest singleton ID in $C(Sview(v, t + H))$. Otherwise, v_{target} is set to *null*.

The third part of the algorithm gets each robot to successfully move to the target node v_{target}, which completes the gathering process. This is the purpose of our Merge subroutine. As above, if a robot starts Merge knowing where in its snapshot view it is located (i.e., $|P_\alpha| = 1$), then it can simply compute a sequence of port numbers that leads to v_{target} and follow it. The difficult case is when a robot α is not sure where in its snapshot it is located at the start of Merge (i.e., $|P_\alpha| > 1$). In this case, α just tries one node from its list of possibilities, computes a sequence of port numbers that leads to v_{target}, and tries to follow it. If it notices any inconsistencies along the way or after it arrives, it deletes the guessed starting node from its list P_α. After each Merge, each robot reverses the steps it took during the Merge in order to go back to where it started so that it can run Merge again. Each execution of Merge finishes in one of two ways: all robots have gathered, or, at least one robot has eliminated one incorrect guess about its starting position. So, after a carefully chosen number of repetitions, we can guarantee that the last performed Merge gathers all robots at the same node. See Algorithm 3 for the pseudocode of Merge.

Algorithm 3. Merge(P_α, v_{target}, n), executed by robot α

1: Using the snapshot view, determine a shortest path π starting at the first node $v_0 \in P_\alpha$ and ending at v_{target}.
2: Attempt to move along the port sequence in π to reach v_{target}.
3: **if** there is a round in which the next port to take along path π does not exist in the local view, or, the port used to arrive at the current node is different than the port specified in path π **then**
4:    Delete v_0 from P_α, then wait $H - t_{\alpha,Move}$ rounds at the current node, where $t_{\alpha,Move}$ is the number of rounds taken to reach the current node
5: **else**   ▷ the port sequence in π was followed with no inconsistency
6:    Wait $H - |\pi|$ rounds at the current node v. In each of these rounds t', consider the current snapshot $Sview(v, t')$:
7:        If the number of nodes in this view is less than n, then remove v_0 from P_α
8:        If l_α is not at v_{target} in $Sview(v, t')$, then remove v_0 from P_α
9:        If the current local view does not match the local view of v_{target} in $Sview(v, t')$ (i.e., a different degree, or a different list of robots), then remove v_0 from P_α
10: **end if**

The pseudocode for the complete algorithm, called the H-View-Algorithm, is provided as Algorithm 4.

Algorithm 4. H-View-Algorithm, run by α starting at node v in round 0

1: Execute **Find-Lookout()**
2: Wait at v_{max} until round $x = (m_{max} + 2) \cdot n_{max}^2$
3: In round x, create a set P_α consisting of the nodes $w \in Sview(v_{max}, x)$ where the degree of w and the list of robot ID's at w are the same as v_{max}'s local view in round x
4: Initialize v_{target} to *null*, initialize *phase* to 1
5: **repeat**
6:    Execute **March-to-Center**(P_α)
7:    *phase* ← *phase* + 1
8: **until** $v_{target} \neq null$
9: **repeat**
10:    Execute **Merge**($P_\alpha, v_{target}, n_{max}$)
11:    Perform the traversals of the previous **Merge** in reverse (returning to v_{max})
12:    *phase* ← *phase* + 1
13: **until** *phase* > $\lceil \frac{m_{max}}{2} \rceil$
14: Execute **Merge**($P_\alpha, v_{target}, n_{max}$)
15: terminate()

2.2   Analysis

We consider three main parts of the algorithm. Our first goal is to show that, immediately after robot α executes **Find-Lookout**, it has moved to a node

v_{max} such that the snapshot view from v_{max} contains $n_{max} = n$ nodes and $m_{max} = m$ robots. The idea is that, in Find-Lookout, robot α will eventually attempt a depth-first search of its snapshot view, which is guaranteed to contain a node in the center of the graph since $H \geq R$. When located at such a node, it will see all n nodes and all m robots, and it will choose such a node as v_{max}.

Lemma 1. *By round* $(m+2) \cdot n^2$, *each non-faulty robot* α *is located at a node* v_{max} *such that the snapshot view at* v_{max} *contains* n *nodes and* m *robots.*

The second part of the algorithm consists of the executions of March-to-Center. Our main goal is to prove that, after at most $f + 1$ executions of March-to-Center, every robot sets its v_{target} variable to the same non-null value. To this end, we first prove that each execution of March-to-Center by the non-faulty robots is started at the same time, and, at the end of each execution, every robot is located at a node such that its snapshot contains all of the network's nodes.

Lemma 2. *At the end of each execution of March-to-Center by any non-faulty robot* α, *the robot resides at some node* v *such that its snapshot view contains all the nodes of* G.

Lemma 3. *For any positive integer* k, *suppose that all non-faulty robots start their* k^{th} *execution of March-to-Center and have* $v_{target} = null$. *For every positive integer* $i \leq k$, *every non-faulty robot starts executing its* i^{th} *execution of March-to-Center in round* $(m+2)n^2 + (i-1)H$.

We now set out to show that all robots set their v_{target} variable to a non-null value within $f + 1$ executions of March-to-Center. The idea behind the proof is to show that, in each execution of March-to-Center that ends with $v_{target} = null$, at least one non-faulty robot makes progress towards determining its correct location within its snapshot view. Once there are enough robots that have determined their correct location (more than the number of Byzantine robots), we are guaranteed to have at least one singleton ID appear in the center of the graph, and all robots will set their v_{target} as the location of the smallest such ID.

To formalize the argument, we introduce a function Φ that measures how much progress has been made by all robots towards determining their correct location within their snapshot view. In what follows, for each $t \geq (m+2) \cdot n^2$, we denote by $P_{\alpha,t}$ the value of variable P_α at robot α in round t. From the description of the H-View-Algorithm, recall that P_α is set by each robot α for the first time in round $(m+2) \cdot n^2$, and the value assigned in this round is the set of nodes in α's snapshot view that match its local view, i.e., the nodes that have the same degree and the same list of robot ID's as α's current location. In subsequent rounds, the only changes to P_α involve the removal of nodes, so $P_{\alpha,t+1} \subseteq P_{\alpha,t}$ for all $t > (m+2) \cdot n^2$. For any fixed round $t \geq (m+2) \cdot n^2$, we denote by Φ_t the sum $\sum_\alpha |P_{\alpha,t}|$, which is taken over all non-faulty robots α. We now prove some useful bounds on Φ_t, and then show that Φ decreases by at least 1 in each execution of March-to-Center that *doesn't* result in all robots agreeing on a v_{target} node. The fact that Φ_t is always bounded between $m - f$ and m implies that at most $f + 1$ executions of March-to-Center can occur before all robots agree on a v_{target} node.

Proposition 1. *In any round* $t \geq (m + 2) \cdot n^2$, *we have* $m - f \leq \Phi_t \leq m$.

Lemma 4. *Consider any execution of March-to-Center by the non-faulty nodes, and suppose that the execution starts in round* t'. *Then, exactly one of the following occurs: (i) all non-faulty robots set their* v_{target} *variable to a non-null value at the start of round* $t' + H$, *or,* (ii) $\Phi_{t'+H} \leq \Phi_{t'} - 1$.

Theorem 1. *There exists a positive integer* $k \leq f + 1$ *such that every non-faulty robot sets its variable* v_{target} *to the same non-null value at the start of round* $(m + 2)n^2 + kH$.

Now we come to the third part of the algorithm which consists of the executions of Merge. Our final goal is to show that all non-faulty robots gather at v_{target} after at most $(f + 2) - k$ executions of Merge, where k is the number of March-to-Center operations executed by the non-faulty robots. Similar to our earlier approach, the key part of the analysis is showing that, at the end of each execution of Merge, either all non-faulty robots have gathered at the same node, or, the value of Φ has decreased by at least 1. After sufficiently many executions of Merge, the value of Φ is guaranteed to be $m - f$, and since this is equal to the number of non-faulty robots (i.e., the number of terms in the sum represented by Φ), it follows that each robot α has $P_\alpha = 1$, i.e., each α accurately knows its location within its snapshot view. Then, all robots will be able to compute and follow a path to v_{target}, which completes the task.

Lemma 5. *Consider any execution of Merge by the non-faulty nodes, and suppose that the execution starts in round* t'. *Then at least one of the following holds: (i) all non-faulty robots are gathered at* v_{target} *in round* $t' + H$, *or,* (ii) $\Phi_{t'+H} \leq \Phi_{t'} - 1$.

Lemma 6. *During the execution of the H-View-Algorithm, if* $k \geq 1$ *executions of March-to-Center are performed followed by* $f + 2 - k$ *executions of Merge, then all non-faulty robots are gathered at* v_{target}.

Finally, we verify that the H-View-Algorithm ensures that Merge is executed at least $f + 2 - k$ times after k executions of March-to-Center. The Merge operation is executed until the value of *phase* is greater than $\lceil m/2 \rceil$, and from the assumption that the number of non-faulty robots is at least $f + 1$, we know that $m \geq 2f + 1$. In particular, this means that the combined number of March-to-Center and Merge executions is at least $f + 1$, and then one more Merge is executed after exiting the 'repeat' loop. This concludes the proof of correctness of the H-View-Algorithm.

Theorem 2. *In any n-node graph with radius R, if the H-View-Algorithm is performed by any team of m robots consisting of f Byzantine robots and at least* $f + 1$ *non-faulty robots with visibility* $H \geq R$, *then Gathering is solved within* $(m + 2) \cdot n^2 + H \cdot m \in O(mn^2)$ *rounds.*

3   Impossibility Results

First, we recall Theorem 4.7 from [10], which states that there is no deterministic algorithm that solves Gathering in the presence of f Byzantine robots if the number of non-faulty agents is less than $f + 1$. This impossibility result was proven in a model where robots have no visibility beyond their local view. However, the same proof works under the assumption that each non-faulty robot has full visibility of the entire graph in every round, which proves that our algorithm is optimal with respect to the number of non-faulty robots in the team.

Theorem 3 ([10]). *There is no deterministic algorithm that solves Gathering if the number of Byzantine robots in the team is f and the number of non-faulty robots is at most f, even if the non-faulty agents have visibility H equal to the diameter of the graph.*

Next, we prove that to solve Gathering in arbitrary graphs, the visibility H of each non-faulty robot must somehow depend on the radius or size of the graph. In particular, it is not sufficient to fix some constant visibility range c. We remark that this does not contradict the existence of previously-known algorithms that work when $H = 0$, as those algorithms make additional assumptions that are not present in our model (e.g., knowledge of the graph size, knowledge of the number of Byzantine robots, or whiteboards at the nodes). The idea behind the proof is to assume the existence of a gathering algorithm $\mathcal{A}$ and obtain a contradiction. First, we construct a cycle graph C_1 that has radius $c + 1$, with two non-faulty robots α and β initially located distance $c + 1$ apart, and no Byzantine robots. As $\mathcal{A}$ is assumed to be correct, the two robots gather and terminate in some round r_1. We construct a cycle graph C_2 that has radius $2r_1 + c + 1$. Robot α is initially located at some node v_0, and two non-faulty robots are initially located at a node at distance $2r_1 + c + 1$ from α. This distance is chosen so that, in the first r_1 rounds, α will not be able to see the other non-faulty robots. Two Byzantine robots with ID's forged to be the same as robot β's are initially located at distance $c + 1$ from α: one in the clockwise direction and one in the anticlockwise direction. When algorithm $\mathcal{A}$ is executed in cycle C_2, the two Byzantine robots move in such a way that α's local and snapshot views in each round are identical to its views when it executes $\mathcal{A}$ in C_1. However, this means that α will terminate in round r_1 (as it did in C_1), and this is before α gathered with the other two non-faulty robots, which contradicts the correctness of $\mathcal{A}$.

Theorem 4. *There is no deterministic algorithm that can solve Gathering when executed in any graph by any team of m robots consisting of $f \geq 0$ Byzantine robots and at least $f + 1$ non-faulty robots if the visibility range H of each non-faulty robot is a fixed constant c.*

We were not able to extend the lower bound argument in Theorem 4 to a non-constant visibility range H. The reason is that, when we change the underlying graph, the visibility radius of a robot is different in the new graph, so we cannot use indistinguishability to conclude that a robot will behave in the same way in both graphs. Establishing a lower bound on H with respect to R is left as an open problem.

Acknowledgements. The authors acknowledge the support of the Natural Sciences and Engineering Research Council of Canada (NSERC), Discovery Grant RGPIN–2017–05936.

References

1. Barrameda, E.M., Santoro, N., Shi, W., Taleb, N.: Sensor deployment by a robot in an unknown orthogonal region: achieving full coverage. In: 20th IEEE International Conference on Parallel and Distributed Systems, ICPADS 2014, pp. 951–960 (2014). https://doi.org/10.1109/PADSW.2014.7097915
2. Barrière, L., Flocchini, P., Barrameda, E.M., Santoro, N.: Uniform scattering of autonomous mobile robots in a grid. Int. J. Found. Comput. Sci. **22**(3), 679–697 (2011). https://doi.org/10.1142/S0129054111008295
3. Bhagat, S., Mukhopadhyaya, K., Mukhopadhyaya, S.: Computation under restricted visibility. In: Flocchini, P., Prencipe, G., Santoro, N. (eds.) Distributed Computing by Mobile Entities, Current Research in Moving and Computing, vol. 11340, pp. 134–183. Springer, Cham (2019). https://doi.org/10.1007/978-3-030-11072-7_7
4. Bouchard, S., Dieudonné, Y., Ducourthial, B.: Byzantine gathering in networks. Distrib. Comput. **29**(6), 435–457 (2016). https://doi.org/10.1007/s00446-016-0276-9
5. Bouchard, S., Dieudonné, Y., Lamani, A.: Byzantine gathering in polynomial time. In: 45th International Colloquium on Automata, Languages, and Programming, ICALP 2018, pp. 147:1–147:15 (2018). https://doi.org/10.4230/LIPIcs.ICALP.2018.147
6. Chalopin, J., Dieudonné, Y., Labourel, A., Pelc, A.: Rendezvous in networks in spite of delay faults. Distrib. Comput. **29**(3), 187–205 (2015). https://doi.org/10.1007/s00446-015-0259-2
7. Chalopin, J., Godard, E., Naudin, A.: Anonymous graph exploration with binoculars. In: Moses, Y. (ed.) DISC 2015. LNCS, vol. 9363, pp. 107–122. Springer, Heidelberg (2015). https://doi.org/10.1007/978-3-662-48653-5_8
8. Cicerone, S., Stefano, G.D., Navarra, A.: Asynchronous robots on graphs: gathering. In: Flocchini, P., Prencipe, G., Santoro, N. (eds.) Distributed Computing by Mobile Entities, Current Research in Moving and Computing, vol. 11340, pp. 184–217. Springer, Cham (2019). https://doi.org/10.1007/978-3-030-11072-D7_8
9. Défago, X., Potop-Butucaru, M., Tixeuil, S.: Fault-tolerant mobile robots. In: Flocchini, P., Prencipe, G., Santoro, N. (eds.) Distributed Computing by Mobile Entities, Current Research in Moving and Computing, vol. 11340, pp. 234–251. Springer, Cham (2019). https://doi.org/10.1007/978-3-030-11072-7_10
10. Dieudonné, Y., Pelc, A., Peleg, D.: Gathering despite mischief. ACM Trans. Algorithms (TALG) **11**(1), 1 (2014)
11. Fischer, M., Jung, D., Meyer auf der Heide, F.: Gathering anonymous, oblivious robots on a grid. In: Fernández Anta, A., Jurdzinski, T., Mosteiro, M.A., Zhang, Y. (eds.) ALGOSENSORS 2017. LNCS, vol. 10718, pp. 168–181. Springer, Cham (2017). https://doi.org/10.1007/978-3-319-72751-6_13

12. Flocchini, P.: Gathering. In: Flocchini, P., Prencipe, G., Santoro, N. (eds.) Distributed Computing by Mobile Entities, Current Research in Moving and Computing, vol. 11340, pp. 63–82. Springer, Cham (2019). https://doi.org/10.1007/978-3-030-11072-7_4

13. Flocchini, P., Prencipe, G., Santoro, N. (eds.): Distributed Computing by Mobile Entities. Current Research in Moving and Computing. Springer, Cham (2019). https://doi.org/10.1007/978-3-030-11072-7

14. Hirose, J., Nakamura, J., Ooshita, F., Inoue, M.: Gathering with a strong team in weakly byzantine environments. CoRR abs/2007.08217 (2020). https://arxiv.org/abs/2007.08217

15. Hsiang, T.-R., Arkin, E.M., Bender, M.A., Fekete, S.P., Mitchell, J.S.B.: Algorithms for rapidly dispersing robot swarms in unknown environments. In: Boissonnat, J.-D., Burdick, J., Goldberg, K., Hutchinson, S. (eds.) Algorithmic Foundations of Robotics V. STAR, vol. 7, pp. 77–93. Springer, Heidelberg (2004). https://doi.org/10.1007/978-3-540-45058-0_6

16. Ooshita, F., Datta, A.K., Masuzawa, T.: Self-stabilizing rendezvous of synchronous mobile agents in graphs. In: Spirakis, P., Tsigas, P. (eds.) SSS 2017. LNCS, vol. 10616, pp. 18–32. Springer, Cham (2017). https://doi.org/10.1007/978-3-319-69084-1_2

17. Pelc, A.: Deterministic gathering with crash faults. Networks **72**(2), 182–199 (2018). https://doi.org/10.1002/net.21810

18. Pelc, A.: Deterministic rendezvous algorithms. In: Flocchini, P., Prencipe, G., Santoro, N. (eds.) Distributed Computing by Mobile Entities, Current Research in Moving and Computing, vol. 11340, pp. 423–454. Springer, Cham (2019). https://doi.org/10.1007/978-3-030-11072-7_17

19. Tsuchida, M., Ooshita, F., Inoue, M.: Byzantine-tolerant gathering of mobile agents in arbitrary networks with authenticated whiteboards. IEICE Trans. **101**–**D**(3), 602–610 (2018). https://doi.org/10.1587/transinf.2017FCP0008

Efficient Dispersion on an Anonymous Ring in the Presence of Weak Byzantine Robots

Anisur Rahaman Molla[1] , Kaushik Mondal[2] ,
and William K. Moses Jr.[3]([✉])

[1] Computer and Communication Sciences, Indian Statistical Institute, Kolkata, India
molla@isical.ac.in
[2] Department of Mathematics, Indian Institute of Technology Ropar,
Rupnagar, India
kaushik.mondal@iitrpr.ac.in
[3] Faculty of Industrial Engineering and Management,
Technion - Israel Institute of Technology, Haifa, Israel
wkmjr3@gmail.com

Abstract. The problem of dispersion of mobile robots on a graph asks that n robots initially placed arbitrarily on the nodes of an n-node anonymous graph, autonomously move to reach a final configuration where exactly each node has at most one robot on it. This problem has been relatively well-studied when robots are non-faulty. In this paper, we introduce the notion of Byzantine faults to this problem, i.e., we formalize the problem of dispersion in the presence of up to f Byzantine robots. We then study the problem on a ring while simultaneously optimizing the time complexity of algorithms and the memory requirement per robot. Specifically, we design deterministic algorithms that attempt to match the time lower bound ($\Omega(n)$ rounds) and memory lower bound ($\Omega(\log n)$ bits per robot).

Our main result is a deterministic algorithm that is both time and memory optimal, i.e., $O(n)$ rounds and $O(\log n)$ bits of memory required per robot, subject to certain constraints. We subsequently provide results that require less assumptions but are either only time or memory optimal but not both. We also provide a primitive that takes robots initially gathered at a node of the ring and disperses them in a time and memory optimal manner without additional assumptions required.

Keywords: Dispersion · Mobile robots · Distributed algorithm · Byzantine faults · Faulty robots · Rings

The work of W. K. Moses Jr. was supported in part by a Technion fellowship. A. R. Molla is supported, in part, by DST INSPIRE Faculty Research Grant DST/ INSPIRE/04/2015/002801, Govt. of India.

C. M. Pinotti et al. (Eds.): ALGOSENSORS 2020, LNCS 12503, pp. 154–169, 2020.
https://doi.org/10.1007/978-3-030-62401-9_11

1   Introduction

The formal study of independent computational agents and their interactions is both a deep and broad area of research, spanning fields such as population protocols [1], mobile robots [30], and programmable matter [17] among others. The specific model of mobile robots on a graph is used to capture the abstraction of agents, limited in their movement capabilities and communication abilities, but free to move in a fixed space. Within this area, problems that are studied take on the form of either having the robots work together to find something in the graph (e.g., exploration [4,11,15,19,22,27], treasure hunting [28]) or form a certain configuration (e.g., gathering [9,10,18,32], scattering [5,21,31,33], pattern formation [35], convergence [12]).

Dispersion is one such problem of the latter category. Introduced in this setting by Augustine and Moses Jr. [3], it asks the following question. Given n robots initially placed arbitrarily on an n node graph, devise an algorithm such that the robots reach a configuration where exactly one robot is present on each node. The original paper looked at the trade-offs between time taken to reach this configuration and the memory required by each robot. It also provided an $\Omega(\log n)$ bit lower bound on the memory required by each robot. Subsequent papers [23–26,29] have expanded the scope of this problem, but have always maintained this focus on time and memory efficiency.

However, none of these previous works consider faulty robots. Thus, a natural question arises: is dispersion possible if there are faulty robots? Specifically, Byzantine faults, which is considered to be the stronger notion among faults.[1] Furthermore, if dispersion is possible, how do the Byzantine robots influence the complexities of the algorithms? In this paper, we answer these questions, showing that dispersion in the presence of Byzantine faults is indeed possible and presenting efficient solutions for Byzantine dispersion on a ring.

The best known algorithm for dispersion on a ring "without faulty robots" is quite straightforward, and takes $O(n)$ rounds and $O(\log n)$ bits of memory per robot [3]. This algorithm and other non-faulty dispersion algorithms do not apply readily when there are Byzantine robots. In fact, the most commonly used techniques for these kinds of problems related to mobile robots on graphs (e.g., dispersion, exploration, scattering) are based on depth first search (DFS) traversals or breadth first search (BFS) traversals–which will not work immediately in the presence of Byzantine robots. The main reason is that it is difficult for a robot to distinguish between a non-Byzantine and a Byzantine robot. We develop new techniques to bypass this difficulty and achieve dispersion in this setting.

---

[1] There are mainly two types of faults–one is "crash fault" which means that once a robot crashes, it is dead and will not be active again thereafter; another one is "Byzantine fault" which means that a robot is alive throughout and may behave maliciously. Note that the Byzantine fault subsumes the crash fault.

1.1 Model

Consider a ring with n nodes. The ring is anonymous in the sense that the nodes are indistinguishable (they do not have identifiers), but the ports have unique labels. Each node in the ring has two ports that correspond to the edges from it, with unique port numbers assigned to each port. Note that an edge between adjacent nodes may have different port numbers assigned to it. Consider n robots initially placed on arbitrary nodes. When all n robots are initially placed on the same node, we call the ring a *rooted* ring.

Robots are distinguishable, i.e., each robot has a unique identifier assigned to it from the range $[1, n^c]$, where $c > 1$ is a constant, unless otherwise stated. Two robots co-located on the same node can communicate with each other. One way to understand this communication between robots is as follows. Each robot has two types of memory: *exposed* and *unexposed*. Any information present in the exposed memory can be read/scanned by the other co-located robots. Information in the unexposed memory is hidden from the others. Since we assumed that a robot cannot change its ID, each robot's unique identifier would be considered to be permanently stored in its exposed memory and not be changeable.

If a robot moves from one node to an adjacent node, it is aware of both port numbers assigned to the edge through which it passed. We also note that a robot present on a node can observe the port through which another robot enters that node. We recursively define the notion of *clockwise* and *counter-clockwise* directions for each robot. Consider that a given robot moves from node u to node v through u's clockwise edge. Now, for node v, the edge $\langle v, u \rangle$ is its counter-clockwise edge and the other edge is its clockwise edge. When a robot first starts the algorithm (before moving anywhere), it assigns the directions of clockwise and counter-clockwise as follows. It observes the port numbers of the node it is initially placed on. Denote the edge with the lower port number as clockwise and the other edge as counter-clockwise.[2] Notice that each robot has its own sense of clockwise and counter-clockwise, but two robots may not agree on this sense.

We adapt the definition of a weak Byzantine robot from [20]. A Byzantine robot may behave maliciously and arbitrarily, i.e., it may share wrong information, perform moves that are deviations from the algorithm, etc. As in [20], we assume that a Byzantine robot cannot fake its ID, i.e., it cannot communicate to a robot that its ID has a value other than the one initially assigned to it. Note that the exposed memory of a Byzantine robot can be read by all other robots co-located with it. Among the n robots, up to f of them are considered to be Byzantine. Some of our algorithms can afford up to $n - 1$ Byzantine robots among n robots. Moreover, our algorithms work without knowing the number of Byzantine robots in the system. That is, each robot knows the value of n, but need not know the value of f, unless otherwise stated.

---

[2] In the algorithms, we mention a robot *resets its sense of direction*, i.e., it resets its notion of clockwise and counter-clockwise. That refers to the robot performing this check again and redefining clockwise and counter-clockwise accordingly.

We consider a synchronous system, where in each round a robot performs the following tasks in order: (i) Robots that are co-located at the same node instantaneously and simultaneously read each other's exposed memory. Robots may perform some local computation and may update information in their unexposed memory. (ii) Robots update their exposed memory as needed. (iii) Each robot either stays at the same node or moves to another node.

Note that task (i) of each round seems to require each robot to have a large memory. However, we have written it this way for ease of understanding. We ensure that our algorithms can simulate task (i) using the memory we allocate to run those algorithms. However, we do restrict the Byzantine robots to not change their exposed memory before we reach task (ii) of a round. We assume that all robots are initially awake and can engage in the algorithms from the beginning.

Considering the fact that a Byzantine robot can settle at any node (we have no control on it), let us now formally define the problem of dispersion on a ring in the presence of Byzantine robots. Let us call this problem *Byzantine dispersion*.

Definition 1 (Byzantine Dispersion). *Given n robots, up to f of which are Byzantine, initially placed arbitrarily on a ring of n nodes, the robots re-position themselves autonomously to reach a configuration where each node has at most one non-Byzantine robot on it and terminate.*

The problem of dispersion on a "rooted ring" is a variation of the above problem statement where all n robots are initially located on the same node.

1.2   Our Contributions

In this paper, we introduce the notion of Byzantine robots to the problem of dispersion of mobile robots on graphs. We first develop an important building block used in subsequent algorithms, the procedure ROOTED-RING-DISPERSION. It achieves Byzantine dispersion on a rooted ring in at most $n-1$ rounds and requires each robot to have $O(\log n)$ bits of memory. This procedure allows $k \leq n$ co-located robots (where all non-Byzantine robots are present) with unique IDs taken from any range to achieve Byzantine dispersion even when n is unknown and f can be as large as $k-1$.

Our first and most important contribution is a time and memory optimal algorithm, OPT-RING-DISPERSION, which solves Byzantine dispersion on a ring in $O(n)$ rounds and uses $O(\log n)$ bits of memory per robot. The algorithm relies on the following four assumptions: (i) the ID space of robots is restricted to the range $[1, n]$, (ii) the upper bound on the number of Byzantine robots f is known to the robots, (iii) f is restricted to $f \leq \lfloor (n-4)/17 \rfloor$, and (iv) *follow* primitive holds, i.e., one robot may follow another robot (refer to Sect. 3 for more details).

Our second contribution is a memory optimal algorithm for Byzantine dispersion on a ring, MEM-OPT-RING-DISPERSION, which requires less assumptions–it only requires the ID space of the robots to be restricted to $[1, n]$. It takes $O(n^2)$ rounds and uses only $O(\log n)$ bits of memory per robot.

Our final contribution is a time optimal algorithm, TIME-OPT-RING-DISPERSION, which requires no assumptions at all. It takes n rounds and uses $O(n \log n)$ bits of memory per robot. It should be noted that this algorithm has a very tight running time. Our results are summarized in Table 1.

Table 1. Our results for Byzantine dispersion of n robots on an n node ring in the presence of at most f Byzantine robots.

Algorithm	Running time (in rounds)	Memory requirement (bits per robot)	Assumptions required
MEM-OPT-RING-DISPERSION	$O(n^2)$	$O(\log n)$	Restricted ID space
TIME-OPT-RING-DISPERSION	n	$O(n \log n)$	None
OPT-RING-DISPERSION	$O(n)$	$O(\log n)$	Restricted ID space, $f \leq \lfloor (n-4)/17 \rfloor$ known, *follow*

1.3   Technical Difficulties and High-Level Ideas

We now highlight some of the key difficulties that make this problem interesting. In doing so, we provide insight into our algorithmic design choices and a high level intuition of our algorithms, though some key details are elaborated upon only in the respective sections.

A fundamental difficulty behind any algorithm for this problem is that Byzantine robots can lie about what they have seen so far. This makes relying on communication between robots risky. One possibility (TIME-OPT-RING-DISPERSION) is to have each robot function independent of the others, with the only real communication between two robots being to see if one of them already settled at the current node. However, this approach requires each robot to develop a way to determine if another robot is Byzantine and remember this information since we do not want two non-Byzantine robots to settle at the same node. Since $O(n)$ robots could be Byzantine, each robot requires $O(n \log n)$ bits of memory.

However, this approach of no communication breaks down when we want each robot to have $o(n \log n)$ bits of memory each. We then require some method for a robot to safely figure out where it can settle, without having to remember the IDs of all the Byzantine robots. In this paper, we have developed a useful primitive (ROOTED-RING-DISPERSION) that allows robots with only $O(\log n)$ bits of memory to achieve Byzantine dispersion. The only catch is that all non-Byzantine robots should already be present on the same node. Thus our problem reduces to one of gathering. How best can we gather robots with limited memory?

If we cannot remember all the robots which are Byzantine, is there a technique to gather where each robot does not need to remember information about all robots all the time? One way to do this is to restrict the rounds in which each robot is allowed to move. Recall that a Byzantine robot cannot lie about its ID. If we restrict a robot with ID x to only move in rounds $f(x, 1), f(x, 2), \ldots$, where $f(x, 1)$ is a function known to all robots, and $f(x, i) \neq f(y, j)$ when $x \neq y$, then we provide a memory-lite way for a robot to identify Byzantine robots. By having robots interact with each other in smart ways and guaranteeing that by a certain round, all non-Byzantine robots have gathered, we solve Byzantine dispersion while requiring robots to only have $O(\log n)$ bits of memory each (MEM-OPT-RING-DISPERSION). However, the algorithm takes $O(n^2)$ rounds and requires the ID space of robots to be restricted to $[1, n]$.

The key reason the previous algorithm took so many rounds is that we restricted $f(x, i) \neq f(y, j)$ when $x \neq y$. This was to ensure that a single robot does not need to keep track of multiple Byzantine robots (and the associated IDs) in a given round. However, when the actual value of f, the upper bound on the number of Byzantine robots is known, then we may be a little clever. By looking for a group of robots with at least $2f + 1$ robots moving together, a robot needs only $O(\log n)$ bits of memory and it can safely follow the group because a majority of the robots in the group are non-Byzantine robots. This helps us eventually gather all non-Byzantine robots together while allowing multiple robots to move at the same time. However, in order to form this initial group of at least $2f + 1$ robots, and ensure that it is the only group that is initially formed requires a bit of work, as seen in OPT-RING-DISPERSION.

1.4   More Related Work

The problem of dispersing mobile robots on graphs was first introduced by Augustine and Moses Jr. [3] and they provided solutions for various types of graphs including paths, rings, trees, and general graphs. After that, the problem was studied by several papers [23–26,29] in various settings to improve the efficiency of the solutions. The best known time-memory efficient algorithm for dispersion of $k \leq n$ robots on an arbitrary n-node graph has time complexity of $O(\min\{m, k\Delta\} \log n)$ rounds and $O(\log n)$ bits of memory per robot [24], where Δ is the maximum degree of the graph. The paper [26] studies dispersion on the grid graph and provides a $O(\sqrt{n})$ time algorithm using $O(\log n)$ memory for each robot, an optimal solution with respect to both memory and time. Randomized algorithms are presented in [29] where random bits are mainly used to break the memory requirement of $\Omega(\log n)$ bits per robot.

Some other problems that are closely related to dispersion on graphs are exploration, scattering, gathering, etc. The problem of graph exploration has been studied extensively in the literature for specific as well as arbitrary graphs, e.g., [4,11,15,19,22,27]. While some of these exploration algorithms (especially those which fit the current model) can be adapted to solve dispersion (with additional work), they, however, provide inefficient time-memory bounds; a detailed comparison is given in [24]. Another problem related to dispersion is *scattering* (also known as uniform-deployment) of mobile robots in a graph and is also studied by several papers, e.g., it has been studied for rings [21,33] and grids [5,31] under different assumptions. Load balancing, where a given load at the nodes has to be (re-)distributed among several processors (nodes) is also relevant to dispersion where robots can be used to distribute the loads. This problem has been studied in graphs, e.g., [13,34].

While it appears that the notion of Byzantine robots is not new to the mobile robots literature in general (e.g., [2,8,14]), it appears that its usage in the context of mobile robots on a graph is fairly recent. To the best of our knowledge, only the problem of gathering has been studied in the context of Byzantine robots in the graph setting. Specifically, Dieudonné et al. [20] introduced the notion of Byzantine robots to the gathering problem. The paper mainly investigates the possibility and impossibility of gathering of mobile robots on graphs in the presence of Byzantine robots. They present some possibility results under certain assumptions on the minimum number of non-Byzantine robots present. Their solution can be adapted to solve Byzantine dispersion on a ring, but gives a time-memory inefficient solution–$\Omega(n^4)$ rounds and $\Omega(n \log n)$ bits of memory per robot. There are some follow-up papers on Byzantine gathering, mostly focused on the feasibility of the solution, e.g., [6,7,16], which can be adapted to solve dispersion on a ring, but result in solutions which are time-memory inefficient.

1.5   Paper Organization

In Sect. 2, we develop a procedure for the rooted ring, which is used as a building block in subsequent algorithms. In Sect. 3, we present our main result, a time and memory optimal algorithm for Byzantine dispersion on the ring. In Sect. 4, we present algorithms which are either only time optimal or only memory optimal, but require less assumptions than our main result. Finally, we present future directions of research in Sect. 5.

2   Building Block

In this section, we present a procedure to achieve Byzantine dispersion on the rooted ring, i.e., when all robots start at the same node initially. This procedure also works when some subset of the robots that includes all non-Byzantine robots are co-located initially. This procedure is subsequently used in our algorithms. The procedure, ROOTED-RING-DISPERSION, is a simple one that finishes in $O(n)$ rounds and requires each robot to have $O(\log n)$ bits of memory. It can handle any number of Byzantine robots, does not require robots to know the value of n, and works even when robots have unique IDs taken from some arbitrarily large range (but still polynomial in n). The procedure works as follows.

In the first round, all co-located robots communicate with each other and determine their position in the total order of IDs as follows. Each robot maintains a $\log n$ bit counter, initialized to 1, which it increments for every robot it sees in this round with a lower ID.[3] Still in the first round, each robot then resets its

---

[3] Note that it is not necessary for a robot to know the value of n in order to maintain a counter using $\log n$ bits of memory given that the robot's total memory is $c \log n$ bits of memory, where c is a sufficiently large constant.

sense of direction so that all robots have the same sense of clockwise direction. Now, a robot whose position in the total order is i, moves $i - 1$ steps in the clockwise direction on the ring (in $i - 1$ rounds) and settles down at that $(i-1)^{th}$ node and terminates the algorithm. Thus, Byzantine dispersion is achieved in at most $n - 1$ rounds.

Theorem 1. *Consider an n-node ring with $k \leq n$ robots placed on a single node such that all non-Byzantine robots are present among the k robots and at most f of them are Byzantine, $f \leq k - 1$. Each robot has a unique ID, $O(\log n)$ bits of memory, and does not have knowledge of the values of n and f. Then Byzantine dispersion can be achieved in at most $n - 1$ rounds.*

3   Time and Memory Optimal Algorithm

We now describe an algorithm, OPT-RING-DISPERSION, that achieves Byzantine dispersion on a ring in optimal time ($O(n)$ rounds) using optimal memory ($O(\log n)$ bits) given that robots' unique IDs are restricted to the range $[1, n]$, robots know the value of f, and $f < n/17$. We also require the following assumption which we call the *follow* primitive. When two robots A and B are co-located on the same node, one robot (say A) can follow the movement of the other robot B. It is important to note that even if B is a Byzantine robot, A can follow the movement of B when they are co-located.

The algorithm has two **Phases**. In **Phase 1**, all non-Byzantine robots gather at a node in $O(n)$ rounds. In **Phase 2**, these gathered robots perform dispersion in an additional n rounds.

Phase 1: The first phase of the algorithm is further subdivided into three **Sub-phases**. We first present intuition for these sub-phases, and then delve into details subsequently. The first sub-phase consists of rounds 1 to n and is used to aggregate the non-Byzantine robots into at most $f + 1$ groups of robots at different nodes. The second sub-phase consists of rounds $n + 1$ to $2n + 1$ and has these groups move in a way so that a sufficient number of non-Byzantine robots gather together, i.e., at least $f + 1$ non-Byzantine robots. The final sub-phase consists of rounds $2n+2$ to $3n+1$ and is used by these at least $f+1$ non-Byzantine robots to move around the ring and collect the remaining non-Byzantine robots.

Sub-phase 1: For the first n rounds, those robots with ID $\in [1, f + 1]$ move along the ring in the clockwise direction. Robots with IDs $\notin [1, f + 1]$, once they see a robot with an ID $\in [1, f + 1]$, follow that robot until the end of round n. If multiple robots from $\in [1, f + 1]$ are seen at the same time, one is chosen arbitrarily and followed.

Sub-phase 2: For the next $n + 1$ rounds, we describe the strategy for each robot depending on who and how many other robots are co-located with them at the start of round $n + 1$. Initially, all robots reset their sense of direction so that all co-located robots have the same sense of clockwise and counter-clockwise. Call the robot with ID 1, R_1. The algorithm instructs R_1 not to move for these $n + 1$ rounds. All robots co-located with R_1 follow it.[4] The goal of this second sub-phase is to have a sufficient number of non-Byzantine robots find and subsequently follow R_1.

We now look at how the other groups of robots not containing R_1 move in this sub-phase. If at some node, there are less than four robots, those robots do not move in this sub-phase. All remaining robots in the ring are present in groups of size 4 or more. Each group is divided into four subgroups $\{G_{LL}, G_{LU}, G_{UL}, G_{UU}\}$, as described below, that move until either the sub-phase ends or they come into contact with robot R_1, in which case they subsequently follow R_1 until the end of this sub-phase. Each group G is first divided into two subgroups: $\lfloor |G|/2 \rfloor$ of the robots with the lowest IDs form G_L and the remaining form G_U. Again $\lfloor |G_L|/2 \rfloor$ of the lowest ID robots of G_L form the subgroup G_{LL} and the remaining form G_{LU}. From round $n+1$ to $2n$, robots in G_{LU} move in the clockwise direction. Robots in G_{LL} do nothing in round $n + 1$, but from round $n+2$ to round $2n + 1$, robots in G_{LL} move in the clockwise direction. Similarly, $\lfloor |G_U|/2 \rfloor$ of the lowest ID robots of G_U form the group G_{UL} and the remaining robots form G_{UU}. They mimic the strategies of G_{LL} and G_{LU} respectively but for the counter-clockwise direction. By the end of this sub-phase, for each of these groups, at least one of the four subgroups comes into contact with R_1.

Sub-phase 3: The third sub-phase, from round $2n + 2$ to $3n + 1$ sees those robots which were co-located with R_1 at the end of round $2n + 1$ move clockwise for n rounds. Each robot X not co-located with R_1 at the end of round $2n + 1$, does not move from its node until a group of at least $f+1$ robots arrive at its node and claim to be robots co-located with R_1 at the end of round $(2n + 1)$. Upon arrival of this group, X does the following. X observes which port the majority of them entered the node through and sets the remaining port as clockwise. X subsequently moves clockwise until the end of round $(3n + 1)$. At the end of round $(3n + 1)$, all non-Byzantine robots are gathered.[5]

Phase 2: Finally, in the second phase of the algorithm, the procedure ROOTED-RING-DISPERSION is called by these gathered robots and Byzantine dispersion is achieved in an additional n rounds.

Theorem 2. *Consider an n node ring with n robots initially arbitrarily placed on it. Each robot has a unique ID in $[1, n]$, $O(\log n)$ bits of memory, and knows the value of f, the upper bound on Byzantine robots. When $f \leq \lfloor (n-4)/17 \rfloor$, the deterministic algorithm OPT-RING-DISPERSION achieves Byzantine dispersion in $O(n)$ rounds.*

---

[4] Notice that we say that other co-located robots are to follow R_1, instead of just staying put. This is to ensure that all robots initially co-located with R_1 continue to stay with R_1, even if R_1 is a Byzantine robot and moves around during the $n + 1$ rounds.

[5] Possibly some Byzantine robots may also be gathered as well, but the presence of these robots does not cause problems as the subsequent procedure, ROOTED-RING-DISPERSION is correct even in the presence of $n - 1$ Byzantine robots.

Proof. The time and memory complexities are obvious from the algorithm. We now prove correctness, i.e., Byzantine dispersion is achieved in $O(n)$ rounds.

The first n rounds (in Sub-phase 1) ensure that all non-Byzantine robots will be partitioned into at most $f + 1$ groups.

There can be at most f groups of 3 robots, hence at most $3f$ non-Byzantine robots do not move from round $n+1$ to round $2n+1$. From the remaining $n-3f$ robots, at least $(n - 6f)/4$ of them should meet and subsequently follow R_1 in these $n+1$ rounds, if they act according to the algorithm. This occurs, regardless of whatever R_1 chooses to do. We prove this below.

Consider one group of ≥ 4 robots G at the start of round $n + 1$. Since robots in G_L and in G_U are visiting all the nodes of the ring from opposite directions, at some point robots from one of the two groups must encounter R_1. Without loss of generality, let the robots in G_U encounter R_1. Recall that we group robots in G_U into two subgroups G_{UL} and G_{UU}. This is to ensure that at least one of the two subgroups encounters R_1 in case R_1 moves in the opposite direction to these two groups, since the groups always occupy consecutive nodes in the ring. Hence, at least $\lfloor (\lfloor |G|/2 \rfloor)/2 \rfloor$ robots from G meet R_1.

If there is only one such group, then at least $\lfloor (\lfloor |G|/2 \rfloor)/2 \rfloor \geq \lfloor (\lfloor (n - 3f)/2 \rfloor)/2 \rfloor \geq (n-3f-6)/4$ robots meet with R_1. However, as the number of such groups increases, the number of robots that eventually meet with R_1 decreases. There can be at most f such groups of robots other than the group containing R_1. Call the groups G_1 to G_f and recall that $\sum_{i=1}^{f} |G_i| \geq n - 3f$. Let G' be the set of robots that eventually meet up with and subsequently follow R_1. We see that $|G'| \geq \sum_{i=1}^{f} \lfloor (\lfloor |G_i|/2 \rfloor)/2 \rfloor \geq \sum_{i=1}^{f} (|G_i| - 6)/4 \geq (n - 3f - 6f)/4 = (n - 9f)/4$.

Since there can be up to f Byzantine robots in these groups, we know that of the robots in G', at least $(n-9f)/4 - f = (n-13f)/4$ of them are non-Byzantine.

According to our algorithm, this group of at least $(n - 13f)/4$ robots move across the ring for the next n rounds to gather all the remaining non-Byzantine robots. Once met, the remaining non-Byzantine robots simply verify that there are at least $f + 1$ robots in this group and subsequently follow this group as described in the algorithm. This is the case when $f \leq \lfloor (n - 4)/17 \rfloor$.

Thus, at the end of round $3n + 1$, all non-Byzantine robots are gathered at the same node. A subsequent call to the procedure ROOTED-RING-DISPERSION guarantees that Byzantine dispersion is achieved in an additional n rounds. Since robots keep track of the current round, they terminate at the end of round $4n+1$ only after the desired configuration of robots on nodes is reached. □

4 Time or Memory Optimal Algorithms with Reduced Assumptions

In the following section, we present two algorithms, a memory optimal algorithm and a time optimal algorithm, which solve Byzantine dispersion on a ring requiring less assumptions than the algorithm presented in Sect. 3. Both the algorithms tolerate up to $n - 1$ Byzantine robots, i.e., $f \leq n - 1$.

4.1   Algorithm with Optimal Memory Complexity

We describe an algorithm, MEM-OPT-RING-DISPERSION, that achieves Byzantine dispersion of n robots, when up to f of them are Byzantine, on an n node ring in $O(n^2)$ rounds requiring each robot to have $O(\log n)$ bits of memory, when robots' unique IDs are restricted to the range $[1, n]$. The robots know the value of n but not f. Intuitively, robots first gather in n^2 rounds, then disperse in an additional $n - 1$ rounds.

The algorithm works as follows. Define stage i as consisting of the rounds from $(i - 1)n + 1$ to in. In stage i, the robot with ID i moves clockwise for n rounds. Any other robot x does nothing until it comes into contact with robot i.[6] On seeing robot i, x communicates with i to see which port i will move through. Subsequently, x moves in that direction until the end of round in. After n such stages, all the non-Byzantine robots are gathered at some node. Subsequently, in round $n^2 + 1$, the algorithm calls procedure ROOTED-RING-DISPERSION to achieve Byzantine dispersion in an additional $n - 1$ rounds.

The following theorem captures the properties of the algorithm. The proof is given in the Appendix.

Theorem 3. *Consider an n node ring with n robots initially arbitrarily placed on it. Each robot has a unique ID in $[1, n]$, $O(\log n)$ bits of memory, and there are at most f Byzantine robots, $f \leq n - 1$. The deterministic algorithm MEM-OPT-RING-DISPERSION achieves Byzantine dispersion in $O(n^2)$ rounds.*

It is clear that if the value of f is known to the robots ahead of time, they can run the algorithm for exactly $f + 1$ stages and subsequently disperse. Thus we have the following corollary.

Corollary 1. *Consider an n node ring with n robots initially arbitrarily placed on it. Each robot has a unique ID in $[1, n]$, $O(\log n)$ bits of memory, and there are at most f Byzantine robots, $f \leq n - 1$. When the value of f is known to the robots, there exists a deterministic algorithm that achieves Byzantine dispersion in $O(fn)$ rounds.*

4.2   Time Optimal Algorithm

We describe an algorithm, TIME-OPT-RING-DISPERSION, that achieves Byzantine dispersion of n robots, when up to $f \leq n - 1$ of them are Byzantine, on an n node ring in $O(n)$ rounds using $O(n \log n)$ bits of memory per robot. Again the robots need not know the number of Byzantine robots in the system.

Each robot, having $O(n \log n)$ bits of memory, can remember all the n robots. It helps to detect Byzantine robot, particularly when a robot deviates the algorithm. Intuitively, this algorithm is easy to explain, though the details are involved. Each robot r moves clockwise in the ring until it finds a node to be

---

[6] This could happen at the beginning of the stage, if the two robots are co-located on the same node.

settled down at. There are two conditions that r checks at a node v before deciding to settle down. One condition is that among the robots on v that claim to already be settled there, there exists a robot that is not known by r to be Byzantine. The second condition is that among all the robots currently at the node v, there exists a robot with ID lower than r's that intends to settle and is not known by r to be Byzantine. If either check succeeds, then r does not settle down at v. Else r settles down. The checking on the second condition involves non-trivial computations. The detailed algorithm is:

Each robot r maintains an array A_r of size $n + 1$, where $A_r[k]$ contains the ID(s) of the settled robot(s) that r encountered in round $k \geq 1$. Note that the total number of settled robots in some node can be more than one, as Byzantine robots may settle with a good robot. $A_r[0]$ is used to represent whether r is settled on the current node or not. Initially $A_r[0] = 0$. Robot r sets $A_r[0] = 1$ when on some node v in order to claim that it is settled on v.

Robot r imposes the local naming convention $\{v_1, v_2, ..., v_n\}$ on the set of all nodes it may see in the ring, where the node it is initially placed on is v_1, then the next node it moves to is v_2, and so on. In any round k, let $G_r'^k = \{s_1, s_2, ..., s_p\}$ be the set of p already settled robots at v_k at the beginning of round k. Let G_r^k be the group of robots on node v_k in round k, excluding those robots in $G_r'^k$. If there is no settled robot at v_k by the start of round k, then $G_r'^k$ is empty. If there are no robots on v_k in round k, excluding those in $G_r'^k$, then G_r^k is empty.

In any round k, let M_r^k be the set of robots whose IDs were written in $A_r[1], A_r[2], ..., A_r[k-1]$. Define $B_r^k = M_r^k \bigcap (G_r'^k \bigcup G_r^k)$ and let its complement be denoted by B_r^{Ck}. Intuitively, B_r^k represents robots that r has identified as acting in a Byzantine manner by claiming to settle at a previous node and now are present at node v_k.

We will shortly describe how robot r determines whether it will settle down at a node v_k in round k. For now, it is sufficient to note that the decision of r to settle down at node v_k in round k is a result of a computation whose input is r's memory and the memories of other robots co-located with it on v_k at that time. This is in fact true of all the robots in G_r^k that may possibly decide to settle down at the node. All these memories can be read by all robots co-located at the node in that round. Thus, robot r can calculate the set $S_r^k \subset G_r^k \bigcup G_r'^k$ of robots that will settle down at node v_k and add it to $A_r[k]$.

We now describe the procedure for r in each round $1 \leq k \leq n$ on node v_k until r settles down.

1. Initialize $S_r^k = G_r'^k \setminus B_r^k$. Robot r performs the following check. If S_r^k is not empty, then r does not settle at v_k.
2. Robot r performs the following calculation to iteratively determine the subset of robots from G_r^k that may decide to settle at the node. Consider all robots s such that $s \in G_r^k$. Order these robots in ascending order of their ID. For each robot s in this list from smallest ID to largest ID, do the following. (Note that $G_s^k = G_r^k$ and $G_s'^k = G_r'^k$.)
   (a) If there does not exist a robot t such that $t \in G_s'^k$ and $t \notin B_s^k$, then proceed to the next step. Else, move to the next robot in the list.

(b) If there does not exist a robot t such that $t \in S_r^k$ and $t \notin B_s^k$, then add s to S_r^k.

Now r performs the following check. If there exists a robot s such that the ID of s is less than that of r, $s \in S_r^k$, and $s \notin B_r^k$, then r does not settle at v_k.

3. If neither of the above two checks are satisfied, then r settles at v_k.
4. If r does not settle at v_k, it writes the robot IDs of $B_r^{Ck} \cap S_r^k$ in $A_r[k]$ and moves clockwise through an edge.

Once r settles down at a node, it waits until the end of round n and then terminates.[7] The following theorem captures the properties of the algorithm.

Theorem 4. *Consider an n node ring with n robots initially arbitrarily placed on it, up to $f \leq n-1$ of which are Byzantine in nature. Each robot has a unique ID and knows the value of n. Algorithm* TIME-OPT-RING-DISPERSION *solves Byzantine dispersion in n rounds and requires each robot to have $O(n \log n)$ bits of memory.*

In order to prove the theorem, we first make an observation and prove a few useful lemmas.

Observation 1. *When r is a non-Byzantine robot, for $1 \leq k \leq n$, the robots in B_r^k are Byzantine.*

Proof. Let robot r encounter a robot s in some round $1 \leq k' < k$ that decides to settle in that round. If s is a non-Byzantine robot, then s never changes its position on the ring and r can only encounter s again in some round $k' + n > n$ (since r only moves in one direction in the ring). Hence, if r finds s in another node, i.e., at some round after k' and before $k' + n$, then s must be a Byzantine robot. In other words, if $s \in M_r^k \cap (G_r'^k \cup G_r^k)$ then r can identify s as a Byzantine robot. $\square$

Lemma 1. *If r does not settle down at node v_k in round k, then there is at least one robot that r currently does not consider Byzantine that is written in $A_r[k]$.*

Proof. Recall that in round k, a robot s that is co-located with r is considered by r to be non-Byzantine iff $s \notin B_r^k$.

Robot r does not settle at node v_k if either of the two checks in Line 1 and Line 2 succeed. Both checks require that a robot $s \neq r$ such that $s \notin B_r^k$ chooses to settle at v_k. Hence, if either of the two checks succeed, then by definition r considers at least one of the robots that settled to be non-Byzantine. $\square$

Note that a robot that appears non-Byzantine to r may in fact be a Byzantine robot. In case r adds more than one robot to $A_r[k]$ for a given round k, we desire that at most one of the robots in $A_r[k]$ may be non-Byzantine. It may in fact be the case that all of the robots in $A_r[k]$ are Byzantine. However, it should not

---

[7] If r terminates prior to the end of round n, it becomes invisible to other robots. Thus, there is the risk of another non-Byzantine robot settling at the same node as r if r terminates early.

be the case that more than one robot in $A_r[k]$ is non-Byzantine, i.e., more than one non-Byzantine robot settles at the same node. The following lemma shows that this is indeed the case.

Lemma 2. *No two non-Byzantine robots settle at the same node v_k in any round k.*

Proof. Let r and s be two non-Byzantine robots co-located on node v_k. If one of them is already settled there, say s without loss of generality, then r will not settle on the node because of the check in Line 1. This is because if s is non-Byzantine, then it would not appear in B_r^k.

If both r and s are in G_r^k, i.e., both are not yet settled at the node, then we show that it is impossible for both of them to settle at v_k. Without loss of generality, let the ID of s be less than that of r. If s passes one of the two checks in Line 1 and Line 2 and thus does not settle at v_k, we do not need to show anything further. However, if s chooses to settle down at node v_k, then it is guaranteed that the check in Line 2 will succeed for robot r, and thus r will not settle at v_k. □

Now we are ready to prove Theorem 4.

Proof of Theorem 4. Let r be a non-Byzantine robot. By Lemma 1, we see that in each round k, $1 \leq k \leq n$, if r is not yet settled, then at least one non-Byzantine robot's ID (from r's perspective) is written in $A_r[k]$. So, by the end of round n, r definitely found a node to settle at as there are only n robots in total. This is true for all non-Byzantine robots. Thus after n rounds, each non-Byzantine robot has settled at some node.

By Lemma 2, no two non-Byzantine robots settle at the same node. Thus, after n rounds, Byzantine dispersion is solved. □

5   Future Work

An interesting open problem is to reduce the assumptions required to achieve dispersion. Specifically, our time and memory optimal algorithm required the following three assumptions: (i) the robots' unique IDs are taken from the range $[1, n]$, (ii) each robot knows the value of f, and (iii) $f \leq \lfloor (n - 4)/17 \rfloor$. Is it possible to develop a time and memory optimal algorithm that drops one or all of these assumptions? An exciting line of research is to study this problem on other types of graphs and eventually develop algorithms that are optimal for any graph. Another generalization relates to time; an understanding of how solutions to Byzantine dispersion look in the asynchronous system warrants study.

References

1. Angluin, D., Aspnes, J., Diamadi, Z., Fischer, M.J., Peralta, R.: Computation in networks of passively mobile finite-state sensors. Distrib. Comput. **18**(4), 235–253 (2006)

2. Auger, C., Bouzid, Z., Courtieu, P., Tixeuil, S., Urbain, X.: Certified impossibility results for byzantine-tolerant mobile robots. In: Higashino, T., Katayama, Y., Masuzawa, T., Potop-Butucaru, M., Yamashita, M. (eds.) SSS 2013. LNCS, vol. 8255, pp. 178–190. Springer, Cham (2013). https://doi.org/10.1007/978-3-319-03089-0_13
3. Augustine, J., Moses, Jr., W.K.: Dispersion of mobile robots: a study of memory-time trade-offs. CoRR abs/1707.05629 ([v4] 2018 (a preliminary version appeared in ICDCN'18))
4. Bampas, E., Gasieniec, L., Hanusse, N., Ilcinkas, D., Klasing, R., Kosowski, A.: Euler tour lock-in problem in the rotor-router model: I choose pointers and you choose port numbers. In: DISC, pp. 423–435 (2009)
5. Barriere, L., Flocchini, P., Mesa-Barrameda, E., Santoro, N.: Uniform scattering of autonomous mobile robots in a grid. In: IPDPS, pp. 1–8 (2009)
6. Bouchard, S., Dieudonné, Y., Ducourthial, B.: Byzantine gathering in networks. Distrib. Comput. **29**(6), 435–457 (2016). https://doi.org/10.1007/s00446-016-0276-9
7. Bouchard, S., Dieudonné, Y., Lamani, A.: Byzantine gathering in polynomial time. In: 45th International Colloquium on Automata, Languages, and Programming, ICALP 2018, Prague, Czech Republic, 9–13 July 2018, pp. 147:1–147:15 (2018)
8. Bouzid, Z., Potop-Butucaru, M.G., Tixeuil, S.: Byzantine-resilient convergence in oblivious robot networks. In: Garg, V., Wattenhofer, R., Kothapalli, K. (eds.) Distributed Computing and Networking. LNCS, vol. 5408, pp. 275–280. Springer, Heidelberg (2009). https://doi.org/10.1007/978-3-540-92295-7_33
9. Cieliebak, M., Flocchini, P., Prencipe, G., Santoro, N.: Distributed computing by mobile robots: gathering. SIAM J. Comput. **41**(4), 829–879 (2012)
10. Cieliebak, M., Prencipe, G.: Gathering autonomous mobile robots. In: Proceedings of the 9th International Colloquium on Structural Information and Communication Complexity (SIROCCO), pp. 57–72 (2002)
11. Cohen, R., Fraigniaud, P., Ilcinkas, D., Korman, A., Peleg, D.: Label-guided graph exploration by a finite automaton. ACM Trans. Algorithms **4**(4), 42:1–42:18 (2008)
12. Cohen, R., Peleg, D.: Robot convergence via center-of-gravity algorithms. In: Proceedings of the 11th International Colloquium on Structural Information and Communication Complexity, (SIROCCO), pp. 79–88 (2004)
13. Cybenko, G.: Dynamic load balancing for distributed memory multiprocessors. J. Parallel Distrib. Comput. **7**(2), 279–301 (1989)
14. Czyzowicz, J., et al.: Search on a line by byzantine robots. arXiv preprint arXiv:1611.08209 (2016)
15. Das, S.: Mobile agents in distributed computing: network exploration. Bull. EATCS **109**, 54–69 (2013)
16. Das, S., Focardi, R., Luccio, F.L., Markou, E., Squarcina, M.: Gathering of robots in a ring with mobile faults. Theor. Comput. Sci. **764**, 42–60 (2019)
17. Daymude, J.J., Hinnenthal, K., Richa, A.W., Scheideler, C.: Computing by programmable particles. In: Flocchini, P., Prencipe, G., Santoro, N. (eds.) Distributed Computing by Mobile Entities. LNCS, vol. 11340, pp. 615–681. Springer, Cham (2019). https://doi.org/10.1007/978-3-030-11072-7_22
18. Degener, B., Kempkes, B., Langner, T., Meyer auf der Heide, F., Pietrzyk, P., Wattenhofer, R.: A tight runtime bound for synchronous gathering of autonomous robots with limited visibility. In: Proceedings of the 23rd Annual ACM Symposium on Parallelism in Algorithms and Architectures (SPAA), pp. 139–148 (2011)
19. Dereniowski, D., Disser, Y., Kosowski, A., Pajak, D., Uznański, P.: Fast collaborative graph exploration. Inf. Comput. **243**, 37–49 (2015)

20. Dieudonné, Y., Pelc, A., Peleg, D.: Gathering despite mischief. ACM Trans. Algorithms **11**(1), 1:1–1:28 (2014)
21. Elor, Y., Bruckstein, A.M.: Uniform multi-agent deployment on a ring. Theor. Comput. Sci. **412**(8–10), 783–795 (2011)
22. Fraigniaud, P., Ilcinkas, D., Peer, G., Pelc, A., Peleg, D.: Graph exploration by a finite automaton. Theor. Comput. Sci. **345**(2–3), 331–344 (2005)
23. Kshemkalyani, A.D., Ali, F.: Efficient dispersion of mobile robots on graphs. In: ICDCN, pp. 218–227 (2019)
24. Kshemkalyani, A.D., Molla, A.R., Sharma, G.: Fast dispersion of mobile robots on arbitrary graphs. In: ALGOSENSORS (2019)
25. Kshemkalyani, A.D., Molla, A.R., Sharma, G.: Dispersion of mobile robots in the global communication model. In: ICDCN (2020)
26. Kshemkalyani, A.D., Molla, A.R., Sharma, G.: Dispersion of mobile robots on grids. In: WALCOM (2020)
27. Menc, A., Pajak, D., Uznanski, P.: Time and space optimality of rotor-router graph exploration. Inf. Process. Lett. **127**, 17–20 (2017)
28. Miller, A., Pelc, A.: Tradeoffs between cost and information for rendezvous and treasure hunt. J. Parallel Distrib. Comput. **83**, 159–167 (2015)
29. Molla, A.R., Moses Jr., W.K.: Dispersion of mobile robots: the power of randomness. In: TAMC, pp. 481–500 (2019)
30. Potop-Butucaru, M., Raynal, M., Tixeuil, S.: Distributed computing with mobile robots: an introductory survey. In: The 14th International Conference on Network-Based Information Systems (NBiS), pp. 318–324 (2011)
31. Poudel, P., Sharma, G.: Time-optimal uniform scattering in a grid. In: ICDCN, pp. 228–237 (2019)
32. Prencipe, G.: Impossibility of gathering by a set of autonomous mobile robots. Theor. Comput. Sci. **384**(2–3), 222–231 (2007)
33. Shibata, M., Mega, T., Ooshita, F., Kakugawa, H., Masuzawa, T.: Uniform deployment of mobile agents in asynchronous rings. In: PODC, pp. 415–424 (2016)
34. Subramanian, R., Scherson, I.D.: An analysis of diffusive load-balancing. In: SPAA, pp. 220–225 (1994)
35. Suzuki, I., Yamashita, M.: Distributed anonymous mobile robots: Formation of geometric patterns. SIAM J. Comput. **28**(4), 1347–1363 (1999)

Conic Formation in Presence
of Faulty Robots

Debasish Pattanayak[1,2], Klaus-Tycho Foerster[2], Partha Sarathi Mandal[1]([✉]),
and Stefan Schmid[2]

[1] Department of Mathematics, IIT Guwahati, Guwahati, India
psm@iitg.ac.in
[2] Faculty of Computer Science, University of Vienna, Vienna, Austria

Abstract. Pattern formation is one of the most fundamental problems in distributed computing, which has recently received much attention. In this paper, we initiate the study of distributed pattern formation in situations when some robots can be *faulty*. In particular, we consider the well-established *look-compute-move* model with oblivious, anonymous robots. We first present lower bounds and show that any deterministic algorithm takes at least two rounds to form simple patterns in the presence of faulty robots. We then present distributed algorithms for our problem which match this bound, *for conic sections*: in at most two rounds, robots form lines, circles and parabola tolerating $f = 2, 3$ and 4 faults, respectively. For $f = 5$, the target patterns are parabola, hyperbola and ellipse. We show that the resulting pattern includes the f faulty robots in the pattern of n robots, where $n \geq 2f + 1$, and that $f < n < 2f + 1$ robots cannot form such patterns. We conclude by discussing several relaxations and extensions.

Keywords: Distributed algorithms · Pattern formation · Conic formation · Fault tolerance · Oblivious mobile robots

1 Introduction

Self-organizing systems have fascinated researchers for many decades already. These systems are capable of forming an overall order from an initially disordered configuration, using *local* interactions between its parts only. Self-organization arises in many forms, including physical, chemical, and biological systems, and can be based on various processes, from crystallization, over chemical oscillation, to neural circuits [7]. Due to their decentralized and self-healing properties, self-organizing systems are often very robust.

D. Pattanayak—Visit to University of Vienna is supported by the Overseas Visiting Doctoral Fellowship, 2018 Award No. ODF/2018/001055 by the Science and Engineering Research Board (SERB), Government of India.

© Springer Nature Switzerland AG 2020
C. M. Pinotti et al. (Eds.): ALGOSENSORS 2020, LNCS 12503, pp. 170–185, 2020.
https://doi.org/10.1007/978-3-030-62401-9_12

We, in this paper, consider self-organizing systems in the context of *robotics*. In particular, we are interested in the fundamental question of how most simple robots can self-organize into basic patterns. This *pattern formation* problem has already received much attention in the literature [6,18,23,24].

A particularly well-studied and challenging model is the *look-compute-move* model, in which each robot, in each round, first observes its environment and then decides on its next move. In the most basic setting, the robots do not have any persistent memory and hence cannot remember information from previous rounds, and they can also not distinguish between the other robots they see: the robots are *oblivious* and *anonymous*. Furthermore, robots cannot communicate. Over the last years, several research lines investigated when robots can and cannot form different patterns [6,13,18,19,23,24,26,27]. However, existing work on pattern formation shares the assumption that robots are non-faulty.

This paper initiates the study of distributed pattern formation algorithms for scenarios where some robots can be *faulty*: the faulty robots do not move nor act according to a specified protocol or algorithm. The setting with faulty robots is particularly challenging, as the non-faulty robots cannot directly observe which robots are faulty. However, even *indirect* observations seem challenging: since all robots are oblivious, a robot cannot remember patterns from previous rounds, and hence, has no information which robots moved recently. In fact, a robot *per se* does not even know whether the current pattern it observes is the initial configuration or whether some rounds of movements already occurred. What's more, the ability to self-organize into a specific pattern seems to require some coordination or even consensus, which is notoriously hard in faulty environments.

Contributions. This paper considers the design of distributed algorithms for pattern formation of most simple oblivious and potentially *faulty* robots. Our main result is an algorithmic framework that allows robots to form patterns which include faulty robots, in a decentralized and efficient manner. In particular, we do not require robots to identify faulty robots explicitly or to remember previous configurations, but require knowledge of the exact number of faults.

For f faults, we show how to form conic patterns in just *two rounds*, for at least $2f + 1$ robots. We form conic patterns such as line, circle and parabola for $f = 2, 3$ and 4, respectively. For $f = 5$, the target pattern are parabola, hyperbola and ellipse. We also prove that this is optimal: no deterministic algorithm can solve this problem in just one round or with less than $2f + 1$ robots. We further discuss several relaxations of our model and extensions of our results, e.g., considering initial symmetric configurations, having at most f faulty robots, or the impossibility of forming the pattern corresponding to f faults. We also discuss an extension where the robots form a line (a circle) for $f = 3, 4, 5$ ($f = 4, 5$).

Organization. After discussing related work in Sect. 1.1, we first provide a formal model in Sect. 2, followed by a study of the special case of $f = 1$ faulty robot in Sect. 3 to provide some intuition. We then give tight runtime and cardinality lower bounds in Sect. 4, and match them for the remaining conic patterns in Sect. 5. In Sect. 6, we show the algorithmic framework and prove the correctness of our algorithm. After discussing further model variations in Sect. 7, we conclude in Sect. 8.

1.1 Related Work

Pattern formation is an active area of research [13,19,27], however, to the best of our knowledge, we are the first to consider pattern formation in the presence of faults: a fundamental extension. In general, pattern formation allows for exploring the limits of what oblivious robots can compute. A "weak robot" model was introduced by Flocchini et al. [18], where the objective is to determine the minimum capabilities a set of robots need to achieve certain tasks. In general, the tasks include *Gathering* [8,9,15], *Convergence* [10,11], *Pattern Formation* [6,19,23], etc. Gathering is a special case of pattern formation, where the target pattern is a point. Gathering has been achieved for robots with multiplicity detection [9,17]. Most gathering algorithms use the capability of multiplicity detection to form a unique multiplicity point starting from a scattered configuration. In the absence of this capability, it has been proved that gathering is impossible in the semi-synchronous model without any agreement on the coordinate system [22].

The objective of gathering algorithms is only to gather the non-faulty robots, not to form general patterns. Moreover, for the specific case of gathering, some interesting first fault-tolerance studies exist. Agmon and Peleg [1] solve the gathering problem for a single crash-fault. Gathering has been solved with multiple faults [4,5] with strong multiplicity detection. Next, gathering has also been addressed for robots with weak multiplicity detection tolerating multiple crash faults [3,21]. For byzantine faults, Auger et al. [2] show impossibility results, and Defago et al. [14] present a self-stabilizing algorithm for gathering. The gathering algorithms only gather non-faulty robots. Since oblivious robots cannot differentiate a faulty robot from a non-faulty one, all the algorithms can be considered to be non-terminating algorithms. In contrast in our paper, we include the faulty robots in the pattern, and as a result, we achieve termination.

Flocchini et al. [18] characterize the role of common knowledge, like agreement on the coordinate system as a requisite for the pattern formation problem, and Yamashita and Suzuki [25] characterize the patterns formable by oblivious robots. Fujinaga et al. [19] present an algorithm using bipartite matching for asynchronous robots. Yamauchi and Yamashita [27] propose a pattern formation algorithm for robots with limited visibility. Das et al. [13] characterize the sequence of patterns that are formable, starting from an arbitrary configuration. Das et al. [12] further extend the sequence of pattern formation problem for luminous robots (robots with visible external persistent memory). As a special pattern formation problem, uniform circle formation has also been considered in the literature [16]. Formation of a plane starting from a three-dimensional configuration has also been solved for synchronous robots [24,26]. The authors characterize configurations for which plane formation is possible. The existing pattern formation algorithms consider the sequential movement of robots.

Since we consider faulty robots in our paper, all the existing algorithms are not adaptable to our cause. A fault-tolerant algorithm has to consider the simultaneous movement of robots and should satisfy the wait-free property to avoid cyclic dependency.

2   Preliminaries

We follow standard model assumptions, inspired by existing work, e.g., [1,3,21].

2.1   Model

Each robot is a dimensionless point robot. The robots are homogeneous: they execute the same deterministic algorithm, are indistinguishable and anonymous (no identifiers), oblivious (no persistent memories), and silent (no communication). The robots do not share a common coordinate system and observe others in their own *local coordinate system*. The robots have unlimited visibility, and the determined locations of other robots are precise.

Each robot follows the *look-compute-move* cycle. A robot obtains a snapshot of relative positions of other robots with respect to its position in the *look* state. Based on the snapshot of other robot positions, it decides a destination in the *compute* state. In the *move* state, it moves to the destination and reaches the destination in the same round. This is known as *rigid* robot movement. The scheduler, which activates the robots, follows a fully-synchronous (*FSYNC*) model, i.e., all the robots look at the same time and finish movement in the same round, i.e., each completion of look-compute-move cycle is one round. We consider that the robots are susceptible to crash-faults, i.e., they stop moving after the crash and never recover. Moreover, the number of f faulty robots is known beforehand, and as such, the robots know which types of pattern to form. In particular, we assume that the following four initial conditions hold:

1. All f faulty robots have already crashed initially.
2. All initial configurations are asymmetric.[1]
3. All robots occupy distinct positions initially.[2]
4. The faulty robots form a convex polygon.

The last assumption needs the faulty robots to be at corners of a convex polygon; the non-faulty robots can lie at any position. The rationale behind the assumption is that four robots forming a triangle with a robot inside the triangle do not correspond to any conic section in $\mathbb{R}^2$, similarly, for five robots. For three or more robots, a collinear configuration is addressed in Sect. 7. For two robots, the assumption trivially holds.

---

[1] This assumption allows us to have a unique ordering of the robots [8].

[2] As any set of non-faulty robots that share a position will always perform the same actions from then on and be indistinguishable from each other.

2.2   Notations

A configuration $\mathcal{C} = \{p_1, p_2, \cdots, p_n\}$ is a set of n points on the plane $\mathbb{R}^2$, where $p_i = (x_i, y_i)$ is a tuple representing the x- and y-coordinates of the robots. Since each robot is initially located at distinct points, it then holds that $p_i \neq p_j$ for any pair of i and j such that $i \neq j$. f is the number of faulty robots. We will always uphold this condition in our algorithms, except for the case of $f = 1$, where the target pattern is a point. The target patterns are conic sections that satisfy the second degree general equation

$$a_1 x^2 + a_2 y^2 + a_3 xy + a_4 x + a_5 y + a_6 = 0 .$$

Depending on the values of a_i for $i \in \{1, 2, \ldots, 6\}$, the equation represents line, circle, parabola, hyperbola or ellipse. We say a set of points form a conic pattern when they lie on the same conic section. Now, we say the conic pattern passes through the set of points. We denote $\mathcal{P}$ as the length of the pattern and u as the uniform distance.

3   Problem Statement and Intuition

Objective. Given a set of robots on the plane as defined in the model (Sect. 2.1), we want the robots to form a conic pattern corresponding to the number of faults.[3]

Point Formation $(f = 1)$. To provide some intuition, we start with the case of $f = 1$. For a single faulty robot, we move all the robots to the center of their smallest enclosing circle. If there is a faulty robot in the center, then point formation is achieved. If the faulty robot is somewhere else, we arrive at a configuration with two robot positions. For a configuration with two robot positions, all robots move to the other robot's position. From Assumption 3., we have all the robots at distinct initial positions. Hence the faulty robot is at a different position from the gathered robots. Moving all gathered robots to the faulty robot's position achieves our objective of point formation, as the faulty robot cannot move.

4   Lower Bound

We saw above that there could be situations where only one round suffices, namely, for the case of exactly $n = 2$ and $f = 1$. However, we can show that for $f \geq 2$, at least two rounds are required. For conic patterns (with $f \in \{2, 3, 4, 5\}$), this bound is tight: we will later provide algorithms that terminate in two rounds.

Theorem 1. *For every $f \geq 2$ and every $n \geq f + 3$ holds: Any deterministic algorithm needs more than one round to make a pattern passing through all f faulty robots.*

---

[3] That is a point for $f = 1$, a line for $f = 2$, a circle for $f = 3$, a parabola for $f = 4$, and an ellipse or parabola or hyperbola for $f = 5$.

Proof. Let φ be a deterministic algorithm that forms the pattern with faulty robots. Suppose φ solves the pattern in one step. Two patterns can have at most f common points[4]. Let $\mathcal{C} = \{p_1, p_2, \cdots, p_{f+3}\}$ be an initial configuration with $f + 3$ robots such that no $f + 1$ robots are in the same pattern.

Without loss of generality, consider two sets of f faulty robots at positions $\{p_1, p_2, \cdots, p_f\}$ and $\{p_2, p_3, \cdots, p_{f+1}\}$ and the corresponding pattern be $\wp'$ and $\wp''$, respectively. The f faulty robots do not move. Let $\wp' = \{p'_1, p'_2, \cdots, p'_{f+3}\}$ and $\wp'' = \{p''_1, p''_2, \cdots, p''_{f+3}\}$. As φ achieves pattern formation in one round, both $\wp'$ and $\wp''$ should be final. We have $p_{f+1} \neq p'_{f+1}$, $p_{f+2} \neq p'_{f+2}$ and $p_{f+3} \neq p'_{f+3}$, since all robots in $\wp'$ are in the pattern. Similarly, we also have $p_1 \neq p''_1$, $p_{f+2} \neq p''_{f+2}$ and $p_{f+3} \neq p''_{f+3}$ for $\wp''$. Since the robots at $\{p_2, \cdots, p_f\}$ did not move to form $\wp'$ and $\wp''$, these $f - 1$ points are common between $\wp'$ and $\wp''$. Since, $p_{f+1} \neq p'_{f+1}$ and $p_{f+1} = p''_{f+1}$, so p_{f+1} cannot be a common point between $\wp'$ and $\wp''$. Out of p_{f+2} and p_{f+3}, at most one can be a common point in the pattern, since there are at most f common points. Since φ is deterministic, the destination for robots at p_{f+2} and p_{f+3} remains the same regardless of the destination pattern being $\wp'$ or $\wp''$. If $\{p'_{f+2}, p'_{f+3}\} = \{p''_{f+2}, p''_{f+3}\}$, then $\wp'$ and $\wp''$ have $f + 1$ common points. This is a contradiction since the patterns are different. Hence no deterministic algorithm can solve the pattern formation problem with faults in one round. The arguments hold analogously for $n \geq f + 3$ robots.   □

Next, we show a lower bound on the number of robots required to solve the pattern formation problem. A configuration with exactly f robots is trivially solvable since the f robots are already in the pattern. Note that for $f \geq 2$, $2f + 1 \geq f + 3$ holds.

Theorem 2. *At least $2f + 1$ robots are required to form a pattern passing through f faulty robots for $f \geq 2$.*

Proof. Consider the number of robots to be $f < n < 2f + 1$. Assume that the configuration of these n robots is such that no $f + 1$ robots are in the same pattern. Let φ be a deterministic algorithm, which decides the destination of the robots given a configuration. Since the robots are oblivious, it is impossible to determine which robots are faulty given a configuration. As we consider patterns from the conic section, a pattern corresponding to f can be uniquely determined through f robots.

Let φ decide the target pattern corresponding to a set of f robots for the given configuration $\mathcal{C}$. So the other $n - f$ robots have to move to the pattern. Since the algorithm cannot determine which robots are faulty, the adversary can always choose the $0 < n - f$ robots to be faulty. Since $n - f \leq f$, none of the robots move. This leads to a stagnated configuration, and the algorithm does not proceed further.

If the algorithm decides a pattern that passes through less than or equal to f points in the configuration, then we choose faulty robots out of the points which

---

[4] Two parabolas intersect at 4 points, which can be the common points between two parabola patterns.

are not on the pattern, and we arrive at a configuration where not all the robots are in the same pattern. Now there are at most $n - f \leq f$ robots on the pattern, which is the same as the previous configuration.   □

5   Detailed Algorithms

In this section, we provide the promised two round algorithms for the different configurations. To this end, we first provide algorithmic preliminaries in Sect. 5.1.

5.1   Algorithmic Preliminaries

In our algorithms, we will perform case distinctions according to the following three types of configurations:

Definition 1 (*Terminal Configuration*). *A configuration is a terminal configuration if all the robots form the target pattern corresponding to f faulty robots.*

Definition 2 (*Type I Configuration*). *If exactly $n - f$ robots are in the target pattern corresponding to f faulty robots, then it is a Type I configuration.*

A Type I configuration can be symmetric or asymmetric.

Definition 3 (*Type O Configuration*). *If a configuration is not Terminal or Type I, then it is a Type O configuration.*

Note that an initial asymmetric configuration can be a Type I or Type O or Terminal configuration. In the following, we also distinguish the configurations based on the uniform spacing between the robots. We use the uniform positions of the robots as a differentiating factor between faulty and non-faulty.

Definition 4 (*Uniform Configuration*). *A configuration is a uniform configuration if the distance between all consecutive pairs of robots in the configuration along the pattern is the same.*

Definition 5 (*Quasi-Uniform Configuration*). *If a uniform configuration with m uniform positions is occupied by n robots, where $n \leq m \leq 2n$, then it is a quasi-uniform configuration.*

With the assumption (Sect. 2.1) that the initial configuration is asymmetric, we can obtain an ordering of the robots using the algorithm by Chaudhuri et al. [8].

Lemma 1. *An asymmetric configuration is orderable [8].*

Using Lemma 1, we can thus always obtain an ordering among the robots. We use this ordering to determine the target pattern in case of a Type O configuration. In general, having an ordering allows us to have complete agreement on the coordinate system, i.e., the robots agree on the direction and orientation.

Let $\mathcal{O}$ be an ordering of the robots that maps the set of robots to a set of integers $\{1, 2, \ldots, n\}$ such that each robot corresponds to an integer. This is the rank of the robot in the ordering. In case of symmetry, two robots can have different orderings. Note that locally, the ordering is unique for a particular robot, but that from a global perspective, different robots can have different orderings.

We use the ordering to determine a target pattern only in cases where there are multiple potential target patterns. We always choose the target pattern passing through the smaller ranked robot in the ordering.

Since the algorithm takes at most two steps to reach a pattern containing all faulty robots, we denote the *initial*, *transitional* and *final* configurations as $\mathcal{C}_0$, $\mathcal{C}_1$ and $\mathcal{C}_2$, respectively.

5.2   Algorithm

We first present a general algorithm with two different strategies for the open pattern and closed pattern. Among the conic patterns, line, parabola and hyperbola are open patterns, while circle and ellipse are closed patterns. The target position of the robots depend on this since open conics have two end points, while closed do not have any. The length of the pattern, $\mathcal{P}$ is determined with respect to the pattern being formed. For line, $\mathcal{P}$ is the distance between the two endpoints. For parabola (hyperbola), $\mathcal{P}$ is the length of the parabola (hyperbola) between the points where the latus rectum[5] of parabola (hyperbola) intersects the parabola (hyperbola). In case of circle and ellipse, $\mathcal{P}$ is the perimeter. We denote u as the uniform distance at which the points on the target pattern are determined. The length u is computed along the pattern. We differentiate between two types of configurations:

Type O Configuration. In this case, we form the target pattern outside the smallest enclosing circle of the configuration. The target pattern can be uniquely determined using the asymmetricity of the configuration, since a Type O configuration can only appear in the initial state. The target pattern size is dependent on the diameter of smallest enclosing circle.

- Compute the smallest enclosing circle of the configuration where O is the center and d is the diameter.
- Let A be the location of the robot with the smallest rank in the ordering. If A is O, then we choose the robot with second smallest rank.
- Find point B such that B lies on $\overrightarrow{OA}$ and $|\overline{OB}| = d$.
- The target pattern corresponding to f passes through B.

Now, we show how we determine the target pattern corresponding to the number of faults (see Fig. 1).

---

[5] The latus rectum is the line that passes through the focus of the parabola and parallel to the directrix.

$f = 2$: The target line is perpendicular to $\overline{OB}$ and has its midpoint at B with
    length d (ref. Fig. 1a).

$f = 3$: The target circle passing through B has radius d and center at O (ref.
    Fig. 1b).

$f = 4$ and $f = 5$: The target parabola has its vertex at B and focus at O. The
    latus rectum of parabola is perpendicular to $\overline{OB}$ and length of latus rectum
    is $2d$ (ref. Fig. 1c).

For an open pattern, we choose the first point at a distance $u/2$ from one end
point and place subsequent $n - 1$ points at distance $u = \mathcal{P}/n$ (ref. Fig. 1a, 1c).

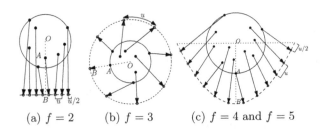

(a) $f = 2$ (b) $f = 3$ (c) $f = 4$ and $f = 5$

Fig. 1. Target patterns (dashed) for Type O configuration

Type I Configuration. The target pattern is determined as passing through
the robots which are not part of the pattern in the existing configuration. The
destinations for robots are at points uniformly positioned at distance u corresponding to the length of the pattern. However, there is a possibility that the
existing pattern and target pattern intersect. We hence avoid using the intersection points as target points. If an intersection point is a target point for a value
of u, then we choose u' depending on the configuration.

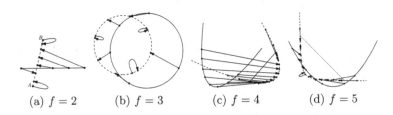

(a) $f = 2$ (b) $f = 3$ (c) $f = 4$ (d) $f = 5$

Fig. 2. Target patterns (dashed) for Asymmetric Type I configurations

Asymmetric Type I: The robots are assigned target points according to their
    rank in the ordering with $u = \mathcal{P}/n$ (ref. Fig. 2). If the target point correspond-
    ing to u overlaps with intersection points, then we choose $u' = \mathcal{P}/(n + 1)$.
    The number of target points with respect to u' is $n + 1$, so we assign two

destinations to the robot with highest rank, which can be chosen arbitrarily (ref. Fig. 5). For $f = 5$, the intermediate configuration can be a parabola, hyperbola or an ellipse. Thus, it can also appear as an initial configuration. We show all the transition between ellipse, parabola and hyperbola in the full version of the paper [20].

Reflective Symmetric Type I: Let k be the number of robots which lie on the line of symmetry. In this case, we choose, $u = \mathcal{P}/(n + k)$. We get k extra target points so that we can assign two target points to the robots on the line of symmetry. A robot on one side (say left) of the line of symmetry finds its destination on the same side. Since the robots on the line of symmetry may not have a common left or right, they can choose one of the two symmetric destinations as their target. This also ensures that the next configuration is not completely symmetric (ref. Fig. 3), since only one of the symmetric points would be occupied. On overlap of target pattern points with existing points, we choose u' similar to asymmetric Type I configuration. We refer the reader to the full version of the paper for more details [20].

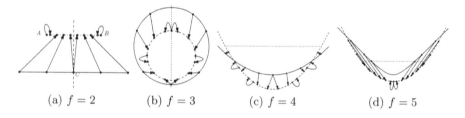

(a) $f = 2$ (b) $f = 3$ (c) $f = 4$ (d) $f = 5$

Fig. 3. Target patterns (dashed) for Reflective Symmetric Type I configurations

Rotational Symmetric Type I: This can occur only in the case of lines and circles. In case of a line, the robots move to the side with smaller angle between the target line m and existing pattern l (ref. Fig. 4a). In case of a circle, the configuration is two concentric circles. We assign two destinations for each robot already on the target circle by choosing $u = \mathcal{P}/(n + k)$, where $k = 3$ (ref. Fig. 4b).

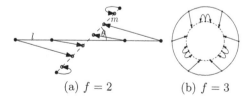

(a) $f = 2$ (b) $f = 3$

Fig. 4. Target patterns (dashed) for Rotational Symmetric Type I configurations

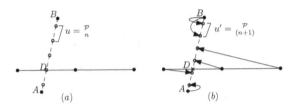

Fig. 5. Choosing Non-overlapping uniform points in the target pattern (dashed)

Choosing Non-overlapping Uniform Points. In case of an asymmetric Type I configuration, we obtain an ordering $\mathcal{O}$. For $f = 2$, the target line passes through A and B. Let A be the robot with smaller rank among A and B. We choose the set of uniform points at a distance $u/2$ from A towards B. Let D be the intersection point of the existing line in the current configuration and the line through A and B (D is marked as a cross in Fig. 5b). If the uniform points overlap with D (ref. Fig. 5a), then we choose another set of points at uniform distance $u' = \mathcal{P}/(n + 1)$. Since, $|\overline{AD}| = 3u/2$, the uniform points overlap with D. We have to choose a set of uniform points corresponding to u' as shown in Fig. 5b. With u', there are $n + 1$ uniform points, the robot B has two potential destinations, one of which can be chosen arbitrarily. We refer the reader to the full version of the paper for the cases of $f = 3, 4, 5$ [20].

6   General Algorithmic Framework

The algorithm broadly has two steps, based on the current robot configuration.

Step 1: Determine the faulty robots.
Step 2: Move to a pattern passing through the faulty robots.

Since the robots are oblivious, they cannot distinguish between Step 1 and Step 2. Hence the properties required for Step 1 have to be applicable to Step 2 and vice versa. For Step 1, a simple process to determine all the faulty robots in a single round is to move all the robots, such that the robots which do not move, will not lie on the pattern points. We determine the pattern points uniformly so that all pattern points are consecutively equidistant along the pattern. This helps us in determining the faulty robots since they would not lie on a pattern point. For Step 2, the pattern determined from the faulty robot positions has to be unique, so that all the robots agree on the pattern. Overall, the algorithm needs to determine a unique pattern such that all robots agree on the pattern, and all robots are required to move to achieve the pattern. We present a transition diagram for configurations in our algorithm in Fig. 6.

Lemma 2. *The destinations of all robots are distinct.*

Proof. We always follow the ordering to determine the destinations for each robot. In the asymmetric cases, we have the ordering, which creates a one-to-one

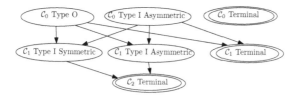

Fig. 6. Transition diagram of configurations

map from the current position of a robot to its destination. In case of symmetric configurations, the robots which are present on the line of symmetry have two potential destinations (from a global perspective) and choose one of them according to their local orientation. Hence the destinations are distinct.   □

Next, we show that there are no overlapping points between the current configuration and the set of destinations. The set of destinations is the set of all potential destination points for the robots in the current configuration. Since some robots are faulty, two consecutive configurations may have those points as common points. Had the robots been non-faulty, then they would have moved to a point that is not in the current configuration. The proof is in the full version of the paper [20].

Lemma 3. *Given configuration $\mathcal{C}$ and a destination set $\mathcal{C}'$, we have $\mathcal{C} \cap \mathcal{C}' = \phi$.*

6.1 Determining Faulty Robots and a Pattern

There are two types of initial configurations where we need to determine the faulty robots, i.e., arbitrary configurations and intermediate configurations. The destinations for the robots are such that no point in $\mathcal{C}_0$ overlaps with any point in $\mathcal{C}_1$. For an arbitrary initial configuration, the target pattern is scaled such that no point in the target pattern lies on or inside the smallest enclosing circle of $\mathcal{C}_0$. Since $\mathcal{C}_0$ is asymmetric, we can always uniquely scale the pattern. We can moreover show that a unique pattern exists that passes through all the faulty robots, and obtain the following three lemmas, with proofs of Lemma 4 and 5 in the full version of the paper [20].

Lemma 4. *It takes one round to determine all the faulty robots for a Type O configuration for $f \in \{2, 3, 4, 5\}$.*

Lemma 5. *It takes one round to determine all the faulty robots for an asymmetric Type I configuration for $f \in \{2, 3, 4, 5\}$.*

Lemma 6. *The target pattern passing through the faulty robots in $\mathcal{C}_1$ can be uniquely determined.*

Proof. The pattern is determined uniquely for a given value of f. For $f = 2$ and 3, the line and circle passing through the points are unique. For $f = 4$, there can be two conjugate parabolas passing through four points. In this case, the parabola with the larger latus rectum is chosen as the target pattern. For $f = 5$, the target pattern is uniquely determined by the five points to be a parabola, hyperbola or an ellipse. Since we assume the faulty robots to form a convex polygon, they can only occupy positions on one side of the hyperbola. From Lemma 3, we know that the destination points do not have a common point with the points in the previous configuration. From the quasi-uniform configuration, we can determine the robots which are not present at a uniform point. Hence we can determine the faulty robots in $\mathcal{C}_1$ and the corresponding pattern.   □

6.2   Termination

We can now show that the algorithm terminates, and we can determine the faulty robots in the terminal configuration. Combining Lemma 4, 5 and 6 yields:

Theorem 3. *Starting from any initial asymmetric configuration, the algorithm terminates in at most two rounds.*

Since the algorithm does not do anything for a terminal configuration, we cannot determine the faulty robots if the initial configuration is a terminal configuration. Moreover, in a terminal configuration, our algorithm designs result in the following distribution of robots on the plane starting from a configuration other than the terminal configuration.

Corollary 1. *Starting from a configuration other than the terminal configuration, the non-faulty robots are at uniform pattern points in the terminal configuration.*

Proof. The destinations are always at uniform points spread over the target pattern. So whenever a non-faulty robot moves, it ends up at a uniform pattern point. Note that the resulting configuration may not be uniform due to the faulty robots. The non-faulty robots occupy the uniform points in a quasi-uniform configuration.   □

From Lemma 3 and Corollary 1, we have the following Corollary.

Corollary 2. *The faulty robots can be determined from a terminal configuration unless it is the initial configuration.*

7   Discussion

In the following, we show how to relax our model and extend the previous results in several directions. In particular, we extend the behavior of the algorithm in the absence of the assumption considered in Sect. 2. We show that with small modifications to the algorithm, we can subvert some assumptions.

Knowing the Number of Faults. We extend the definition of Type I configuration to include configurations where at most f robots are not in the pattern in the current configuration. As we need exactly f robots to determine the target pattern, if $f' < f$ are not in the pattern, we choose a target pattern passing through those f' and the first $f - f'$ robots in the ordering to set the pattern.

Initial Configuration with Reflective Symmetry. For a configuration with a single line of symmetry, we can always follow the strategies described for Type I symmetric configurations in the algorithms from Sect. 5. The robots on the line of symmetry have two destinations on either side of the line of symmetry. According to their local orientation, they choose one of the destinations.

Lower Order Patterns for Higher Number of Faults. We add special cases if the robots are collinear (resp. co-circular) for $f \in \{3, 4, 5\}$ (resp. $f \in \{4, 5\}$). In this case, the robots form a line (resp. circle). If the initial configuration is this situation, then it is impossible to determine the faulty robots. Hence the configuration in the next step becomes an arbitrary configuration. We thus need three steps to achieve pattern formation instead of two.

8   Conclusion

This paper initiated the study of distributed algorithms for pattern formation with faulty robots. In particular, we presented an algorithmic framework that allows solving many basic formation problems in at most two rounds, which is optimal given the lower bound also presented in this paper. We regard our work as a first step and believe it opens several interesting avenues for future research. In particular, it will be interesting to study pattern formation problems for more advanced robots under failures, as well as randomized algorithms. It will also be interesting to generalize our failure model, e.g., to support transient crash faults and byzantine faults.

References

1. Agmon, N., Peleg, D.: Fault-tolerant gathering algorithms for autonomous mobile robots. SIAM J. Comput. **36**(1), 56–82 (2006)
2. Auger, C., Bouzid, Z., Courtieu, P., Tixeuil, S., Urbain, X.: Certified impossibility results for byzantine-tolerant mobile robots. In: Higashino, T., Katayama, Y., Masuzawa, T., Potop-Butucaru, M., Yamashita, M. (eds.) SSS 2013. LNCS, vol. 8255, pp. 178–190. Springer, Cham (2013). https://doi.org/10.1007/978-3-319-03089-0_13
3. Bhagat, S., Mukhopadhyaya, K.: Fault-tolerant gathering of semi-synchronous robots. In: Proceedings of the 18th International Conference on Distributed Computing and Networking, Hyderabad, India, 5–7 January 2017, p. 6 (2017)
4. Bouzid, Z., Das, S., Tixeuil, S.: Gathering of mobile robots tolerating multiple crash faults. In: IEEE 33rd International Conference on Distributed Computing Systems, ICDCS 2013, Philadelphia, Pennsylvania, USA, 8–11 July 2013, pp. 337–346 (2013)
5. Bramas, Q., Tixeuil, S.: Wait-free gathering without chirality. In: Scheideler, C. (ed.) Structural Information and Communication Complexity. LNCS, vol. 9439, pp. 313–327. Springer, Cham (2015). https://doi.org/10.1007/978-3-319-25258-2_22

6. Bramas, Q., Tixeuil, S.: Brief announcement: Probabilistic asynchronous arbitrary pattern formation. In: Proceedings of the 2016 ACM Symposium on Principles of Distributed Computing, PODC 2016, Chicago, IL, USA, 25–28 July 2016, pp. 443–445 (2016)
7. Camazine, S., Deneubourg, J.L., Franks, N.R., Sneyd, J., Bonabeau, E., Theraula, G.: Self-organization in Biological Systems. Princeton University Press, Princeton (2003)
8. Chaudhuri, S.G., Mukhopadhyaya, K.: Leader election and gathering for asynchronous fat robots without common chirality. J. Discret. Algorithms **33**, 171–192 (2015)
9. Cieliebak, M., Flocchini, P., Prencipe, G., Santoro, N.: Distributed computing by mobile robots: gathering. SIAM J. Comput. **41**(4), 829–879 (2012)
10. Cohen, R., Peleg, D.: Robot convergence via center-of-gravity algorithms. In: Proceedings of SIROCCO, pp. 79–88 (2004)
11. Cohen, R., Peleg, D.: Convergence properties of the gravitational algorithm in asynchronous robot systems. SIAM J. Comput. **34**(6), 1516–1528 (2005)
12. Das, S., Flocchini, P., Prencipe, G., Santoro, N.: Forming sequences of patterns with luminous robots. IEEE Access **8**, 90577–90597 (2020)
13. Das, S., Flocchini, P., Santoro, N., Yamashita, M.: Forming sequences of geometric patterns with oblivious mobile robots. Distrib. Comput. **28**(2), 131–145 (2014). https://doi.org/10.1007/s00446-014-0220-9
14. Défago, X., Potop-Butucaru, M.G., Clément, J., Messika, S., Parvédy, P.R.: Fault and byzantine tolerant self-stabilizing mobile robots gathering - feasibility study. CoRR abs/1602.05546 (2016)
15. Flocchini, P., Prencipe, G., Santoro, N.: Distributed Computing by Oblivious Mobile Robots. Synthesis Lectures on Distributed Computing Theory. Morgan & Claypool Publishers, San Rafael (2012)
16. Flocchini, P., Prencipe, G., Santoro, N., Viglietta, G.: Distributed computing by mobile robots: uniform circle formation. Distrib. Comput. **30**(6), 413–457 (2016). https://doi.org/10.1007/s00446-016-0291-x
17. Flocchini, P., Prencipe, G., Santoro, N., Widmayer, P.: Gathering of asynchronous robots with limited visibility. Theor. Comput. Sci. **337**(1–3), 147–168 (2005)
18. Flocchini, P., Prencipe, G., Santoro, N., Widmayer, P.: Arbitrary pattern formation by asynchronous, anonymous, oblivious robots. Theor. Comput. Sci. **407**(1–3), 412–447 (2008)
19. Fujinaga, N., Yamauchi, Y., Ono, H., Kijima, S., Yamashita, M.: Pattern formation by oblivious asynchronous mobile robots. SIAM J. Comput. **44**(3), 740–785 (2015)
20. Pattanayak, D., Foerster, K., Mandal, P.S., Schmid, S.: Conic formation in presence of faulty robots. CoRR abs/2003.01914 (2020). https://arxiv.org/abs/2003.01914
21. Pattanayak, D., Mondal, K., Ramesh, H., Mandal, P.S.: Gathering of mobile robots with weak multiplicity detection in presence of crash-faults. J. Parallel Distrib. Comput. **123**, 145–155 (2019)
22. Prencipe, G.: Impossibility of gathering by a set of autonomous mobile robots. Theor. Comput. Sci. **384**(2–3), 222–231 (2007)
23. Suzuki, I., Yamashita, M.: Distributed anonymous mobile robots: Formation of geometric patterns. SIAM J. Comput. **28**(4), 1347–1363 (1999)
24. Tomita, Y., Yamauchi, Y., Kijima, S., Yamashita, M.: Plane formation by synchronous mobile robots without chirality. In: 21st International Conference on Principles of Distributed Systems, OPODIS 2017, Lisbon, Portugal, 18–20 December 2017, pp. 13:1–13:17 (2017)

25. Yamashita, M., Suzuki, I.: Characterizing geometric patterns formable by oblivious anonymous mobile robots. Theor. Comput. Sci. **411**(26–28), 2433–2453 (2010)
26. Yamauchi, Y., Uehara, T., Kijima, S., Yamashita, M.: Plane formation by synchronous mobile robots in the three-dimensional euclidean space. J. ACM **64**(3), 16:1–16:43 (2017)
27. Yamauchi, Y., Yamashita, M.: Pattern formation by mobile robots with limited visibility. In: Moscibroda, T., Rescigno, A.A. (eds.) SIROCCO 2013. LNCS, vol. 8179, pp. 201–212. Springer, Cham (2013). https://doi.org/10.1007/978-3-319-03578-9_17

Author Index

Printed in the United States
By Bookmasters